Drift

Drift

Illicit Mobility and Uncertain Knowledge

Jeff Ferrell

UNIVERSITY OF CALIFORNIA PRESS

University of California Press, one of the most distin-
guished university presses in the United States, enriches
lives around the world by advancing scholarship in the
humanities, social sciences, and natural sciences. Its
activities are supported by the UC Press Foundation and
by philanthropic contributions from individuals and
institutions. For more information, visit www.ucpress.edu.

University of California Press
Oakland, California

Library of Congress Cataloging-in-Publication Data

Title: Drift : illicit mobility and uncertain knowledge /
    Jeff Ferrell.
Description: Oakland, California : University of
    California Press, [2018] | Includes bibliographical
    references and index.
Identifiers: LCCN 2017044533 (print) |
    LCCN 2017051505 (ebook) | ISBN 9780520968271
    (ebook) | ISBN 9780520295544 (unjacketed cloth : alk.
    paper) | ISBN 9780520295551 (pbk. : alk. paper)
Subjects: LCSH: Tramps—United States—History. |
    Homelessness—United States—History. | Tramps—
    United States—Social conditions. | Tramps—Political
    aspects—United States. | Railroads—United States—
    History. | Social values—United States—History.
Classification: LCC HV4505 (ebook) | LCC HV4505 .F47
    2018 (print) | DDC 305.5/690973—dc23
LC record available at https://lccn.loc.gov/2017044533

Manufactured in the United States of America

26 25 24 23 22 21 20 19 18
10 9 8 7 6 5 4 3 2 1

In memory of Bob Waldmire,
drifter extraordinaire

Contents

Acknowledgments

My thanks to Claudio Altenhain, Michael Boudreau, Frank Gemert, Mark Hamm, Willem de Hann, Keith Hayward, John Lennon, Travis Linnemann, Dragan Milovanovic, Gavin Morrison, Laura Naegler, Susan Phillips, Simon Springer, Fraser Stables, Lucia Trimbur, and Ken Tunnell. My thanks also to Maura Roessner and the fine staff at the University of California Press. And to all the freight hoppers out there? Thanks for your time—I'll see you down the line.

. . .

Portions of the book were previously published in the following:

Jeff Ferrell. "Postscript: Under the Slab." In *Liquid Criminology*, edited by Michael Jacobsen and Sandra Walklate, 221–29. London: Routledge, 2017. Reprinted by permission of Taylor and Francis/Routledge.

Jeff Ferrell. "Drifting through Space: An Epistemology." *Lo Squaderno*, no. 39 (March 2016): 21–25.

Jeff Ferrell. "Drift: A Criminology of the Contemporary Crisis." *Radical Criminology*, no. 5 (2015): 139–68.

Jeff Ferrell. "Manifesto for a Criminology beyond Method." In *The Poetics of Crime*, edited by Michael Jacobsen, 285–302. London: Ashgate, 2014. Reprinted by permission of Taylor and Francis/Routledge/Ashgate.

Jeff Ferrell. "Outline of a Criminology of Drift." In *New Directions in Criminological Theory*, edited by Steve Hall and Simon Winlow, 241–56. London: Routledge, 2012. Reprinted by permission of Taylor and Francis/Routledge.

Jeff Ferrell. "Anarchy, Geography, and Drift." *Antipode* 44, no. 5 (2012): 1687–1704.

Jeff Ferrell. "Disciplinarity and Drift." In *What Is Criminology?*, edited by Mary Bosworth and Carolyn Hoyle, 62–75. Oxford: Oxford University Press, 2011. Reprinted by permission of Oxford University Press.

Jeff Ferrell. "Kill Method: A Provocation." *Journal of Theoretical and Philosophical Criminology* 1, no. 1 (2009): 1–22.

PART ONE

Illicit Mobility

1

Drift Dialectics

This is a book about drift and drifters in their many forms—a book about the ways in which dislocation and disorientation can become phenomena in their own right. In it I sketch at least something of drift's long history, while also situating contemporary drift within the particular economic, social, and cultural dynamics of the present day. In this I also try to show that drift is today a global phenomenon—perhaps even the defining trajectory of a globalized world. Throughout, I explore the contested politics of drift—both the ways in which legal and political authorities work to control drift and drifters and the ways in which drifters and those who embrace drift create their own slippery strategies of resistance. I also trace the use of drift as a conceptual orientation within sociology, criminology, and other disciplines, and I propose that we can bring these and other disciplines into closer engagement with the contemporary world by learning the theoretical and methodological lessons offered by those adrift.

For all that, though, there's something I must admit; you'll see it soon enough in this first chapter anyway. This is the fact that, despite my best efforts to maintain a broad, global perspective on drift, I'm drawn to one particular sort of drift: that undertaken historically by the North American hobo, and in contemporary times by the hobo's bastard descendant, the train-hopping gutter punk. There are a number of reasons for this. First, as has been my habit in other research projects (Ferrell 1996, 2001, 2006), I prefer to do research as independently and immersively as possible and with as few resources as I can manage—and, based as I am in the United States, it was certainly more feasible to undertake research with North American drifters than it was with, say, Syrian war refugees in Turkey or North Africans crossing the Mediterranean to southern Europe. As will become clear throughout the book, drifting also tends to be highly uncertain and distinctly episodic, so this too necessitated a lengthy, loose research strategy more readily undertaken from my home turf. But really, as long as I'm being honest, it's more than that. It's that the music and culture of hobos, High Plains drifters, blues travelers, and gutter punks are part of who I am and were so long before I began to understand the shadowy links between them. It's the fact that this book was written late in the North American night, with the rumbling thuds and booming train horns of the nearby rail yard echoing through my windows, reminding me of the train hoppers and gutter punks out there rolling through the darkness. Most of all, as I'll explain in chapters 5 and 6, it's because I stumbled into my research with gutter punks and contemporary hobos right in the middle of writing this more general book on drift and drifters. Unintended and unplanned, this accidental association led me to all sorts of historical and contemporary insights regarding drift; it took me beyond my own expectations, to places I otherwise couldn't have found or imagined.

And if that's not drift, I don't know what is.

UNCERTAIN TRAJECTORIES

For those caught up in them, particular historical moments trace distinctly different trajectories across the arc of prospects and perception. Among certain adherents to the mythology of Western modernity, one moment after another has often seemed connected along a straight and ascending line to a better future—a future fulfilled by the insights of science, the convenience of technology, and the satisfactions of material prosperity. Within and against this modernist ascension, fundamentalists have often sought to reverse its trajectory, to return the social order to the past principles of founding fathers and founding documents. Reactionaries all, they push back against what they see as prevailing myths of progress, afraid that, if left unchecked, the social order will move only toward accumulating moral decay. Political revolutionaries often see, or long for, a trajectory that resembles that of a rocket launch—a new social order, blasting free from the old, taking flight, roaring upward toward a firmament of previously unimagined possibility. When, on the other hand, a social order fails of its own accord, from inside its own rotting contradictions, some find themselves caught in an opposite trajectory, descending quickly and deeply into economic ruin and existential despair; others ride a sad social spiral, a process of circling back time and again on recurring problems, each time a bit farther from their solution; and some, Durkheimians especially, sense a dispersal out from the middle, a centrifugal failure of social bonds and cultural cohesion. From the view of certain non-Western religious and cultural traditions, of course, it might be added that all these trajectories are soundly inconsequential, if not entirely illusory, subsumed as they are within an endless, circling trajectory of time and space reincarnated.

In any case, all such trajectories remain entangled in the messy course of human history and likewise remain contested and compromised in the practice of everyday social life. Because of this, the notion of a historical moment's trajectory is probably most useful when thought of not as some sort of teleological determinism but as a narrative device by which certain stories can be told, or perhaps an analytic metaphor by which certain historical tendencies can be understood. Adopting this more modest sense, I argue here that the present historical moment is tracing a trajectory that is, oddly enough, defined largely by its insistent lack of definition. This is the trajectory of drift. Drift follows neither the straight-line, forward motion of progress nor the stern reversals of fundamentalism. It neither ascends nor descends, and it remains too uncertain a motion to maintain even the circling arc of a spiral. Sometimes drift comes close to the unraveling trajectory of a failed Durkheimian social order—but even here it is uncertain in its uncertainty, since as we shall see, drifters sometimes consider their unsettled circumstances a new sort of social and moral map. Likewise, drift is often the trajectory of the disengaged and the dispossessed—but disengaged from what, dispossessed of what, and on whose terms? Certainly drift suggests some sort of disruption, some degree of spatial and temporal dislocation—yet this in turn implies some degree of certainty, some coordinates of time and space, against which to measure drift's disruptions.

"Nowadays men often feel that their private lives are a series of traps," C. Wright Mills (1959, 3) said a half century ago, catching as he did something of modern society's overwhelming intrusion into the everyday spheres of lived experience. Today we might say that more and more women and men feel that their lives are an accumulation of radical uncertainties, sensing as they do that they are left to negotiate a world that seems less a series of traps than a series of slippages (Cooper

2014; J. Young 2007). If for Mills and others the defining critical meta-phor was the trap, and with it personal trajectories that were stalled out, stuck in the stasis of unexamined assumptions and social inequal-ity, the more useful metaphor today is drift, and with it a scattershot trajectory through assumptions that seem always in the process of fad-ing away, with or without examination. Sometimes the streets are too dead for dreaming; other times there are no sure streets on which to dream, no signposts and no destination, no paths to anywhere. Some-times you stand still, waiting for your education or your next job or the revolution, but waiting at least for something; sometimes, as Tom Kromer (1935) wrote of his life adrift as an impoverished hobo during the Great Depression, you wander for no reason, on the way to nowhere, while waiting for nothing.

Lives adrift, folks waiting for nothing or on the way to nowhere known—these circumstances circle the world today. A global crisis that interweaves economic inequality and ecological decay with conflicts over immigration, development, and consumption has set these circumstances in motion. Within this crisis drift has come to pervade everyday experi-ence, incorporating both normative and spatial dislocation, resulting from both economic development and economic collapse, and flourish-ing precisely in those situations meant to contain it. Ongoing civil and transnational warfare continues to spawn swelling refugee populations. Repressive governmental regimes engage in the forced expulsion of dis-sidents and minority groups—and when these regimes are confronted, even successfully, further dislocation often results. Within China, across Europe, and around the globe, economic migrants wander in search of work, or are simply moved en masse from one work locale to another as economic demands change. In the United Kingdom, Europe, and the United States, the corporate criminality of the past decade's mortgage/banking crisis, the ongoing destruction of low-cost housing as part of urban redevelopment schemes, and the proliferation of part-time and low-wage service work all conspire to preclude certainties of home, shel-ter, or destination. Moving from house to house or country to country, sleeping in cars or temporary encampments, haunting streets and train stations, those cut loose from certainty find little in the way of spatial or social stability.

In this world, impoverished Central Americans—many of them unac-companied minors—risk assault, extortion, and police apprehension to hitch rides through Mexico atop a US-bound freight train, variously known as La Bestia—the Beast—or El Tren de la Muerte—the Death

Train (see Nazario 2006). Sometimes they make it to within sight of the US border but no farther, holing up indefinitely in drainage canals or river beds; other times they drown in the Rio Grande or end up in emergency shelters or US migrant detention centers that mostly resemble jails, waiting to be sent back. Cubans traverse eight Central American countries in their attempts to get to the United States, "in an exodus that some officials have likened to a stampede"; a group of Haitians, part of "an extraordinary wave of Haitian migrants streaming to the U.S.," crosses nine countries, only to find the final border closed (Robles 2016, 8; Semple 2016 A1). Trafficked children and migratory sex workers around the world subsist as perpetual "new arrivals," dislocated both from home communities and new areas of residence; in Italy, nuns intercede on their behalf. Migrants from rural areas pour into sprawling encampments outside Rio de Janeiro, Mumbai, and Ulan Bator or find themselves shuttled between one country and the next by political and economic upheaval. Young Arabs find a failure of opportunity and dream of moving abroad. Millions of battered Syrian refugees, remnants of Syria's "lost generation," flood across Europe, some by way of a Norwegian border outpost 250 miles north of the Arctic Circle. African refugees in search of work or safety brave the lawlessness of Libya to crowd rickety boats across the Mediterranean, only to find themselves bounced back and forth between southern European borders—if they are lucky enough to survive the sea crossing in the first place. Other African refugees—a half million, mostly Somalis—languish in Kenya's Dadaab refugee camp, said to be the world's largest.

In southern Europe, a native-born generation finds that today, even advanced degrees leave them lost between dead-end jobs and unemployment—and so they sleep in their cars, when they are not considering driving them into a wall. Young Portuguese professionals look to relocate to Brazil or Mozambique. In Spain, home evictions leave people on the streets and hungry, so they dig in urban trash bins for food; in the countryside battles erupt over the gleaning of harvest leftovers. Migrants meanwhile storm Spain's North African city of Melilla, desperate to reach a migration center. Italian authorities try to intercept migrant ships that were on a course for Italy and then abandoned by traffickers. Sicilian towns care for arriving migrants and bury those who don't survive—though the Identification and Expulsion Center outside Rome is described as an inhumane prison. In Greece young migrants camp in an abandoned furniture factory, looking to move on toward Northern Europe.

But Northern Europe harbors instabilities of its own. In Germany, a "shadow labor market" of poorly paid temporary workers is now seen as essential to the country's global standing. And as regards refugees, the country confronts an ongoing problem after a recent terrorist attack—"a vexing problem, common in Europe: how to handle hundreds of thousands of virtually stateless wanderers who are either unwilling or unable to return home" (Smale, Gall, and Pianigiani 2016, A1). France puts its own citizens on trial for assisting refugees, and eventually razes the sprawling migrant camp at Calais, from which migrants sought entry into the United Kingdom; evicted Calais migrants now relocate to camps in Paris instead. Meanwhile, even well-educated young people find themselves jobless: French undercover journalist Florence Aubenas (2011) writes *The Night Cleaner*, a bestseller about the existential and social costs of pervasive part-time work. Also in this context the eclectic, unstructured *Nuit Debout* (Night, Standing Up) movement emerges against labor market inequities, and inequities in general.

In Japan—even before the 2011 tsunami and nuclear crisis—almost half of the country's young workers are consigned to temporary, "irregular" jobs amidst a collapsing career structure. Chinese officials announce a plan to move 250 million rural residents into Chinese cities and smaller, newly built towns; some 330,000 "ecological migrants," victims of global warming and other environmental problems, have been moved to fabricated "villages." Already, rural migrant workers make up a third of Beijing's population, and with no place to live, occupy abandoned air-defense tunnels underneath the city. In Beijing and other East Asian cities, other homeless people shelter inside McDonald's restaurants, in the process earning the nickname "McRefugees"; elsewhere in China, gangs of grifters lure isolated, impoverished men into mining work, then murder them so as to collect compensation from mining companies. Hundreds of thousands of Rohingya, a Muslim ethnic group, are confined to governmental camps in Myanmar. Those who manage to leave find themselves abandoned at sea, held for ransom, often unable to find a country that will accept them as refugees. When 3,000 do make it to Malaysia, they find themselves "lost in time"—"our lives are just waiting," says one (quoted in Buckley and Ramzy 2015, A1). Waiting also afflicts the thousands of refugees Australia holds in off-shore island detention centers—as does sexual abuse, ill health, and pervasive despair. Onshore, homeless "gypsy kids" camp illegally near the resort town of Byron Bay, dodging police and hoping to avoid fines for public drinking.

In the Philippines "informal settlers" make up a quarter of Manila's population, with thousands of them living and sleeping among the dead in Manila's North Cemetery; as part of a beautification plan ahead of a regional forum, officials round up and detain the homeless by the hundreds. In post-Soviet, free-market Russia, "the *bomzh*—a homeless person in dirty clothes, begging in the metro underpasses, at churches, lying on park benches or scavenging near train stations—has become omnipresent in Russian cities and towns" (Stephenson 2006, 113). Two hundred thousand civilians flee a Pakistani military campaign in North Waziristan; tens of thousands of Afghans are forced out of Pakistan a year later after a terrorist attack. Israel expels thousands of Sudanese and Eritrean migrants. By 2014, Lebanon has taken in over one million registered Syrian war refugees. A ship filled with five hundred migrants from Gaza sinks off the coast of Malta, after being rammed by another human trafficker's boat. Hundreds of thousands flee the economic collapse in Venezuela, some of them aboard smugglers' boats bound for Curaçao.

Meanwhile, in the United States, migrant farmworkers continue to face family disruption, limited educational opportunities, and deportation (Holmes 2013). Graduate students, part-time instructors, and non-tenure-track instructors, some of them so poor they receive food stamps, now make up three quarters of college faculty The newly homeless and unemployed drift from city to city, sleeping in flood drains beneath the streets of Las Vegas or squatting in the countless Las Vegas houses lost to foreclosure. Others sleep in New York City's Penn Station or become semipermanent residents of cheap mid-American motels (Dum 2016). US national parks fill not with recreational campers but with the down-and-out and the displaced—"Tensions Soar as Drifters Call National Parks Home," headlines the *New York Times* (Healy 2016: A9)—and retirement-age "workcampers" travel in mobile homes and old campers from seasonal job to seasonal job, looking to make late-life money. Amidst all of them drift the shell-shocked, sometimes suicidal veterans of the wars in Iraq and Afghanistan,

Unsurprisingly, then, Zygmunt Bauman (2002, 343) described refugees, even fifteen years ago, as "perhaps the most rapidly swelling of all the categories of world population," and Saunders (2010, 1, 21) more recently estimated current worldwide rural-to-urban migration as involving "two or three billion humans, perhaps a third of the world's population," with China alone already producing some "150 to 200 million . . . peasants 'floating' between village and city." The United Nations in turn estimates that some sixty million people, the majority of them children, have now been made refugees by war and other upheavals; in this context it warns of a "lost generation" of children deprived of schooling. With ongoing global warming, other reports suggest, those cast adrift will only increase in number (Chan 2015; Sengupta 2016).

FOUR DIALECTICS OF DRIFT

As suggested by this brief tour of the contemporary world, being cast adrift is no simple matter; it invokes a tangle of switchbacks and uncertainties, a sort of sideways skittering across the surfaces of social life. My attempts to make sense of drift, and to explore its underlying dynamics, have followed a similar course; appropriately enough, they've unfolded as a series of mistakes, hesitations, and reconsiderations, leading me down one wrong road and then another. Through all this intellectual wandering, my sense of drift has taken shape not in a straightforward manner but in terms of contradictions, or perhaps more accurately, dialectics. Time and again, I've discovered in drift dynamics that work against themselves, that run on tension and irony, and that undermine any effort to overcome their essential confusion. The dialectical pairings that follow, then, might be thought of as ways of thinking about a contemporary world adrift, and as an orientation—or disorientation—to the remainder of the book.

Drift Then and Again

In some ways the drift this book explores and theorizes is a distinctly contemporary phenomenon. Pervasive dislocation constitutes a new and immediate problem of astounding magnitude—one brought on by the growing inequities of globalized capital; the collapse of housing and financial markets; population shifts to urban areas; land and water crises associated with global warming; and upheavals in the Middle East, North Africa, North and South America, and elsewhere. In this sense drift is the consequence and condition of late modernity, the price to be paid for the predations of neoliberal social policy, global social inequality, and high-speed social change. "The vertigo of late modernity," Jock Young (2007) calls it—the fear of falling, the dizziness of endless cultural offerings, the sense that the solid foundations of work and community are melting into air. And carrying all this along? The literal dis-location of millions, the spatial disruption of social life, the placeless refugee camps, the migrants always on the move away from one crisis and toward the next.

And yet some scholars concerned with the uncertain dynamics of contemporary social life argue that this widespread dislocation is in fact not
a recent aberration spun off from the conventional world of durable certainty. Instead, they argue, it was the period of twentieth-century Fordism—with its regulatory controls, relative stability, and social welfare
state—that constituted the exception within the long and chaotic history
of modern capitalist development (Neilson and Rossiter 2008; Fantone
2007). From this perspective, itinerant labor, unstable career opportunity, and spatial dislocation are not simply dimensions of "late capitalism" or "liquid modernity" (Bauman 2000); likewise, a vertiginous sense
of disorientation is not only symptomatic of the late modern condition
(J. Young 2007). Rather, they are a return to the sort of predatory uncertainty that has long defined capitalism and that was interrupted, briefly
and partially, by the decades of Fordism in the United States and Europe.

Widening this view, it might be argued that modernity itself, with its
corporate nation-states and perpetual war machines, has produced and
continues to produce profound and ongoing dislocation—and with it an
endless stream of migrants, refugees, and lost souls—as much as it has
produced bureaucratic stability, rationalized labor, and regimes of political power. Certainly, if we look past the masking ideologies of social
stability and social progress, there is evidence for all of this—from the
aggressive dislocations of early industrial capitalism to the lost generation of World War I, from Soviet collectivized farms to Nazi death trains,
from Depression-era drifters in the United States and displaced persons'
camps in post–World War II Europe to homeless vets from Vietnam and
Iraq. Add to this the moral and intellectual decentering brought about by
modernity, and it seems that theorizing drift takes on even greater
urgency, as a way of understanding both where we may be heading and
where we've been.

In this light it's worth noting that when C. Wright Mills began to
develop his metaphor of the trap a half century ago, the trap had already
begun to take on an atmosphere of drift. "In what period have so many
men been so totally exposed at so fast a pace to such earthquakes of
change?" asked Mills (1959, 4). "The very shaping of history now out-
paces the ability of men to orient themselves in accordance with cher-
ished values. And which values? Even when they do not panic, men
often sense that older ways of feeling and thinking have collapsed and
that newer beginnings are ambiguous to the point of moral stasis. . . . Is
it any wonder that they come to be possessed by a sense of the trap?"
Here, at the very historical and geographic apex of Fordist stability,

Mills's sociological seismograph was picking up "earthquakes of change" and echoes of profound moral uncertainty. Likewise, as I will discuss in chapter 2, Gresham Sykes and David Matza ([1957] 2003) began to sense during this same Fordist period that the seemingly stable social order carried within itself the everyday seeds of its own illegitimacy—seeds that could spawn drift and sprout into crime and delinquency. If we understand drift to embody both spatial and normative disorientation, then in normative terms, at least, even Fordism provided at best only a flawed stability, hiding underneath its unifying myths deep currents of uncertainty and unrest. Mills's clangingly gendered language offers another hint as well: however ambiguous and contradictory was the normative order for "men," the trap of uncertainty was worse for women, ethnic minorities, and others excluded from most forms of sanctioned stability.

Thinking in this way about drift as both a historical and a contemporary phenomenon, I've come to reconsider the very dynamics of social order and social disorder, and I've come to realize something else: drift and dislocation constitute a kind of secret history (Marcus 1989) underlying some of North America's most distinctive and evocative cultural forms. For a time, cowboys, trappers, and Native Americans battled over the American frontier, but they shared something, too: a dedication to nomadic living in often violent opposition to settlers of all sorts. "An undertold story in American history," Richard Grant (2003, 126) calls it—this panoply of cowboys, hunters, trappers, and runaways who "went native" by embracing the nomadic ways of Native Americans, and often Native American communities themselves. The historian John Mack Faragher argues that, "the Americans and Indians who lived in these backwoods hunting communities shared a set of general social values," including geographic mobility and "personal freedom and independence"—not to mention a strong dislike for settlers (quoted in Grant 2003, 124). When the residues of this life found their way into music, distinctively American musical forms like country and country blues took shape with the likes of Jimmie Rodgers—the Traveling Brakeman, who sang of leaving, loss, and life a thousand miles from home—and Hank Williams and His Drifting Cowboys. And speaking of distinctively American musical forms: when the Mississippi Delta blues migrated with African Americans up Highway 61 to Chicago, it exploded into an electrified and electrifying sound that would, among other things, lay the sonic foundation for rock and roll. Then there's Route 66, flowing west with displaced Okies and the ghost of Tom

Joad, following the lonesome soundtrack laid down by Woody Guthrie; the Beats, rolling high and lonesome back and forth across the continent; the Hell's Angels, the Comanche nomads of post–World War II America; American film noir, which emerged awash in shadowy currents of moral ambiguity and a vertiginous sense of fate. And all this is not to mention the hobos, an enduring subculture and cultural exemplar of American drift, if ever there was one, and a subculture that will appear, disappear, and reappear throughout this book.

This list offers a couple of clues for thinking about drift as both historical thread and contemporary phenomenon. The first is the way in which drift accelerates as part of one crisis or another. The unfolding conquest of the American frontier, the cataclysms of the American Civil War and the Great Depression, the desperation and disorientation spawned in Europe during and after World War II, the economic and ecological calamities of the present day—such historical moments mix moral and spatial upheavals into earthquakes of change that leave millions refugees from their own past and present. In this sense drift constitutes the consequence, the collateral damage, of historical crisis—but drift also constitutes the lived experience of such crisis, the manner in which people suffer from it but also suffuse it with their own meanings and motivations. And here then is the second clue: in the low moans of the American blues and the lonesome yodels of Jimmie Rodgers, in the dark beauty of film noir and the hardscrabble literature of the Great Depression, we can catch the ways in which drift forces open new ways of thinking and being and forms a fluid countercurrent to the crisis that produces it.

Drift as Dependency and Autonomy

Attending to the music, literature, and cinema of drift—or for that matter simply listening to the accounts of those who wander—two contradictory portraits of drift and drifters emerge. In the first, drifters have forfeited, or been forced to forfeit, the most basic elements of human agency: control of their own bodies, control of the times and spaces they occupy, control even of their own decisions and desires. Cut loose from stabilities of place or community, their victimization surpasses even that of others who suffer discrimination or disempowerment; they are not only dependent on the wills of others but made to be dependent time and again, to abandon even the certainty of their own sad circumstances as they drift from situation to situation. "Looking back at it, it seems to me that I was blown here and there like a dead leaf whipped about by the autumn winds till at last it finds lodgment in some cozy fence corner," remembered the old hobo and road thief Jack Black ([1926] 2000, 17) in his book *You Can't Win*. And indeed Black and other wanderers couldn't win; they could only lose and then move on from one fence corner or the next to lose once more. In the equation between the individual and society, drifters are in this sense among those individuals most overwhelmed by, and beholden to, the social order of which they are nominally a part; when they survive at all, they survive at the whim of strangers—and lacking stable community or spatial foundation, drifters will assuredly meet only strangers. "Wandering," said the sociologist Georg Simmel ([1908] 1971, 143), could be "considered as a state of detachment from every given point in space." We might say that wanderers are likewise detached from, and serially dependent on, every given social arrangement.

Yet this same detachment can be read in a different way: as radical self-determination, with drifters less victims of the social order than escapees from it. Here drifting becomes an ongoing exercise in autonomy; torn loose from the everyday structures and strictures of a sedentary existence, drifters take charge of their lives in ways that no settled homeowner or successful community stalwart can understand—or endure. "There's nothing nobler than to put up with a few inconveniences like snakes and dust for the sake of absolute freedom," said Jack Kerouac ([1960] 1970, 173) in his mid-twentieth-century ruminations on "the vanishing American hobo"—and for drifters, endured "inconveniences" can also include physical and sexual assault, economic exploitation, and endless exile. Kerouac was himself a sort of cultural hinge, his train hopping and hoboing during the 1940s and 1950s connecting those allegedly vanishing hobos to the Beats, who would soon enough take up the hobo habit of transcontinental wandering. For those hobos and Beats, and for other drifters before and after, their hard-earned and sometimes dangerous status as serial outsiders was understood to bring with it critical insight cut with existential independence. "Where are all these freedoms they talk about?" asks the El Paso Kid, one of the old hobos that Bill Daniel (2008, 91; 2005) came to know while hopping freight trains a couple of decades ago. "'I don't see 'em. You start criticizing and suddenly they wave the flag in your face. You're supposed to shut up. My history goes way back, being a misfit, an outcast, and outsider. 15 years old I jumped my first freight train." Robert, another of the hobos that Daniel (2008, 99; 2005) met, is even more explicit:

They want you to work 35 years then pay a price for it and then you only got 10 more years to live. That's cold the way things is set up, man, I don't even believe in this here. They say this country is based on hard work and integrity and worshipping God. That's a lie. It's built on murder, man. Mayhem, slavery, oppression, lies, stealin' and killin'. That's what it's based on. And you can't change it after it started. Just stay away from it. Try to get away from it. Be independent of it. Cause if you try to deal in it, you become part of it. Stay away from it, you diminish it by one. By one.

Listening to the El Paso Kid and Robert, the equation by which the social order overwhelms hapless drifters is reversed; instead, drifters' gritty escapes from the social order are seen to position them above and beyond it, and to underwrite a resolutely outsider perspective on it.

The question then becomes, to whom is drift a danger? From the first view, drift produces profound and ongoing danger for drifters themselves, as they are serially stripped of their own autonomy, denied their standing in the social order, and exposed to all manner of exploitation. Adrift, they are without control over themselves or their situations, left always vulnerable to the emerging crises of their lives. But from the second view, drift seems mostly a danger to the social order, and to those individuals and institutions invested in the stability of current arrangements—with drifters embodying in their attitudes and in their ongoing movement a bit too *much* autonomy for the liking of the sedentary and their guardians. Of course this tension plays out differently among different groups of drifters—a young woman fleeing a war zone may escape it but in so doing engage with a very different sort of drifting vulnerability than does a well-practiced male wanderer traversing a familiar route—and much of this book attempts to explore these differences. Yet this tension regularly remains unresolved as well, animating drift, responses to it, and perceptions of it. As later chapters will show, for example, legal and political authorities sometimes aim to assist drifters on the grounds that they have been victimized by their uncertain circumstances; more often, and even at the same time, the authorities aim to control drifters and to contain the threat they pose to social stability and orderly social change.

Part of what determines whether drifters are understood as dependent victims or autonomous escapees, whether they are seen as unfortunate folk much like everyone else or outsider threats to social order, is the issue of planning. At times this is a matter of origins and intent: Did the Syrian immigrant now confined to a Greek refugee camp plan this as part of a strategy to enter the European Union, or did she simply find herself desperate to escape her homeland for any new opportunity? Did the teenager living on the street plan to run away from home, or was she thrown out and thrown away by abusive parents? Of course sociologists would remind us that such questions are seldom so simple. Personal plans are made or left unmade in social situations, in interactions with others who share those situations, and as part of longer trajectories of personal life and social history. And it is just this complexity that takes us beyond the origins of drift to the day-to-day lives of those adrift.

Here I'll admit to one of my own assumptions. Before I began hanging out with drifters, and listening to and reading their accounts, I assumed that such folks were either unable or unwilling to engage in the intentionality of planning—that in fact their unplanned existence defined the nature of drift itself. The fear-swept war refugee and the proudly independent wanderer might lead vastly different lives, I thought, but they surely shared one trait: an absence of planning, whether forced or voluntary. Now, this *can* be the case—as later chapters will show, drift is sometimes embraced as a sort of unplanned politics of liberation—but what I discovered among most drifters was something significantly different. Drifters make plans all the time—but what distinguishes their planning is the unpredictable and often brief trajectory from plan to execution to revised plan. Serially disempowered, susceptible to every new contingency, drifters generally have little time between setting a course and engaging in course corrections. Pick whatever metaphor you like—the sailor constantly tacking and retacking into a strong wind, the surfer continually resetting her course across the face of a monstrous wave—but this is the life of the drifter, dependent on larger forces but intentional in response to them. If "the best laid schemes of mice and men oft go astray," as Robert Burns wrote, then the best-laid schemes of drifters almost *always* go astray—but they are schemes nonetheless, to be recalibrated and reinvented along the way. In chapter 6, a train hopper will be heard to point out, "You've got a general direction, but it doesn't have much glue on it. The plan has equal weight to every new direction that comes along." Echoing the El Paso Kid, Douglas Harper (1982, 153) likewise argues, "The tramp takes none but his own rules seriously and even those are negotiable. . . . The tramp remains free of and unrepentant to a society which he perceives as a set of pressures to conform, to take orders, and to be unadventuresome." Harper in this way links the fluid negotiability of drifters' rules and plans with their status outside conventional society, and if we reverse this link, we can think about yet another sort of dialectical question: perhaps long-term planning is mostly the privilege and the curse of those with settled lives, stable arrangements, and bureaucratic affiliations; and perhaps for such people—which would of course include city planners, police officials, and economic investors—the necessary ephemerality of drifters' planning seems only haphazard, mindless, and dangerously unpredictable.

Drift Apart, Drift Together

Much of the mythology surrounding drift has to do with "the drifter"— the lone wanderer, isolated from others, moving episodically through one community or another but never fully part of any. You catch a bit of this in the accounts of hobos like the El Paso Kid and Robert. You see it in the title of Jack Kerouac's 1960 book *Lonesome Traveler,* and in his description there of the hobo as being "born of pride, having nothing to do with a community but with himself and other hobos and maybe a dog" (176). You notice it time and again in Jack London's (1907) now century-old recollections of his own tramping days, and his self-promotion as a lone "tramp-royal" able to best not only homeowners and police but all other tramps (see Lennon 2014). And you certainly watch it take shape in the iconography of the free-riding American cowboy and in Hollywood films like *High Plains Drifter* (Eastwood 1973), with the drifter who is its lead character lacking even a name by which others might come to know him.

There's more than a little truth to all this; as already seen, some drifters are in fact willing escapees from the confines of conventional community—lonesome travelers indeed—and even those who aren't find that drifting presents some serious impediments to sociality. The spatial instability and ongoing contingency of drift mean that people come and go, wander off, find themselves pulled away by border guards or cops or hunger. The social calculus of such a world can be maddeningly imprecise— a favor may not be returned or a social debt not repaid if the recipient is no longer around to do so—and so in anticipation of this failure, the sorts of mutual obligations that bind many groups and communities may not emerge. The immediacy of plans and their implementation often creates what seems to nondrifters to be only the barest shell of shared enterprise, all but certain to dissolve sooner than later. If we are curious about the dynamics of subcultures, or the limits of community affiliation—or for that matter the most fundamental sociological question of how individuals and groups relate—then drifters in their fluid isolation provide a distinctive sort of test case (see Goldsmith and Brewer 2015).

As before, though, the answer to the sociological question of the drifter seems more dialectical than direct; drifters embody not so much the mythic lone individual as they do a different sort of dynamic linking individual and group. In my experience, drifters do in fact come together but mostly in occasional communities—or perhaps more to the point, communities of occasion. Like drifters themselves, these communities come and go; they are social groups but decidedly unstable ones, a volatile mix of on-the-fly individuals who share spaces and agendas that can evaporate on the spot—or evaporate as the spot is itself abandoned owing to some emerging contingency. In such communities the social calculus tilts toward the individual, even toward the value of individual autonomy and isolation, but with mutual support and assistance as needed. The emotional calculus is distinctive as well, reflecting what I've come to call *intensities of ephemeral association*. After perhaps a few moments of defensive posturing—an understandable strategy among those new to each other and lacking stable markers of social identity— members of these groups seem to accelerate toward acute experiences of social bonding. The long process by which the more sedentary might establish trust and shape other mutual emotions is necessarily compacted; contingencies of time and place, uncertainties as to durability and duration, preclude leisurely negotiations.

Yet even amidst these intensely shared experiences, and as befits the nature of drift and drifters, the free-floating individual remains. Among the hallmarks of tramp life, Douglas Harper (1982, 98, 100–101) found, was a commitment to "retain a constant guard over establishing anything but immediate, uncommitted yet not unserious relationships with others. . . . One lived in the moment; one did not defer gratification; one did not base . . . happiness and satisfaction on the accomplishing of abstract goals." Harper concluded that "this produced both an intensity and a sense of relaxation." Even after many months out hoboing, Ted Conover (1984, 178) likewise found "devastating" the speed with which his relationships with other hobos fell apart, and he concluded that, even when they are together, hobos remained more "partners" than friends. These dynamics also account for a phenomenon that both Harper and Conover experienced, and that I've experienced and heard tales of countless times among drifters: the missing goodbye. A night of hardcore partying, a week of shared survival, a fortnight together in a refugee camp, a month of collective labor . . . and suddenly someone's gone, without explanation or farewell or apology, to be seen again, or not, sometime down the road. Ephemerality shadows intensity in the lives of drifters, and the equation of individual and community is recalibrated once again.

Early on, I found this all odd, if not a bit off-putting, but then I began to think: by what standards do we measure the social strength or moral validity of community? Must a community be durable to be viable? Or could it be that durability and intensity form the twin poles of community—and more than that, that they form dialectical poles, such that an increase in one tends to decrease the other? Theater performers on tour, new-in-town street musicians, itinerant harvest workers, day laborers, temporary residents of cheap motels (Ferrell 2001; Dum 2016)—all seem particularly adept at making connections with strangers as needed, finding the joy in each other's occasional company, holing up in hotel rooms or alleyways to hit it as hard as they can, and then being on their way. "Fifteen minutes with you, oh, I wouldn't say no," sang the Smiths (Morrissey and Marr 1984)—and how many fifteen-minute moments have I shared with drifters over the past few years, on buses and in bus stations, in and around rail yards, in back-alleys, and back up under shade trees in the summer heat, many of these moments fiercely pleasurable or deeply informative, and all of them over soon enough? More to the point, how many such moments are shared among drifters of all sorts each day? In this sense the world of drift and drifters begins to seem like some loosely shifting social web, the scattered beads for a necklace that never quite gets strung, a world defined neither by isolated individuals nor by stable social groupings but by some amorphous space in between. As later chapters will show, this is of no small consequence; when political authorities or scholarly researchers mistakenly assume that their own models of sedentary stability must surely apply to drifters, problems ensue.

Later chapters will suggest something else as well: that the intense ephemerality of drifters' communities and the fluid flexibility of their planning might offer some important lessons for surviving a contemporary world that is itself increasingly adrift. Forms of human organization and collective behavior flourish or fade in particular historical circumstances; perhaps those forms developed by drifters can provide some hope for progressive change, or at least some tentative models for mutual survival, in the contemporary historical moment of part-time work, pervasive spatial dislocation, and social inequality. The forms of affiliation and intentionality favored by drifters might even provide a corrective of sorts to big data's digital police state and to a social world suffused with surveillance, where the perpetual knowability and predictability of place and movement are now the primary dangers. Contemporary train hoppers sometimes produce their own little pamphlets and zines, and one of them is titled *Let's Get Lost.* Maybe we should, if only we can. In any case, given the dynamics of the contemporary world, the prevalence of drift doesn't seem to be in question. The only question is *how* we'll drift, and whether we'll drift apart or drift together.

Drift as Hope and Despair

All of this suggests a final, deep-running dialectic regarding drift: its powerful interplay of hope and despair.

For many the despair is undeniable. Especially when the dislocations of drift are enforced by economic ruin or political conflict, the consequences—a sense of abandoned stability and mounting uncertainty, a fear that the future may hold little but hollow hope, a wariness of falling into one downward danger or another—coalesce into a profound sense of living lost in the world. Caught up in such situations, trapped in a refugee camp or a human smuggler's safe house or a factory full of immigrant workers, the sense of "waiting for nothing" echoes from the 1930s and into the present. For those who would cherish a little home and a stable life, then, a drudgerous slog through failure and fear; and for those dislocated from family and community, a tragic experience of emotional alienation. One of the migrant workers interviewed by Lee and Pratt (2011, 225, 232), a migrant employed as a janitor in the United States, who sent money to the children she left behind with her mother in Mexico, makes this clear from the first: "I want to start by saying that I am here, but I did not want to come here. Do you know of any mother who wants to leave their children? I could not find a job in Mexico and I could not afford to send my children to school. Or buy food for my family. My mother was getting weaker. Every day we ate so little—just beans—and that is when I knew I had to cross." And on the occasions when she is able get away from her paying job in the United States for a return visit to Mexico, the family is not restored; instead, the tragedy only deepens. "I feel panic," she says. "I want to be with them in Mexico, but I cannot help them while I am with them." For her and millions of others adrift, spatial and normative dislocation combine to deliver a double blow to one's sense of self; the dispersed geography of drift intertwines with its emotional and cultural disruptions to shape a distinctly painful sort of dislocated isolation. This is drift suffused not with possibility and adventure but with layer upon layer of loss and sorrow.

Countless such individual and family tragedies circulate in a contemporary world awash in migrants, refugees, homeless and landless populations, and casual workers. As subsequent chapters will document, contemporary drift and its accompanying despair are at the same time tragedies, whose origins extend past the individual and the family and into global substrata of power, domination, and inequality. The damaging potency of these forces lies in their complexity; as with drift itself, they can best be understood in terms of irony and contradiction. The first of these contradictions centers on the economic circumstances of the contemporary global world. The dramatic accumulation of power and profit at the very top of this global economy means that, for more and more people below this top tier, economic insecurity and eventual economic ruin await—and with this ruin, propulsion into lives of dislocation, instability, and despair. In this sense we can outline a simple and perhaps predictable equation, and one that does indeed often apply: economic inequality and economic failure spawn drift. Yet as the following chapters will show, the deformities of the contemporary global economy are such that the opposite is true as well: what now passes for economic growth and economic success also promote drift. In fact, such "successes" are often built on it. Local models of urban revitalization, national models of economic recovery, international models of globalized development— all cast millions of people adrift as surely as economic failure and stagnation. A damnable system indeed: win or lose, the majority of its inhabitants gain mostly spatial and cultural insecurity.

A second underlying contradiction is of particular interest to a criminologist like myself; in fact, criminologists have over the years documented its maddening dynamics in a variety of historical circumstances (Becker 1963; Young 1971). This is the contradiction of law and law enforcement. On the one hand, as subsequent chapters will highlight, the law and its enforcers in Western societies have for centuries criminalized the activities and identities of drifters and vagabonds, constructing them as a social danger and undertaking to halt their alleged disruptions of the social. This is as much the case, and perhaps more the case, today; from the neighborhoods of small cities to the long fronts of international borders, legal and political authorities deploy new statutes and new enforcement strategies in aggressive attempts to halt unregulated movement and transitory occupation. Save for its technological specificities, Jack Kerouac's 1960 consideration of the legal circumstances behind the "vanishing American hobo" could as well be written in 1880, or 2018:

> They [sheriffs] pick on the first human being they see walking. . . . They just don't know what to do with themselves . . . except pick on anything that moves in the night and in the daytime on anything that seems to be moving independently of gasoline, power, Army or police. I myself was a hobo but I had to give it up around 1956 because of increasing television stories about the abominableness of strangers with packs passing through by themselves independently. . . . There ain't a sheriff or fire warden in any of the new fifty states who will let you cook a little meal over some burning sticks in the tule brake or the hidden valley or anyplace any more because he has nothing to do but pick on what he sees out there in the landscape moving independently of the gasoline power army police station. (180–82)

On the other hand, these same sheriffs and fire wardens and border guards—and these same statutes and enforcement strategies—serve to contradict themselves quite thoroughly; as with contemporary economic forces, their apparent successes in policing drifters only cast more and more people adrift. Destabilizing communities by policing them, enforcing spatial and social exclusion along with the law, pushing people from one newly off-limits location to another, the law and its enforcers perpetuate the current generation of vagrants and vagabonds and all but ensure the next one.

Economically and legally, drift's despair doubles down. Achingly personal, existential even in its dislocation of people from their past and future, it is also evidence and consequence of the worst sorts of contemporary social arrangements. If for many people around the world contemporary drift constitutes a hard road without resting place or discernable destination, it's a road built on injustice and inequality and laid out along the lines of the contemporary global crisis.

And yet amidst these desperate circumstances, and as part of them, drift produces distinct sorts of hope, insight, and possibility. To begin with, drift is often defined as precarious and problematic in contrast with what we imagine to be its opposite: satisfying stability of occupation and career, enduring membership in institutional and community life, and long-term acquisition of status and comfort. For more and more people, of course, such stabilities have long since disappeared as viable solutions to a life adrift. But perhaps more to the point, such stabilities continue to mean for many others not satisfaction but the accumulating degradations of demeaning labor, the slow-death entrapment of bureaucratic identity, and the stultifications of traditional family and gender roles. Seen in this way, social structures that inhibit a drifting existence can seem more like anchors around one's ankles than open avenues toward steady self-realization. Instead of drift denoting despair and social stability signaling the corrective to this despair, then, it may be that contemporary forms of drift and stability *both* spawn despair—but that the despair of drift at least holds out the possibility of changing circumstances. When the solidity of social arrangements is productive and affirming, uncertainty looms as a threat, a bad gamble against the guarantees of day-to-day life. When those arrangements are constraining, or increasingly unworkable, uncertainty can begin to take on the hue of hope.

To consider such matters is of course not to think only about drift and drifters but to consider the nature of contemporary society itself, and beyond that to invoke the whole intellectual history of sociology and sociological criminology. Is a stable capitalist work life a sign of occupational success or, as Karl Marx would have it, more often a marker of ongoing alienation and dehumanization? Is membership in a variety of bureaucratic organizations an essential aspect of community integration or, as for Weber, more a multiplying captivity played out in a series of iron cages? As with Merton, Sykes and Matza, and others, does deviance constitute a drifting away from the social order, or is it more an understandable response to its inherent contradictions? The remainder of the book will try to address such questions, with one theme recurring: the distance that drift puts between the drifter and the social order is often a place of deprivation and despair but also a hard-earned space for critique and imagination.

In a contemporary world suffused with consumerism and its overwhelming ecological consequences—towering landfills, ocean islands of discarded plastic, rampant deforestation, global environmental degradation—drift offers yet another hue of hope (Ferrell 2006). For centuries now, drifters of all sorts have eschewed material possessions and material comfort, learning to make do on less and to practice various forms of radical self-reliance. Again, the dynamic is dialectical: this antimaterialism has emerged as a consequence of and necessity for ongoing, uncertain mobility but also as a cultural orientation underlying and promoting such mobility. The roguish, vagabonding pícaro of sixteenth- and seventeenth-century Spain, Cresswell (2011, 243) writes, had "no faith in material possessions and consider[ed] freedom and happiness to be the product of lack of roots and attachment." Concluding his account of traveling with tramps and hobos in the 1970s and 1980s, Harper (1982, 155) likewise recalls a time that he and Carl, a tramp with whom he was train hopping, spotted a fancy travel trailer being pulled behind a car:

> Carl spoke for all tramps when he said: "Would you like to live like that? They're afraid to sleep on the ground; they'd turn up their noses at the perfectly good food we've been eating—they live for those things and they can't live without them." This kind of independence means both the ability to live with few possessions and it means defining oneself apart from the material things people surround themselves with. . . . It may be easy to idealize or overemphasize this quality of life. But on the other hand tramps exist without most of the props we put between ourselves and our environments, and they laugh at the ends we go to maintain them. I found extremely disconcerting the realization that most of my plans and accommodations were socially constructed and could be easily left behind, and I admired the way the tramps live more directly, more immediately, and with fewer rationalizations.

The material possessions, the "props we put between ourselves and our environments," are of course today far more numerous—and from a drifter's view, far more needlessly consumed—than they were decades or centuries ago. Because of this, the need for a sociological imagination—for an understanding of how consumerist needs and wants are "socially constructed," and might be deconstructed—is ever-more critical as well. In a world pervaded by advertised images and seductive "consumption spaces," such an imagination can be hard to come by—unless, by choice or necessity, one drifts away from those seductions and learns instead the allure of less. Because of this, drifters' long-standing antimaterialist ethos may offer some contemporary environmental understandings and might even harbinger forms of floating sustainability by which the planet can yet be salvaged.

As suggested already, it seems that drift and drifters also put forth the broader possibility for alternative forms of community and epistemology. Throughout the book, this possibility will be explored: the notion that drift itself can constitute a collective common ground, and on this ground can emerge new ways of knowing the world. In the same way that drift is both a historical and contemporary phenomenon, so are its politics; as I'll show in the following chapters, drift has more than once been embraced as a fragile but resilient form of human community, deployed as a strategy for flowing around and beyond existing authority, and celebrated as a process of ongoing spatial enlightenment. Now, as millions drift though a contemporary world of growing social and spatial uncertainty, these politics have come again. Facing the inevitability of dislocation, some head off on their own; others find ways to recalibrate the need to control and be controlled, to retune their social expectations to shifting circumstances. Left with little that endures, they manage to make situational magic out of structural malaise and so to reimagine the very nature of social order and social change. For them, drift takes shape, not as a failure of determination, but as a determination to fail, a determination to embrace a form of "assertive desertion" (Carlsson 2002) from the built-in inequities of social stability. Consequence of the contemporary crisis, drift can at the same time constitute resistance and alternative to it.

Almost a century ago, the sociologist Robert Park (1928, 882, 887–88) published an essay on migration and marginality. In it, he quoted Carl Bucher's claim that, "every advance in culture commences, so to speak, with a new period of wandering."' Park explained,

> Migration as a social phenomenon . . . may be envisaged in its subjective aspects as manifested in the changed type of personality which it produces. . . . Energies that were formerly controlled by custom and tradition are released. The individual is free for new adventures, but he is more or less without direction and control. . . . The emancipated individual invariably becomes in a certain sense and to a certain degree a cosmopolitan. He learns to look upon the world in which he was born and bred with something of the detachment of the stranger. He acquires, in short, an intellectual bias.

More recently, the philosopher Costica Bradatan (2014, SR12) made a similar argument regarding "the wisdom of the exile." Compensating for the "existential earthquake" that comes with exile, Bradatan argued, is "the greatest of philosophical gifts"—"the insight that the world does not simply exist, but it is something you can dismantle and piece together again, something you can play with, construct, reconstruct and deconstruct. As an exile you learn that the world is a story that can be told in many different ways." Together, Park and Bradatan suggest a radical epistemology of drift, and one that is radically sociological as well—a comparative epistemology by which the drifter, on the move between social settings, comes to see the construction of social convention and to see past it as well. Dislocation and disruption in this way spawn not only desperation but alternative ways of understanding the world, and they produce a kind of free-floating liberation through which new worlds can be imagined and undertaken. In the following chapters I'll explore this dynamic, and I'll propose that this dynamic is both an appropriate subject matter for social inquiry and a way of revitalizing social inquiry itself.

2

Drift Contexts

The previous chapter closed with American sociologist Robert Park's (1928) provocative theoretical suggestion, offered almost a century ago, that migration serves to liberate those involved in it from the conventions of custom, and in so doing sparks a cosmopolitan "intellectual bias" toward new ideas and interpretations. As part of this emerging epistemology, Park argued, the migrant begins to see the world from which she came with "something of the detachment of the stranger"— and arriving as a newcomer in a new world as well, the migrant acquires a double estrangement from the taken-for-granted security of the familiar, past and present. In making this argument Park drew on the German sociologist Georg Simmel and his 1908 essay "The Stranger." In this essay Simmel ([1908] 1971, 143, 145–46) described the sort of person who relocates to a new community but never fully becomes a part of it—the "potential wanderer" who "has not quite got over the freedom of coming and going." The stranger's latent mobility, Simmel argued, creates a "synthesis of nearness and remoteness" within the new community and produces for the stranger a subversive sort of perceptual freedom; with the stranger's actions "not confined by custom, piety or precedent," he is able to assess his new situation in a more general and, in Simmel's terms, "objective" manner.

A SOCIOLOGY OF DRIFT

Situated both inside and outside the social order, the stranger, the migrant, and the drifter are perceptually oriented in a way that does indeed seem to produce what Simmel ([1908] 1971, 146) called "many dangerous possibilities." As he and Park were beginning to see, the transitory outsider inhabits a world of potent cultural marginality. Even when fixed for a time in one locale, the drifter is never fully situated; unlike the lifelong member of the community, the drifter remembers a previous life and can't help but anticipate another. Because of this, the discomfort is mutual; the longtime community member sees in the drifter a lack of socialization and social commitment, and the drifter sees in her present circumstances not an ideal or innately superior social order but only one situation among many. The drifter in this way occupies a position fraught with pain and possibility; able to contextualize and compare what others take for granted, unable to feel fully at home, the drifter does indeed offer up "many dangerous possibilities" to those who would prefer that the present social order remain unexamined and its inequities unexposed. Such defenders of the social order often refer to an influx of migrants or drifters as an "invasion," backing up this pejorative characterization by citing the number of recent arrivals or the increase in social service recipients. The insights of Park and Simmel suggest that in fact the real issue, the real invasion if you will, is more a matter of epistemology and perception than of human bodies; to the extent that new arrivals are "not confined by custom, piety or precedent," they bring with them a distinct sort of cultural distance and cultural disruption.

Other sociologists have noticed this same distance and disruption but have come at it from different directions. Emile Durkheim's ([1893] 1984) classic sociological concept of "anomie" denotes a breakdown of social order, a rupture in moral regulation, in such a way that members of society are left in a state of ill-defined identity and normless uncertainty. In times of economic disruption or social conflict, then, Durkheim's cultural drifter doesn't arrive from the outside but rather emerges from the inside, shaped by a society's own institutions and institutional failures. Her dislocation is not so much spatial as it is normative, a jarring disconnection from the moral stability on which she once relied, an uncertain path toward the next moral decision. Here Durkheim's notion of anomie, and Robert Merton's (1938) subsequent interpretation of it, suggests that any unraveling of social order can produce extremes of cultural estrangement and disorientation, so that people are left with what Garfinkel (1967, 45) would later call "amnesia for . . . common sense knowledge of social structures." Pushing further still to understand drift as an interior social phenomenon, Merton emphasizes that this tendency toward normative disorientation may, ironically, be embedded not only in social crisis but in the very normative structure of society itself. As part of the everyday social order, a society offers its members both culturally approved aspirations and the legitimate means to achieve them. But if the mismatch between the two is sufficiently great—if the strain of aspirations unattained and unattainable through legitimate means is sharply enough felt—then the social order carries within itself the seeds of its own failure, its own potential for producing members afflicted by desperation and moral drift. The travelogue of despair sketched in the previous chapter suggests something of this; from Syria to southern Europe, from Japan to the United States, young people today report that their deeply inculcated goals of education and career have been blocked—betrayed, actually—through no fault of their own, and so they are left to innovate, to retreat, or to wander away. Here we begin to see also a dynamic that will thread itself through subsequent discussions: the way normative drift and spatial drift can intertwine in the lives of those cut loose from social certainty, such that they remain strangers wherever they go.

Within the history of criminology and sociology, these themes of normative uncertainty, strangeness, and drift have been most fully explored by David Matza and Gresham Sykes ([1957] 2003), most famously in their article "Techniques of Neutralization: A Theory of Delinquency." On one level their model sets out to explain how would-be delinquents go about temporarily neutralizing their bonds to a shared moral order—how, that is, they employ various techniques of neutralization—with successful neutralization then leaving them free to drift toward delinquent behavior. Yet on another level theirs is more a critical theory of the normative order itself. For them, the seeming solidity and consistency of the collective moral order are illusory; in reality, this moral order is haunted by cultural contradictions, interpretive ambiguity, and situational variability. "The normative system of a society is marked by . . . *flexibility*," they contend. "It does not consist of a set of rules held to be binding under all conditions" (233–34; emphasis in original). Significantly, then, potential delinquents neutralize their bonds to an ambiguous social order by employing the same moral ambiguities already extant in social life—and, as Sykes and Matza (234) note, these ambiguities themselves constitute "cultural constructions" closer to Mills's (1940) vocabularies of motive than to isolated individual beliefs. As they explicate more fully in subsequent works (Matza and Sykes 1961; Matza 1964: 60–61; see also Velarde 1978), the social order in this way incorporates its own self-made contradictions—and so, as with Merton, the seeds of its own disorder. Like Park's migrants and Simmel's strangers, Sykes and Matza's potential delinquents notice and negate taken-for-granted cultural assumptions, developing along the way a sort of critical exteriority. But like Merton's subjects, theirs is nonetheless an interior operation in which the social order's own contradictions become the lever for drifting from it.

In developing this model, Sykes and Matza were arguing against Al Cohen's (1955) theory of subculturally grounded delinquency—contending, that is, that while some delinquency takes shape and endures within oppositional delinquent subcultures, other forms of delinquency emerge in an uncertain and episodic manner. Yet writing in mid-1950s America, at the pinnacle of America's presumed postwar, normative consensus and Fordist success, they were also arguing against the very reality of this successful and consensual order. Even *within* the Fordist period, the mechanisms of drift were present; even here, Sykes and Matza were saying, the boundaries between normal and abnormal, law and crime, were slippery and shifting. "Thou shalt not kill," undermined at every turn, exemptions endlessly taken, by patriotic war reports and the state's own death penalty, not to mention the "fantasies of violence in books, magazines, movies, and television [that] are everywhere at hand" (Matza and Sykes 1961, 717). "Thou shalt not steal," except that every commercial encounter constitutes a swindle and a con, and with this the growing realization that what the large print giveth the small print taketh away (Waits 1976). Oh, and young people, know your rights: "You have the right not to be killed—murder is a crime—unless it was done by a policeman or an aristocrat. . . . Young offenders, know your rights. You have the right to free speech, as long as you're not dumb enough to actually try it" (Strummer and Jones 1982). By Sykes and Matza's reckoning, then, drift is *inherent* in an already compromised moral order, awaiting only the neutralizing touch of the potential delinquent. The prerequisites for drifting away from the illusion of moral certainty are structurally in place: the ambiguity of dominant moral claims, the situational flexibility of allegedly absolute legal statutes, the everyday abrogation of supposedly sacred religious codes. The potential delinquent senses these contradictions and hypocrisies, draws on them—but does not invent them. Seeing the holes in the moral order, the potential delinquent only wedges them open a bit wider so as to set a course of autonomous social action, making manifest existing moral contradictions in an attempt to exit, if momentarily, existing social constraints. The moral compromises and subterranean values (Matza and Sykes 1961) that circulate through daily life in this way constitute the shifting cultural milieu from which crime, delinquency, and drift emerge.

In this sense a compromised moral order spawns drift as surely as a constipated social order spawns strain. Mixing Merton with Sykes and Matza, we can say that the moral order of contemporary society is itself anomic—not only at the level of the structural contradictions that Merton charted but within the experience of everyday moral uncertainty. Echoing Merton's analysis, Sykes and Matza ([1957] 2003, 237) speculate that, "on a priori grounds it might be assumed that these justifications for deviance [techniques of neutralization] will be more readily seized by segments of society for whom a discrepancy between common social ideals and social practice is most apparent." Or, it may be that "this habit of 'bending' the dominant normative system—if not 'breaking' it—cuts across our cruder social categories." In either case the gap between "social ideals and social practice"—that is to say, the *strain* of pronounced moral absolutes grinding against the reality of everyday moral contradictions—opens a path to delinquency and drift. Of course the path may not be taken—in the same way that for Merton the structural contradictions that spawn strain may or may not be addressed through theft or drugs, so the moral contradictions that underlie drift may or may not result in delinquency—but there can be no doubt as to its origins. The path is paved with cultural contradictions.

Like Merton, Sykes and Matza locate the potential for drift within the order of society—or, more particularly, in the tensions and contradictions that suffuse it. Consequently, to understand the drifter—the temp worker, the unemployed college graduate, the global migrant—we must first understand the prerequisites of their drift: the host of gaps and contradictions that permeate social and cultural arrangements, spawning disorientation and dislocation. When played out in a social order that offers little in the way of productive work or financial stability, a deeply inculcated cultural commitment to providing for one's family can actually propel a mother or father away from that family and toward some foreign world where money might be earned and sent back. When it emerges that a college education is more likely to produce lifelong debt than a lifelong career, young people can abandon not only formal schooling but the foundational notions of education, career, and achievement that they have been taught. As crises accumulate, those caught up in them can begin to imagine the unimaginable. Together with Park and Simmel's approach, then, the work of Merton, Sykes, and Matza produces a useful sociology of knowledge and sociology of drift. Arriving from outside the social order or emerging from inside it, the drifter is both the consequence and the carrier of cultural liminality. A stranger in a strange land, the drifter lives in between—between places past and present, between marginality and belonging, between proscribed morality and immorality, and within the spaces left open by ambiguity and contradiction. As in the previous chapter, if the sociological question is the place of the individual in the social order, then the drifter offers some distinctly odd, uncertain, and revealing answers.

By Sykes and Matza's logic, the drifter in turn offers some answers that are distinctly sociological in nature. After all, the same social order that harbors these moral contradictions also embodies a host of mechanisms operating to mask them. For some young people, the accumulated entreaties of the priest, the parent, and the teacher—and in the United States, the school police liaison—may suffice in sustaining the moral straight and narrow. For others, the pre-scripted morality of the televised police procedural or the moral drama of the athletic spectacle may, for a time, paper over emerging doubts. For still others, the busy hum of a youthful life may itself be sufficient to keep contradictions at bay. Even when moral contradictions do begin to bubble up through these layers of cultural containment, delinquency still may not occur; certainly not every young person who senses the social order's moral inadequacy turns this sensation into neutralization, drift, and delinquency. Just as for Merton the structural contradictions that spawn strain may or may not be addressed through theft or drugs or conformity, so too the moral contradictions that underlie drift may or may not result in delinquency. For Merton and for Sykes and Matza, sociological criminology preserves human agency while critically situating it at the intersection of social structure, culture, and crime.

But for Sykes and Matza, the delinquent is precisely the sort of young person who *does* see past mechanisms of cultural containment—past the moral proclamations of various authorities and the simplistic scripts proffered by popular morality tales—so as to perceive the inherent contradictions and inconsistencies underlying the moral order. Moreover, the successful delinquent then acts on these insights, invoking them as techniques of neutralization so as to engineer a temporary exit. In this sense the young delinquent is a *natural social critic and activist,* perhaps because she is not yet fully socialized into the shared illusions of moral certainty, but in any case stands sufficiently outside the taken-for-granted dualities of good and bad, law and crime, to see them as forms of cultural artifice.

That is, the delinquent operates *as a critical sociologist.*

Regarding "denial of responsibility" as a technique of neutralization—the claim that "delinquent acts are due to forces outside of the individual and beyond his control"—Sykes and Matza ([1957] 2003, 234, 238) note that "the similarity between this mode of justifying illegal behavior assumed by the delinquent and the implications of a 'sociological' frame of reference or a 'humane' jurisprudence is readily apparent." They then add in a footnote, "A number of observers have wryly noted that many delinquents seem to show a surprising awareness of sociological and psychological explanations for their behavior and are quick to point out the causal role of their poor environment." Perhaps Sykes and Matza are here being "wry" themselves. But even if so, they are also confirming the trajectory of their own analysis toward a "surprising" affinity between the delinquent's worldview and the sociologist's. The technique of neutralization that involves "denial of injury"— that is, the delinquent's sense that "his behavior does not really cause any great harm despite the fact that it runs counter to the law" (235)— likewise sounds suspiciously similar to the critical criminologist's critique of low-order criminalization, punitive drug laws, and victimless crime. As for the "condemnation of the condemners"—the delinquent's claim, that is, that those in power are often "hypocrites, deviants in disguise"; police are often "corrupt, stupid, and brutal"; and teachers and parents are "always" inclined toward favoritism and abuse—well, that's certainly not always the case, but as any good sociologist would tell you, it's the case more often than those police and teachers and parents would have us believe. And as regards the delinquent's "appeal to higher loyalties"? "The conflict between the claims of friendship and the claims of the law, or a similar dilemma," Sykes and Matza (236) remind us, "has of course long been recognized by the social scientist (and the novelist) as a common human problem."

Sykes and Matza, it turns out, have undertaken far more than a simplistic theory of moral order and deviance from it—have accomplished more even than a sophisticated and nuanced "theory of delinquency. In proposing that the delinquent mindset time and again mirrors that of the sociologist or criminologist—embodies, even, something of the sociological imagination—they have also suggested that the sociological and criminological mindset embodies something of the delinquent's. Wryly or otherwise, Sykes and Matza have aligned sociological criminology not with agents of social control *but with the drifters and the delinquents.*

Of course there are other issues as well beyond the tensions explicated by Park, Merton, Sykes and Matza, and others; to contextualize contemporary drift, it seems to me, we must construct some further analytic edifices on this sociological foundation. A first concerns the particular dynamics by which contemporary law and economy engender drift. A second attempts to account for the spatial dimensions of drift and to imagine the ways in which normative and spatial drift intertwine. A third, explicated in the following chapter, explores the experiential and collective politics of drift—on the assumption, following Merton and Sykes and Matza, that while structural contradictions may set the conditions for social action, they do not determine its course or its meaning for those engaged in it.

A POLITICAL AND SPATIAL ECONOMY OF DRIFT

As the previous chapter outlined, a plethora of contemporary social dynamics serves to cast people and populations adrift; the many tragedies of contemporary times flow beyond and across the various borders that once contained everyday life.

Within this flow, there are multiple political economies of contemporary drift, each shaped by the distinct intersections of global and local dynamics. Here I begin with one of particular salience: the degree to which, amidst the dynamics that define late capitalist economies, both failure and success engender dislocation. The links between economic failure and drift are perhaps easier to imagine and have, to some extent, already been glimpsed in the previous chapter. Over the past decade the corporate criminality of a multicountry financial crisis evicts millions from their overmortgaged homes and leaves millions more unemployed or piecing together part-time work. Ecological crises brought on by global warming, global oil, and global agribusiness push small farmers off their land, turn fishing communities into welfare/subsistence economies, and force itinerant farmworkers into ever-wider arcs in search of work. Amidst collapsing national economies and crippling civil wars, refugees—some of them already migrants from elsewhere—leave belongings behind to flee in crowded boats or on commercial airlines. With economic failure comes, often enough, the anomic disorientation and structural strain of Durkheim and Merton, accompanied by profound moral and spatial disorientation—a conspiracy of despair that precludes certainty as to home, shelter, or destination.

And yet with contemporary economic "success" arrive many of the same problems. With the withering of urban industrial production in many American and European cities, and the global exportation of production to developing countries, urban areas increasingly build their economies around service work, entertainment, tourism, and high-end consumption. Researchers like Markusen and Schrock (2009, 345, 353) argue for this sort of "consumption-driven urban development," noting that "superior local consumption-based offerings help to attract skilled workers, managers, entrepreneurs, and retirees," and emphasizing that "economists and geographers have recently stressed the significance of lifestyle preferences of skilled workers as an important determinant of economic development." Confirming this economic trajectory, if less enthusiastically, David Harvey (2008, 31) concludes that "quality of urban life has become a commodity, as has the city itself, in a world where consumerism, tourism, [and] cultural and knowledge-based industries have become major aspects of the urban political economy." To paraphrase Marx, cities built the first time on the tragedy of industrial labor are now rebuilt on the farce of image and impression; Monterrey, California's Cannery Row today offers Steinbeck-themed shops and a world-class aquarium, and Fort Worth, Texas's bloody stockyards and slaughterhouses now process only the kitsch recollections of cowboy boots and cattle. In such worlds urban authenticity, like urban quality of life, emerges as an upscale commodity (Zukin 2010).

But if these commodified "lifestyle preferences" and retail markers of urban quality benefit the managers and entrepreneurs privileged enough to consume them, they are distinctly less helpful to a far larger population: the growing army of low-end retail and service workers who provide them. For them, the Fordist model of occupational stability and advancement is finished; their work lives are now defined by the uncertainty of part-time and temporary employment, flex scheduling, missing medical and retirement benefits, and aborted careers. For them the old social contract has been annulled, as has the link between long work hours and long career. And so, a lesson we're meant to miss amidst the glitz of fancy shops and valet parking: accompanying every "successful" urban redevelopment scheme, every old factory converted into high-end lofts and retail spaces, is an increase in the number of workers left with few options but to drift between unstable employment, unaffordable housing, and economic failure.

Once western cities took shape around the economic interests of industrial capitalists and the relative stability of long-term employment; now they are reshaped by developers and city planners, who carve from them integrated lifestyle zones of high-end consumption. Within existing urban arrangements, though, these "consumption spaces" (Zukin 1997) are rarely developed from open land; instead, they're built on the revanchist reclaiming of urban space for privileged populations (N. Smith 1996). Invoking the ghosts of those displaced by Haussmann's sweeping reconfiguration of nineteenth-century Paris, and by the "brutal modernism" that Robert Moses applied to twentieth-century New York City, David Harvey (2008, 28, 34) emphasizes that this sort of contemporary urban development is predicated on "the capture of valuable land from low-income populations that may have lived there for years." For Harvey, this dispossession constitutes a sort of spatial imperialism, and an abrogation of "the right to the city"—and this is certainly so. With this working-class land captured, with its low-cost housing obliterated and its local shops bought out, ongoing spatial and normative consequences develop for those dispossessed—put simply, the great likelihood that they and their neighbors will now be cut loose and cast adrift in ways that they were not before. Noticing a high-end condominium complex, where once there was a historic working-class neighborhood, we see the physical evidence of the revanchist city (N. Smith 1996); less easily seen, less in focus, are the neighborhood's former residents, many now scattered ghost-like throughout the city, often moving between one short-term abode and another. The boutique hotel put up in place of the old SRO flophouse stands still for observation; the SRO's one-time residents, now homeless on the streets, do not. As historian Coll Thrush says of Seattle's sharp decline in SRO housing owing to high-end development, "The people who remained downtown tended to be poorer, sicker, more often homeless and unemployed, and less likely to be white" (quoted in Beckett and Herbert 2009, 27). It's not just that the new day spa, built in place of the old warehouse or neighborhood center, signals a shift in the city's class character and the terms of its employment; it's that its built stability mocks and masks the drifting instability of those it has displaced. For many in the economically "successful" global city, the fragility of occupation is echoed in the dislocation of neighborhood and home.

The inequitable spatial and economic instability inherent in consumption-driven urban development is not merely a matter of economics, though; it is quite literally enforced and reinforced by the law as well. As I and others have documented (Ferrell 1996, 2001, 2006; Amster 2008; MacLeod 2002; Mitchell 2003; Benjamin and Smithsimon 2011), the policing of these new consumption spaces—more broadly, the policing of these late modern urban economies—emerges as a form of aesthetic policing. The goal is to police the meaning and appearance of the city and its new consumption spaces, to protect the city's "quality of life" from those whose public presence would intrude on its ensemble of attractions and profitability. Here policing comes to focus on perceptions as much as populations, on minimizing risk and intrusion as much as solving crimes (O'Malley 2010). So, for example, an economic official in the United States argues during an urban revitalization campaign that panhandling is a problem precisely because "it's part of an image issue for the city"—and an American legal scholar agrees, positing that "the most serious of the attendant problems of homelessness is its devastating effect on a city's image" (quoted in Ferrell 2001, 45; quoted in Mitchell 2003, 201). As Aspden (2008, 13) concludes in regard to the recent transformation of a decaying British industrial city into a "corporate city of conspicuous consumption, . . . there seems to be no place in the new Leeds for those who disturb the rhythms of the consumer-oriented society." Twenty years ago Staughton Lynd argued that "American capitalism no longer has any use for, let's say, 40 per cent of the population. . . . They're now superfluous human beings. They're nothing but a problem for the people who run the society" (quoted in Slaughter 1994, 35). Today, the urban consumer economies of the "luxury city" (Chronopoulos 2011) likewise have no use for those lacking the will or means to consume—or worse yet, lacking the good graces to remain invisible to those who do. They're nothing but a problem to be policed.

This policing of panhandlers, homeless populations, and other undesired populations in turn rests on an ascendant late-modern model of risk-based urban crime control. Developed and supported by major insurance companies—and in the case of programs like Neighborhood Watch, even funded by them (O'Malley 2010, 26–27)—this model emphasizes a rationalized, actuarial approach to crime prevention through systematic surveillance and "the collection of information in order to make predictions, and the formation of preventative interventions based on these" (31). By this model's logic—"the military and neoliberal logic of security," as Shukaitis (2009, 157) calls it—surveillance cameras and tightly controlled public spaces function to prevent crime in the present and to provide the sorts of calculable big data on people and their movements that can be used to curtail crime in the future. By the same logic, the unregulated, the unpredictable, and the unmeasurable—the leftover bit of unused land, the homeless drifter, the impromptu street party, the unregistered bicyclist—stand not as markers of urban vitality but as open invitations to criminality and the breakdown of crime control. In fact, for conservative criminologists like Wilson and Kelling (1982), the presence of homeless panhandlers or the public paintings of graffiti writers are defined *only* as signs of social disorder—as metaphorical "broken windows" that serve to dispirit citizens and to invite more violent forms of criminality. What some might see, or might once have seen, as hallmarks of vital urban life—open public space, unregulated occupation of it, fluid interaction within it, unfettered movement through it—a new generation of politicians and police officials sees as unacceptable components of urban risk. Risk-based policing and consumer-based urban economies coalesce around a central consequence: intolerance toward unregulated urban space and those who would occupy or traverse it inappropriately.

At times this ideology is implemented with startling simplicity. In the United States, existing streets, sidewalks, or parks are deeded to private developers, and so made unavailable to the unprofitable and the unregulated (Amster 2008). In the United States, the United Kingdom, and beyond, new urban developments or redeveloped urban spaces, which might at first appear to incorporate swaths of public space or networks of public squares, are in fact increasingly private affairs, managed by property groups and patrolled by private security forces. So pronounced is this trend that some observers conclude that "privatisation of space is now the standard price of redevelopment" (Vasagar 2012, 16); indeed, even London's city hall and its surroundings are now privatized, and a patch of East London streets and squares is now owned by J.P. Morgan. Along with endless shopping opportunities, such spaces feature "high-security, 'defensible' architecture and strict rules and regulations governing behavior. Cycling, skateboarding and inline skating are often banned. So are busking, filming, taking photographs and political protest" (Minton 2012, 17). The results are as predictable as they are profitable. "It is a vision of society in which you work and shop," says Naomi Colvin. "At times when you are not working or shopping, you may go to restaurants. You may possibly go to some officially sanctioned kind of entertainment activity which is sponsored by X but there's no scope for people to do something of their own—to do something spontaneous" (quoted in Vasagar 2012, 16–17). A more precise description of the contemporary consumerist city and its controls would be difficult to imagine.

This risk-managed urban consumerism is in turn enforced though a host of popular crime control strategies. In Britain, authorities use dispersal orders and curfews to push undesirables away from consumerist havens and profit-driven nighttime economies. Under the auspices of the 2014 Antisocial Behaviour, Crime and Policing Act, they also have at their disposal public space protection orders, which criminalize otherwise legal activities, like public sleeping or the gathering of young people, within defined geographic areas. Enforceable by private security personnel, as well as by police officers, the public space protection orders are often used in concert with consumerist urban development schemes and, as one developer put it, as part of "cleaning up the town centre" (quoted in Garrett 2015). In the United States, Britain, and elsewhere, built-environment policing programs like CPTED (Crime Prevention Through Environmental Design) seek to reduce particular forms of crime by building social control into the spatial environment; such programs are regularly employed, for example, to discourage "loitering" by the homeless and other vulnerable populations in public areas or transit stations. By removing waiting facilities, installing uncomfortable benches, and closing public toilets, authorities are indeed often able to force such populations from public parks or town squares, thereby "cleansing" these spaces for preferred populations of tourists and short-stay retail consumers. Of late, applications of this approach have begun to take on the aura of medieval torture chambers—or perhaps Artaud's theater of cruelty—with the use of water sprinklers to soak homeless loiterers and the installation of sharpened spikes in front of buildings and under bridges to prohibit sitting or lying down (Andreou 2015; *New York Times* 2015). In this way CPTED approaches encode mean-spirited class conflict in the everyday spatial environment. In this way they also undermine even the fragile spatial communities that emerge among the vulnerable populations that occupy such spaces—the temporary encampments, the shared sleeping spaces—and so put these populations back on the move once again. Chapter 4 will revisit the US "move on" laws that were used to roust laborers and labor organizers a century ago; today, CPTED programs and associated laws against "public sleeping" and "public camping" likewise force vulnerable populations to move on, again and again, in search of even minimal comfort or convenience (Ferrell 2001).

The contemporary criminal justice emphasis on "broken windows" policing and "place-based" crime prevention (Eck and Eck 2012) redoubles this designed disruption. Former New York City mayor Rudolph Giuliani, who with his police chief William Bratton pioneered this approach in New York City, summarizes its intent. As regards the homeless and others on the street, Giuliani says, "you chase 'em and you chase 'em and you chase 'em and you chase 'em, and they either get the treatment they need or you chase 'em out of the city" (quoted in Bellafante 2015, 24). This approach produces enforcement campaigns that continually roust the homeless, dismantling their temporary shelters and destroying or confiscating their possessions (Onishi 2012). In Santa Ana, California, for example, an official's memo states that city policy is that "vagrants are no longer welcome in the city of Santa Ana . . . the mission of this program is to move all vagrants and their paraphernalia out . . . by continually removing them from the places that they are frequenting in the City" (quoted in Mitchell 2003, 197). Programs like the Los Angeles Safer Cities Initiative (SCI) institutionalize this approach further. This "place-based policing intervention" deploys police officers to move through Skid Row areas with entrenched homeless populations, "breaking up homeless encampments, issuing citations, and making arrests for violations of the law" (Berk and McDonald 2010, 813, 817) for the purpose of dispersal. Such initiatives are designed specifically to address the alleged problem of "spatial concentration" among the homeless—with such initiatives to be complemented by the "dispersal of homeless facilities" and support services throughout urban areas as well (Culhane 2010, 853). Vitale (2010, 868, 870) argues that, owing to aggressive fines and arrests, such initiatives only further entrap those targeted in homelessness. To this I might add that such initiatives also force the homeless into ever-more dislocated and disoriented ways of living; as before, they are "moved on" whenever and wherever they settle. Revealingly, Vitale also wonders if "the primary goal of the SCI [is] really to reduce crime and homelessness or instead to remove a large concentration of poor people forcibly from Skid Row in hope of encouraging the subsequent gentrification of the area. . . . A major effort to gentrify Skid Row has been underway for years."[1]

In this climate Fort Worth, Texas, undertakes "a new program [that] is paying for a private security company to patrol the area to keep the homeless moving" (Hirst 2015, 1AA). "Redevelopment officials" in Honolulu, Hawaii, disperse a homeless tent colony so as to "encourage development" and over concern that such colonies are a "threat to the image of the state that is central to tourism"; tent colony resident Douglas Sencio reports that "I have no idea where I'm going to go" (Nagourney

2011, A21). Three years later, the Honolulu mayor declares an all-out "war on homelessness," arguing that "we cannot let homelessness ruin our economy and take over our city," because when tourists come to Honolulu, "they want to see their paradise. They don't want to see homeless people sleeping in parks or on sidewalks on the beach." Concerned as the mayor is over the "visual impact" of homelessness, those living on the streets amidst closed parks, camping bans, and police harassment are concerned about something else. "We're so sleep-deprived, we're running around," says one homeless man. "We ask them, 'Where do you want us to go?' and they just say, 'Get out of Waikiki'" (quoted in Nagourney 2014, A1, A13; *New York Times* 2015). Sacramento, California, evicts 150 homeless people from tents along the American River; media coverage notes that "it was not clear where the campers would go" (*New York Times* 2011, A26). San Jose, California, razes a sixty-eight-acre homeless encampment, believed to be the largest in the United States; with median rents in the area around three thousand dollars, and a shortfall of some sixteen thousand affordable housing units, the consequences remain predictable. "When asked where they would go that night, 'I have no idea' was the common refrain" (Grady 2014, A13). As Denver, Colorado, officials outlaw "urban camping" and aggressively clear homeless encampments, residents of the camps and their advocates even take to wearing buttons that ask, "Move along to Where?" (Healy 2017, A8; see Langegger and Koester 2016, 2017). Rousted, displaced, moved on, the undesirables of the new urban economy are kept in perpetual motion, sent on an endless slow-motion death march toward nowhere. Some are even forced to remain in motion as they catch a few minutes' sleep, riding all-night city buses that have become de facto sleeping quarters for those with no place else to rest, rolling dormitories for the displaced (Lo 2015). As Kristina Gibson (2011, 3–4) says of homeless young people in New York City, and of the case workers who have tried to defend them,

> What social workers tried to prove was not just that the young people being displaced had as much right to be in a public space as did any other member of society and, furthermore, had nowhere safe to "move on" to but also that many of the youth were on the streets because they had been abused and, more often than not, had been kicked out by their own families and communities. . . . Public-space regulations that pushed street youth out of the West Village were not helping them get off the streets, for they did not go home. Rather, constantly being moved around only narrowed their options. . . . When kids are pushed out of public spaces around the city, their plight not only is worsened, it also is made invisible.

The proliferation of banishment orders, buffer zones, and exclusion zones in New York, Los Angeles, Seattle, Portland, and other US cities further enforces these strategies of spatial exclusion and the hard reality of having nowhere to go. Cities today have at their disposal a full arsenal of exclusion laws and statutes: antibegging buffer zones around bus stops, theaters, and cafes; Stay out of Drug Area (SODA) and Stay out of Areas of Prostitution (SOAP) orders and injunctions; city park exclusion ordinances; updated trespass laws; public housing exclusions; off-limits orders; civil injunctions; and "no contact orders" (Beckett and Herbert 2009; Liptak 2014). Once they are caught up and convicted in aggressive homeless dispersal campaigns, or in "broken windows" legal campaigns against those who allegedly commit low-order, street-level offenses, those on the urban margins are then subject to banishment and exclusion orders as conditions of sentencing, deferred prosecution, or community supervision. For homeless folks and others, the result is an urban archipelago of overlapping and often ill-defined exclusion zones—from city parks, from downtown areas, from the neighborhood where one's family lives—the violation of which results in further criminalization and disenfranchisement. Coupled with CPTED, "place-based" policing, and other contemporary legal strategies, the result is an experience of profound, prolonged dislocation. "No, you know I don't understand these zones . . . they're everywhere," says one homeless denizen of Seattle. "They try to tell you that you can't walk around, can't be in them, but where can I go, I'm homeless, I got no place to go. They're everywhere" (quoted in Beckett and Herbert 2009, 130).

In these ways a political economy of drift becomes also a criminology of drift. Global corporate criminality in the form of mortgage fraud and insider trading costs millions their homes and their livelihoods, cutting them loose from neighborhood and career; others lose home, neighborhood, or career to the economic bulldozer of "consumption-driven urban development." Cast adrift, they find themselves pushed off privatized sidewalks, driven from public spaces, cited for loitering or trespass, rounded up and arrested for the crime of spatial concentration, banished from neighborhoods and parks. As criminologists, we might note in such situations the iatrogenic effects of law and economy, and as with the cultural contradictions already seen, the "ironies of social control" (G. Marx 1981). The spatial controls meant to contain urban space, to protect it from transient populations, serve only to make such populations more transient; the closure of urban space to drifters exacerbates urban drift. The reconstitution of urban economies around managed meaning and market-driven consumption dislocates the very sorts of citizens whose peripatetic presence is thought to threaten consumption and its meanings in the first place.[2]

In these ways a political economy of drift also complements a sociology of drift. While classic works in sociology and criminology can usefully attune us to the social and cultural contradictions that are the progenitors of drift, they nonetheless tend to conceptualize drift as an oddly de-spatialized phenomenon. For Durkheim, Merton, Matza, and Sykes, the dislocations brought about by structural contradictions are normative in nature, and the fixed locations from which the normative drifter departs are conceptualized primarily in terms of moral certainty or social cohesion. In this sense such conceptualizations are essentially metaphorical; they draw evocatively from the physicality of the rudderless boat lost to the ocean, even the wayfaring stranger wandering town to town, but decline to situate this metaphorical drift in the physical spatiality of human action. Other threads in existing sociological and criminological theory—theories of social ecology and social disorganization, for example, with their ecological metaphors, "zones of transition," and grounding of crime in place rather than person—certainly introduce spatiality into criminological analysis. Yet despite their invocation of "disorganization" and "transition," these are primarily analyses of locations—humanly constructed locations, certainly, but locations nonetheless—rather than analyses of drifting human movement through and beyond them (see Hayward 2012a, 2012b). It remains, it seems, to suggest some of the dynamics linking drift as normative anomie and drift as dislocated spatial experience.

One dynamic has already been glimpsed more than once: the likelihood that normative dislocation and spatial dislocation will intertwine in the lived experience of drift. Bankrupt economic aspirations lead young people to imagine a better life elsewhere and often to set out in search of it; the dissolution of agricultural economies, and with them long-standing ways of village life, drives rural families toward urban slums or *maquiladoras*. Retail temp workers and part-time university instructors forfeit both their career aspirations and their ability to settle in any one job setting or neighborhood. As a civil war unravels ideologies of national unity and multigenerational familial ties, it also pushes those so afflicted to seek refuge beyond its borders. But more than this, the economic migrant, the war refugee, the banished beggar now arrives in a new spatial environment, whose symbolic coordinates, unreadable and unknowable to the culturally uninitiated, confirm the anomic experience of being a stranger in a strange land. As seen in the previous chapter, Robert Park (1928, 887) argued that for the migrant, "energies that were formerly controlled by custom and tradition are released. The individual is free for new adventures, but . . . more or less without direction and control." Thought of in spatial terms, this insight holds. Social space is cultural space (Ferrell 1997), encoded with meaning and memory, and to flee from Tunisia to southern Italy, to cross from rural Mexico to a North American metropolis, to wander one country or the next chasing employment, is to lose oneself in ways that are at the same time spatial and normative.

Other dynamics directly interweave the pains of cultural and spatial dislocation with the dangers of legal marginality, and so create a redoubling of initial drift. For the homeless of Los Angeles and Portland, for Tunisian refugees lost along and between the Italian-French border, for Bangladeshi migrants idling off the coast of Malaysia, there is often by law simply no legitimate place to settle. Beyond this, the strict household-registration system in China means that the hundreds of millions of citizens now moving illicitly from village to city occupy "an uncomfortable world that is neither urban nor rural, isolating them from their own children, [and] preventing them from becoming full members of the country's economy" (Saunders 2010, 16). In Russia, a similar system of "administratively organized territorial affiliations" guarantees that for homeless populations "a lack of place also means a lack of any social recognition, employment rights or recourse to public welfare" (Stephenson 2006, 145). The millions of global refugees, whose drifting journeys pause in refugee aid camps, nonetheless remain adrift in similar ways. As Bauman (2002, 344; 2000, 102) argues, such "non-places" or "nowhere-evilles" originate as "a totally artificial creation located in a social void," and so incorporate an "extra-territoriality" absent meaning or belonging for those forced to occupy them. Describing these massive collectivities as "city-camps" (*camps-villes*), Agier (2002, 322) notes that they are designed to induce "the social and political non-existence of the recipients" of their aid, and, quoting Michael Pollack, he sketches a striking intersection of spatial and normative drift that occurs within them: "Identity becomes a preoccupation . . . only where it is no longer taken-for-granted, when common sense is no longer given in advance and when the actors involved can no longer agree on the meaning of the situation and the roles they are supposed to be playing in it."

A particularly complex intersection of cultural, spatial, and legal drift emerges with the global mass migration of rural populations to urban areas. As such populations begin to accumulate in an urban area, they often first settle in the relatively unplanned, unregulated zones that surround it—thereby forming emergent "arrival cities," as Saunders (2010) calls them. These areas function as tenuous, informal footholds for those seeking a life in the city and, with their links to both rural areas and the city itself, operate as ongoing conduits for subsequent generations of migrants. Unlike the often-anonymous dependency of refugee camps, they generally operate as do-it-yourself cultural and economic accomplishments, with their warrens of homemade architecture, their cultural affirmations of urban life and rural tradition, and their networks of informal aid and economic innovation. At the same time, they suffer from the benign neglect of urban authorities; allowed to exist, they nonetheless remain outside the orbit of water and sanitation services, legal protection, and urban citizenship. In this sense such arrival cities are not so much illegal as *extralegal;* and over time, this legal and spatial marginality may move either in the direction of incorporation into the formal urban grid or outright criminalization and demolition. Adding further complexity is Saunders's argument that the occupants of such areas are generally not aimless wanderers but highly motivated seekers of a better life in the city; adapting Merton, we might say that they respond to the strain of blocked aspirations through a form of *spatial innovation.* In doing so, though, they often spend generations connected only tenuously to the city of their aspirations, moving back and forth between rural village and city as a result of economic failure or deportation and left to semiurban spaces of marginality and fluctuation. The arrival city is "both populated with people in transition . . . and is itself a place in transition"—yet it is also "a place of upward mobility—or at least a calculated grasp for the best hope of mobility" (Saunders 2010, 11, 50).

Two concepts would seem of some utility for thinking through these interplays of normative and spatial drift in the context of law and crime. The notion of alienation, in both its Marxian formulations and its more general usage, has long denoted the social distance that separates people from their work, their family, or their identity; alienation denotes the experience of deep estrangement, the sense of being a stranger in one's own life and activities. For the drifter, this experience of alienation from past associations or stable community—or, with Simmel, alienation even from those communities of which the drifter is currently a part—is amplified by the ongoing experience of *spatial alienation.* The drifter occupies space temporarily and provisionally, passing through it, in it but not of it, distanced from it by unreadable cultural codes and enforced anonymity.

The drifter's physical presence hides a cultural and legal absence, and portends eventual physical absence as well—and for those who control and profit from such space, the drifter is already invisible, a noncitizen, at best a problem of law enforcement or risk management. In the context of common street narratives among homeless youth like "moving on" and 'just arrived," Gibson (2011, 15, 170–73) points out that "becoming homeless" is not a "fixed state" but rather "a progression in which kids run away and/or are kicked out, stay on a friend's or a relative's couch, go home again, leave again, couch-surf until their welcome has worn out, stay at crisis shelters and drop-in centers, and, in some cases, live on the streets." For young people, then, drifting into and through the streets is indeed a progression—a spiraling progression of social and spatial alienation. And as refugee camps remind us, even when drifters secure the relatively long-term occupation of social spaces, it is seldom a matter of self-affirming spatial stability—more a matter of being stuck, of waiting with little hope or prospect. "I don't understand the word future," says Mohammed Salim, a young Burmese refugee lodged, indeterminately, in an Indonesian migrant camp. Putting his future in the past tense, he explains, "In the future, I wanted to learn computers, but in Burma, all I was thinking about was how long would it be before I'm dead" (quoted in Cochrane 2015, A12).

Drift also invokes multiple dimensions and multiple moments of *transgression*. Transgression suggests a crossing over, a breaching of boundaries established by law or custom, map or morality. Drifting takes its participants across such boundaries as they are encoded in individual identity, as they are enforced within sedentary associations— and as they are mapped into spatial arrangements. In drift the morality and spatiality of transgression intersect and interweave; stepping away from the cultural codes by which she once navigated, stepping over and into worlds whose cultural codes she has yet to decipher, the drifter time and again crosses into uncertain terrain. And as her trespasses accumulate, authorities find in the drifter all kinds of trouble. After all, to dig for survival in a retailer's trash bin is to transgress not one cultural code but many, to violate the assorted sanctities of private property, consumption, cleanliness, and law. To leave Syria and wash up in Greece, uninvited, is to breach not just national borders but bigger boundaries of ethnicity, economy, and national sovereignty.

Yet all this is mostly what others make of the drifter. What might the drifter make of herself and others, amidst the experience of serial alienation and transgression?

3

Drift Politics

Contemporary drift can be understood as a product of cultural contradictions, economic arrangements, and emerging strategies of legal
enforcement; the drifter can in turn be thought of as a cultural stranger,
or in the eyes of the state, an apparitional problem taking shape as outlaw or legal nonentity. The human agency of the drifter, though, suggests something more: that the drifter might transgress boundaries with
an emerging intentionality, might begin to see the world differently as a
result of so many borders breached—might even learn to turn marginality and estrangement back on those whose arrangements have engendered it. You'll recall from the first chapter Robert Park's (1928, 887)
claim that migration must be studied generally but also "in its subjective aspects as manifested in the changed type of personality which it
produces." The same can be said of drift and drifters—and those who
have considered their "subjective aspects" have found in them some
explosive potential. Park and Simmel suggested that drifters attain a
kind of epistemic exteriority, an ability to see past situations and past
otherwise unexamined social customs and conventions. Durkheim and
Merton found in the drifter's anomie a fraught suspension of the moral
code, and so a potential openness to adaption and innovation. Sykes
and Matza discovered in the drifting delinquent-to-be a young person
able to identify moral hypocrisy, an emergent sociologist as well—a
person ready to utilize this sociological awareness in engineering a temporary exit from the everyday order of things. Notably, the work of

these social theorists on migrants, strangers, and potential criminals wasn't at all oriented toward subversive politics or radical social change—but talk of freedom from enforced conventions and suspension of existing moral codes surely suggests that drift harbors the potential for a transformational politics of some sort.

TOWARD AN EXPERIENTIAL POLITICS OF DRIFT

Whatever the forces that cast and keep one adrift, whatever the mix of structural victimization and human agency, drifting tends to produce at least one sort of transformation: that which results from the sequenced experience of exclusion and alienation. The drifter exists as a perpetual outsider—outside the boundaries of home country, outside the conventional labor market, outside the protection of legal citizenship. As this drifting continues across time and space the exclusions accumulate, and in so doing reinforce the drifter's identity as always outside the frame—an outsider many times over. Here is the drifter's sorrow, loss, and alienation, the emptiness of anomie as well—but here also is the hard-earned potential for living and learning beyond the usual bounds of the social order. A serial transgressor by law or by choice, the drifter is able to see—forced to see—the order of things from the other side, over and over again, and so to understand that the truth claims of one gatekeeper are as suspect as those of the next. Like Sykes and Matza's neutralized delinquent, the drifter experiences social and cultural contradictions, sees them manifest in her own life, and in seeing them escapes them—at least sometimes, for a while.

Little wonder, then, that the economic and legal dislocations forced on people around the globe lead them to imagine radical alternatives, to think beyond the previous generation, to make seemingly absurd plans for negotiating escape or surviving the contingencies of continued confinement. Even amidst a crisis of prison overcrowding and abuse brought on by budget cuts, prisoners in Portugal nonetheless refuse to apply for prison leave—since at least inside the prison they can eat regularly. Says one ex-convict, now departed for part-time work in Switzerland, "If you come out of jail in Portugal now, you've got almost zero chance of not going straight back in. There's just nothing for you to do except sit around and stay poor and depressed" (quoted in Minder 2012, A12). In Kosovo, the "stifling sense of uncertainty" (Smale 2015, 6) is such that many Kosovars who fought for their land are now eager to leave it, desperate to migrate to Germany or to Hungary or beyond. In the United

States, gutter punks and other impoverished young travelers find themselves "blackened and hollow," made that way by the exclusions of the contemporary city: "It's never your city when you are locked out of it by the system of the city itself. It's easy to become contemptuous of a place which has no room for you, which bars you from the most basic needs" (CrimethInc. 2003, 97). Consequently, they squat in buildings, sleep rough, Dumpster dive, hitchhike, shoplift, and run little scams, since "to revolt against work and thus boredom, routine, wage slavery, the exchange economy with your *body* as well as your mind, to recognize and legitimize your heart's longing to escape by *trying to,* is to declare openly that we are *not* crazy for wanting more than the scraps of self [that] capitalism leaves us" (Commando 2003, emphasis in original).

Choosing prison over Portugal, abandoning the land for which you fought, launching a low-order assault on work and the city—these are indeed the acts of serial outsiders, acts that constitute, if not transformations of the social and spatial order, then at least desperate inversions of it. Richard Grant (2003, 263) spent years wandering North America with itinerant rodeo cowboys, freight train hobos, peripatetic neohippies, and other "American nomads"; he found a similar sort of outsider mentality, and one similarly underwritten by accumulated inequities of law and spatial arrangement. "They have a quintessentially nomadic attitude toward sedentary society," he concluded. "They don't pay taxes, they don't vote, and they don't consider themselves bound by the social contract. And thanks to vagrancy laws, begging laws, laws against sleeping in parks, laws against hitchhiking and riding freight trains— laws, in short, that make it illegal to be poor and nomadic—they are locked into conflict with the sedentary state and its coercive power." As with other drifters, a particular sort of experiential politics can be seen among Grant's nomads—one whose critical distance, like the drifter's own experiences, emerges from the interplay of living outside the dominant social order while continually being roped back into it by law and regulation. His notion of a "nomadic attitude" hints at a perceptual dynamic as well—at the possibility that drifting can create commonalities of alternative knowledge and perception for those caught up in its various manifestations.

Cultural geographers and literary scholars have noted similar possibilities, both in studies of spatial mobility and attitude (Prince 1973) and in their broader invocation of the *flâneur* (Baudelaire [1863] 1964; Benjamin 1999; Keith 1997). A strolling urban explorer, a dawdling urban drifter who encounters the city as a series of unplanned episodes, the flâneur embodies a subversive model of urban citizenship that emerges from her ongoing, uncertain movement within the city's life. In Baudelaire's ([1863] 1964, 9) classic conceptualization, this fluidity of movement produces also a fluidity of knowledge and perception:

> For the perfect *flâneur*, for the passionate spectator, it is an immense joy to set up house in the heart of the multitude, amid the ebb and flow of movement, in the midst of the fugitive and the infinite. To be away from home and yet to feel oneself everywhere at home; to see the world, to be at the centre of the world, and yet to remain hidden from the world. . . . Thus the lover of universal life enters into the crowd as though it were an immense reservoir of electrical energy. Or we might liken him to a mirror as vast as the crowd itself; or to a kaleidoscope gifted with consciousness, responding to each one of its movements and reproducing the multiplicity of life and the flickering grace of all the elements of life.

Adrift in the city, lost amidst its swirl of people and situations, the flâneur engineers a form of urban engagement based not on settled boundaries or official knowledge but on ephemeral urban encounters and a holistic, comparative understanding of the city's spaces. In Keith's (1997, 145) estimation, this form of engagement and understanding carries the potential for undermining the accepted order of urban life—since, "spatially, the order of things is never more clearly revealed than through disruption, the striking juxtapositions of the street walk." In Elkin's (2016, 2017) estimation, it holds the potential to subvert the gendered order of urban life as well. De Certeau (1984, 101) agrees: "The long poem of walking manipulates spatial organizations, no matter how panoptic they may be," he says. "It creates shadows and ambiguities within them."[1]

Raising the political stakes, Situationists and psychogeographers likewise emphasize the subversive politics and transformational potential of the *dérive*. A fluid drifting through urban space, a "rapid passage through varied ambiances," in order "to study a terrain or to emotionally disorient oneself," the *dérive* mixes abandonment of the "usual motives for movement and action" with a reorientation toward possibility (Debord 1958; see Makeworlds 2003). For Situationists, that possibility is no less than a revolution of everyday life (Vaneigem [1967] 2001)—an effort to undermine taken-for-granted exercises of power while simultaneously fomenting anarchic situations, with the effect of reinventing the world as a landscape of uncertainty and surprise. Developing this approach a half century ago, the Situationists intended to disrupt societies designed for consumerism and passivity—to "trigger stoppages in the factories of collective illusion" (Vaneigem [1967] 2001, 271)—and to dismantle the urban spatial arrangements in which such consumerism flourished and was enforced. By this logic, the *dérive*—the process of getting lost while not looking to be found, of making one's way sans map or manufactured meaning—in turn provides a precise counterpoint to the sort of risk-managed, consumerist cities seen in the previous chapter. If, as Naomi Colvin (quoted in Vasagar 2012, 16–17) has already said, the privatized city incorporates "a vision of society in which you work and shop . . . but there's no scope for people to do something of their own—to do something spontaneous," then the *dérive* is the countervision, the fever dream of those who find in abandonment and disorder an experiential politics of liberation.

Suggesting something of this lived politics, Raoul Vaneigem ([1967] 2001, 195) argues that the nature of the *dérive* is such that "in losing myself I find myself; forgetting that I exist, I realize myself. . . . The traveler who is always thinking about the length of the road before him tires more easily than his companion who lets his imagination wander as he goes along." Here we glimpse not just the intentional Situationist politics of the *dérive* but once again the latent politics of Park's migrants, Simmel's strangers, and Matza's delinquents—the sense that for drifters of all sorts, the move away from structural certainty can produce not only disorientation but new possibilities for personal and political transformation. Guy Debord (1958) makes this experiential inclusivity explicit, arguing that for him and his associates the *dérive* was less a singular technique than an overarching practice: "Our rather anarchic lifestyle and even certain amusements considered dubious that have always been enjoyed among our entourage—slipping by night into houses undergoing demolition, hitchhiking nonstop and without destination through Paris during a transportation strike in the name of adding to the confusion, wandering in subterranean catacombs forbidden to the public, etc.—are expressions of a more general sensibility which is no different from that of the dérive."

Debord's list of amusements offers an uncanny foreshadowing of activities that would emerge a half century later under the general heading of "place hacking" or "urban exploration." As documented by Bradley Garrett (2013; Kindynis and Garrett 2015) and others, place hackers explore abandoned buildings and disused transit stations, scale under-construction office towers and perch atop urban bridges, with the intent of illicitly reclaiming the city and its spaces for unfettered play and unregulated public engagement. In this sense, they drift through an urban environment that otherwise demands predictability and obedience, along the way problematizing who and what constitute "public" space and public citizenship and embracing the sort of illicit, adrenaline-charged disorientations that a Situationist would admire. If we add to this list still other such activities—nocturnal graffiti writing, subterranean wall painting, alley-to-alley trash scrounging—we begin to see in drift an inclusive and expanding realm of experiential politics (see Ferrell 1996, 2006, 2013; Ferrell, Hayward, and Young 2015, 213–14; Ferrell and Weide 2010).

Throughout this realm, drifting regularly produces a kind of critical, comparative exteriority by which drifters are able—or are forced—to see beyond the certainty of any one situation. Here perhaps the pain and potential of drift intertwine. The sorrows of a global migrant's endless journey, the outrage of a homeless person caught between urban exclusion orders, the fluid insights derived from the long walking poem of the *dérive* or the flâneur—each is profoundly different, yet each is built from the recurring experience of radical dislocation. In each case the experience of drift seems also to produce an emerging intentionality, and with it a sense of the self as somehow separated from the more static social order. Sharply subversive lessons are interwoven with this loss and pain, and with them a recalibration of self and society unavailable to the sedentary. Whether drift's ongoing normative and spatial alienation is imposed by contemporary arrangements or embraced for its liberatory possibilities, it in this way creates at least the potential for a progressive critique of the existing order of things. This critique captures something of the sociologist's critical eye for social arrangements, the anthropologist's keen eye for comparison, and the geographer's cartographic eye for spatialities of power (Ferrell 2012a). Further, the recurring, radical exteriority of drift seems to promote the sort of anarchic epistemology that Feyerabend (1975) has outlined—an epistemology attuned to dimensions of power and authority embedded in otherwise taken-for-granted understandings and perceptions. Of course, for the impoverished temp worker or the banished street denizen or the stateless migrant, all such insights may be regularly overwhelmed by the daily task of simply surviving ever-more exclusionary spatial, legal, and economic regimes; for them, the lesson of Sisyphus may mostly be that the rock always rolls back down.

That's the thing about drift: it's innately uncertain, less a dead end than a detour. Conventional maps of meaning come undone. Spatial maps unravel, too, the certainty of their grid subject to continual trespass. For those adrift, disorientation emerges as a way of life—a way of life whose accumulated experiences write shadow histories of cities, governments, and social change. A moveable famine of loss and despair, an ongoing experience of having nowhere to go, drift also spreads a moveable feast of possibility, a hope at least of anywhere but here. And oddly enough, these slippery, shifting experiences of drift sometimes even coalesce into shared endeavors by which the experiential politics of drift becomes a collective politics as well.

TOWARD A COLLECTIVE POLITICS OF DRIFT

Michel De Certeau (1984, 96, 105) saw and celebrated a "rich indetermination," a "proliferating illegitimacy" amidst the collective movement of the city's citizens—a "poetic geography" of free space. Echoing De Certeau's (1984, 93) notion that urban walkers "follow the thicks and thins of an urban 'text' they write without being able to read it," Massey (2006, 40, 46) likewise argues that "both space and landscape could be imagined as provisionally intertwined simultaneities of ongoing, unfinished stories." The contemporary proliferation of privatized urban spaces, surveillance cameras, and exclusionary spatial controls seen in the previous chapter reveals on the other hand an ongoing attempt to negate these very dynamics—an attempt to make the text of urban life all too visible and readable, to script the stories of social space from beginning to end. Here the poetic geography of the city becomes a forced march of everyday life, a prearranged interplay of people, places, and products. In this way the emerging structural economy of the contemporary city undermines the very viability of urban social life itself, by encoding ever-more restrictive controls in the spatial environment and by containing the unpredictability and disorder essential to an emergent, democratic urbanism (Ferrell 2001).

As powerful and pervasive as this antidemocratic urbanism may now be, though, it is not without opposition from various contemporary social groups and social movements that imagine something better than an obituary for urban space. Understanding the threats of surveillance and exclusion, these groups are committed to keeping urban spatial arrangements open, dedicated to breathing life back into those spaces that have been suffocated. While orbiting around a diversity of social and political issues, they share an understanding of open public space as essential to a democratic society—that is, as the primary forum in which directly democratic processes and collective cultures can be invented and negotiated (Springer 2011). "The conceptual link that I operate from is trying to preserve spaces that are historically dedicated to the public," says anarchist activist and scholar Randall Amster, "because it's my belief that without public spaces, any kind of talk about democracy basically goes out the window" (quoted in Ferrell 2001, 52). Likewise, such groups conceptualize public space as an ongoing and collective cultural accomplishment, and so understand it to be a primary venue of contested symbolism and cultural progress (Amin 2008). Linking these concerns with issues of environmental sustainability and social justice, these groups engage particular public space issues—road building, automotive domination, spatial exclusion of the homeless, urban privatization—within a broader ethos of spatial justice. Chris Carlsson, one of the founders of the Critical Mass urban bicycling movement, argues, for example, that collectively abandoning the automobile to embrace public bicycling is not only an act of spatial democratization but "an act of desertion from an entire web of exploitative and demeaning activities, behaviors that impoverish the human experience and degrade planetary ecology itself" (Carlsson 2002, 82). Pushing back against the closure, containment, and privatization of urban space, such groups valorize the sorts of direct, everyday democracy that can flourish in accessible urban space—and they employ DIY (do-it-yourself) activism, "direct action," and other anarchist and antiauthoritarian strategies both to liberate this space and to reanimate it with just such democratic activity.

Confronting an Arizona plan to privatize public sidewalks and criminalize the public presence of the homeless, for example, Randall Amster and the Project S.I.T. movement called on traditions of "anarchist direct action, the I.W.W. . . . the civil rights movement . . . the philosophies of Gandhi and King . . . passive resistance, civil disobedience . . . [and] the burgeoning WTO, World Bank anti-globalization movement" to stage sidewalk sit-ins and create "a kind of space for spontaneity" and resistance (quoted in Ferrell 2001, 51–52; see Amster 2008). Over the past couple of decades, Reclaim the Streets activists in the United States and Europe have likewise blocked urban automotive traffic, held illegal street parties, and otherwise launched "ephemeral festivals of resistance"—all while referencing and reinventing the Paris Commune's 1871 "festival of the oppressed," the Situationist interventions of Paris 1968, and other moments in antiauthoritarian history (Jordan 1998, 139). During the 1996 Democratic National Convention in Chicago—itself preceded by homeless roundups and the destruction of low-income housing—the anarchist group Active Resistance "highlighted the significance of the spatial dimensions of conflict and the territoriality of social struggle" by ignoring designated protest areas and staging an illegal "festival of the oppressed" in the streets around the convention (Shantz 2011, 70). In New York City, Bike Lane Liberation Clowns attempt to "bridge the space between the joy of riding free and possibilities for public-space environmental activism" by playfully ticketing drivers parked in bicycle lanes (Shepard and Smithsimon 2011, 188). In New York City, Madrid, and cities around the world, Jordan Seiler and the always-changing members of PublicAdCampaign undermine the commodification of public space by illicitly removing corporate advertising from public areas and replacing it with independent art, in this way striving to help "communities regain control of the spaces they occupy"; of late they've even developed a mobile app designed to digitally transform urban advertising into street art (www.publicadcampaign.com). In these ways, these and other groups work to uproot the conventional signposts that define and delimit urban space—legal statutes and police lines, automotive traffic, corporate advertising—and to institute instead spontaneously self-made encounters within public venues.

The widespread practice of "dis-organizing" and "dis-organization" further exemplifies this anarchic orientation. As does Kropotkin (1975), these groups see the immobility of rule and regulation as inhibiting human freedom and human progress—even if the rules and regulations are their own. As a result, they emphasize dis-organization—that is, just enough coordination to propel social activism forward but not so much that it becomes a static end in itself. In this way they seek not only to reintroduce indetermination and uncertainty into the spaces of urban life but to do so by means that are themselves indeterminate and uncertain. Chris Carlsson has, for example, noted his pleasure at overhearing Critical Mass participants explaining the essential meaning of a Critical Mass ride, especially when their explanations differ from his own and those of others. The anonymous punk/anarchist author of the book *Evasion,* a chronicle of squatting and street living, has likewise written, "I always secretly looked forward to nothing going as planned. That way, I wasn't limited by my own imagination. That way anything can, and always did, happen" (quoted in White 1999; Anonymous 2003, 12). More pointedly, Reclaim the Streets, which describes itself as "a direct action network seeking the rediscovery and liberation of the city streets," felt compelled at one point to issue a press release, "On Disorganization," in response to media attempts to report on Reclaim the Streets "leaders." Reclaim the Streets (2000), they announced, "is a non-hierarchical, leaderless, openly organized public group. No individual 'plans' or 'masterminds' its actions and events. RTS activities are the result of voluntary, unpaid, co-operative efforts from numerous self-directed people attempting to work equally together." A recent public event, they added, was put together in this way "in part previously, in part spontaneously on the day itself." As the Situationists said back in 1963, "We will only organize the detonation. The free explosion must escape us and any other control forever" (quoted in Marcus 1989, 179–80).

A global urban bicycling movement intent on challenging automotive dominance and restoring public spaces for human interaction, Critical Mass embraces this sort of dis-organization, both in preparing for its collective rides and in conducting them. In preparation for Critical Mass rides, participants are encouraged to create and distribute their own media promoting the ride and to communicate using alternative networks. The route the ride will take is left upon to discussion, or simply allowed to emerge in transit; if a map materializes, it is considered provisional at best. Likewise, those involved offer up no leaders with whom public officials might negotiate and disavow any need for police protection or assistance. During the course of the rides—"open-ended, leaderless and democratic free-for-alls," as Shepard and Smithsimon (2011, 171) describe them—the bicycles' collective flow trumps the rigidity of traffic laws. As riders approach an intersection, a few will break off to temporarily "cork" the intersection—to block it from cross traffic as the ride progresses through it, whether or not stop signs are present or traffic lights are green or red—and then rejoin the ride; at the next intersection, other riders may or may not voluntarily take on the corking (Ferrell 2011a). Unlike other forms of urban traffic—hurried, hyper-regulated, anxious—Critical Mass rides are meant to drift through urban space as organic, on-the-move collectivities. In their drifting uncertainty, they are in turn meant to embody the dis-organization and spontaneous self-determination that produced them and to demonstrate that such fluid direct action can effectively replace the usual policing of public space. As David Graeber (2007, 378) argues, Critical Mass participants and other anarchist activists dedicated to direct action understand "mass mobilizations not only as opportunities to expose the illegitimate, undemocratic nature of existing institutions, but as ways to do so in a form that itself demonstrated why such institutions were unnecessary, by providing a living example of genuine, direct democracy."[2]

Operating within this ethos, the group Food Not Bombs dis-organizes the direct salvaging of wasted or surplus food in urban areas, which it then serves to the homeless, recent immigrants, and others cut loose from the security of home or career; put differently, Food Not Bombs attends directly to those cast adrift by the contemporary urban and global crises, understanding itself as intervening in a system that "values wasteful consumption over common sense" (CrimethInc. 2004, 248). Hundreds of Food Not Bombs chapters reclaim and serve food throughout North America, Europe, Africa, Southeast Asia, and other places around the globe—and they do so not through centralized organizations but in ways that are intentionally fluid, imprecise, and unstable. As "an anarchist dis-organization" (Clark 2004, 28), Food Not Bombs disavows hierarchical structures and political authority, promoting only the general principles of consensus, nonviolence, and vegetarianism while emphasizing that "the core of [its] philosophy is that each local group is autonomous" (Butler and McHenry 2000, 73). In this way Food Not Bombs itself drifts along with others cast adrift, open to changing circumstances and emerging problems. But by doing so—by openly feeding the hungry in public urban areas, with a minimum of organization, and with neither the permission nor the assistance of legal and political authorities—Food Not Bombs itself becomes part of the problem for those invested in consumer-driven urban development and its attendant legal controls. Legal harassment, like the arrest of hundreds of Food Not Bombs food servers in San Francisco or the arrest of Orlando, Florida, Food Not Bombs "food terrorists," as they were labeled by the local mayor, is common (Butler and McHenry 2004; Ferrell 2001, 2006; Donohoe 2011; Bradshaw 2017).

Graeber (2009, 258, see 526–28; 2007, 394) has argued that the "Situationist legacy is probably the single most important theoretical influence on contemporary anarchism is America," and indeed the Situationist notion of creating a "revolution of everyday life" from ephemeral situations that disrupt and reverse dominant arrangements echoes in the performative spatial politics of these groups as well. Reclaim the Streets' illegal street parties incorporate the playful subversions of social and spatial coordinates that have long animated carnival (see Presdee 2000). Critical Mass participants emphasize that their rides are not manifestations of traditional political protest but instead playful, celebratory enactments of alternative spatial community and alternative gender and identity relations (Ferrell 2001, 105–21). In gathering and feeding the needy openly and in public spaces, Food Not Bombs both directly addresses hunger and stages for public view the outrageous inequities of contemporary society. In all of this the goal is to create what Bey (1991) calls "temporary autonomous zones"—spaces of momentary community that at the same time subvert (*détourn*) the taken-for-granted assumptions undergirding the present order, allow for the ephemeral flowering of alternatives, and invite others into the process.

In this light a seemingly straightforward dualism—activist groups battling legal and economic authorities for control of urban space—can be seen to harbor a more subtle dynamic. To the extent that these groups found their spatial activism in anarchic and antiauthoritarian approaches, their goal is not so much to take control of urban space as it is to obliterate spatial domination and spatial control in the first place, all in the interest of spontaneity and emergence. To paraphrase the old anarchist cry, their goal is not to seize spatial power but to destroy it; as Ward (1973, 38–39) says, their belief is in the "revolutionary" potential of "leaderless groups" to unravel, not replace, everyday arrangements of power and control. The temporary autonomous zones created by fluid Critical Mass rides or unregulated Food Not Bombs events aren't new urban settlements; they're forms of ephemeral community that undermine the long-term control of urban space. When PublicAdCampaign illicitly removes advertising from urban public space, the intent is not to enforce a new spatial aesthetic but to open such space to aesthetic and cultural conversation. As Jordan Seiler (author interview, 2016) says, his hope is that PublicAdCampaign "contributes to a larger social movement that is anti-consumerist, wildly skeptical of capitalist propaganda, concerned with self-determination, [and] interested in locality and relationship building"—and he hopes that the direct action of on-the-ground advertising removal will open public space not only to independent art, but to "public messaging, opportunities for political dialogue, all of those civic conversations that have a rightful home in public. . . . Removal of advertising would come with a public negotiation of what should follow." These and other groups imagine a city whose constellations of activity are ephemeral and invitational, a city animated by creative urban disorder, a city of the flâneur and the *dérive*—a city in which De Certeau's "rich indetermination" and "proliferating illegitimacy" are breathed back to life. That is, they seek a city adrift.

Within this sort of collective politics drift emerges as both method of engagement and model of urban living. Put differently, and as widely noted in discussions of contemporary anarchist and antiauthoritarian politics (Ferrell 2001; Naegler 2016; Brisman and South 2013, 89–116), an open and intentionally dis-organized process is meant to presage, and move toward, an equally open and emergent world of possibility. For many forms of collective politics the model of social change is a long march toward preset goals, led by those best able to define them; here the notion is more the undermining of domination and control, so that people are free to drift toward goals that will only emerge collectively from the journey itself. By this notion, drift is to space as anarchy is to order—not so much a head-on confrontation as an illicit disruption of the map itself. By this logic, the opposite of a straight line is not an oppositional straight line but a wandering and uncertain one; the counterpoint to marching north is not marching south but dispersal. Drift suggests a type of comparative, outsider politics especially attuned to the tension between critical engagement and radical disengagement, in harmony with what Carlsson (2002, 75) calls "assertive desertion." Assertive desertion is direct action adrift, an intentional and defiant wandering away from authority that usurps its legitimacy in ways that direct engagement with it does not.

Here emerges a culture of drift, and with it a cultural politics. Drift may be the consequence of contemporary economic and political arrangements, but when it is invested with collective agency and meaning it reemerges in alternative styles of spatial activism and cultural resistance to those arrangements. These styles are as fluid, ambivalent, and disorganized as the lives of those who create them. They drift across spaces, situations, and social categories as readily as those whose lives they reflect, drawing on the sorts of portable skills that they carry with them from job to job—when a job is to be had. All the while, such approaches confront the spaces of law and commerce glancingly, subversively, even playfully—much as drifters themselves move though urban space. Because of this, these approaches also hint at alternative orientations for knowing the world, for moving through it, and for living collectively in it—orientations that pulse with progressive political possibility.

PRECARIOUS POSSIBILITIES

Over the past few years "precarity" has emerged as shorthand for a form of social life pervaded by uncertainty, dislocation, and precarious situations—a life lived sans safety net or ontological certainty. Then again, it's not clear just whose shorthand precarity is. Precarity can be taken as a summary description of a particular historical period—the present period of global crisis and structural disintegration—though it can also reference the contemporary recurrence of longer historical trends toward dissolution and risk. It can be understood as describing the particular problems of a new and largely youthful social class—the "precariat"—as well as the ways this new class is organizing around and against these problems. It can also be read in academic books and journals as a conceptual apparatus, a lens through which to make sense of a plethora of contemporary social conditions. Yet to the extent that precarity both denotes a contemporary world adrift and emerges from it, this ambiguity is perhaps less problematic than appropriate; as Tavia Nyong'o (2013) says of precarity and our multiple understandings of it, "the contagious sense that something might be happening, that another world might be not only possible but indeed be actually coming into view, seems to have been occasioned by street theorizing as much as by straight theorizing." A concept denoting drift and dislocation, a practice still being born from today's circumstances, precarity itself remains fluid and ill-defined (Arnold and Bongiovi 2013).[3]

In any case, in southern Europe, in Latin America, and increasingly in North America, something does indeed seem to be happening. Those involved with precarity as a loose-knit social movement, or perhaps as a general organizing concept, seek to confront the inherent uncertainty of the post-Fordist, consumer-driven economies seen in the previous chapter. They focus especially on a young generation lost between the twin instabilities of long-term unemployment and "flexible," part-time work. For these service-industry "chainworkers" (Colleoni, Marino, and Galetto 2014), the global economy of the late capitalist city leaves little but aborted careers, low-wage service work, unpredictable work scheduling, unaffordable housing—in short, a life defined by precarious prospects and constant uncertainty. As Braverman (1974) has documented, the degradation of work in the twentieth century resulted from the systematic de-skilling of material labor and imposition of Taylorist models of scientifically managed efficiency; such is the degradation of work in the twenty-first century that "immaterial" labor is now subject to algorithmic regulation and de-skilling, without even the small compensations of Fordist security and social welfare that accompanied parts of this earlier process (De Angelis and Harvie 2009). As a result, a new generation confronts a present and a future cut loose from the social contract—a present and future without conventional anchors of education, career, and identity. In this way contemporary consumer-driven cultural economies not only dislocate impoverished urban residents and close public spaces; they also spawn a young, peripatetic army of low-wage service and retail workers drifting between part-time jobs and temporary housing, negotiating irregular work schedules and unpredictable child care, and finding little hope for spatial or social permanence (Seligson 2011).

Theorists of this social condition, and of the movements that are emerging within and against it, speculate that today the sheer extent of precarious circumstances permeating the lives of young people, migrants, refugees, and others may be such that the "precariat" is now emerging globally as "the post-Fordist successor to the proletariat." Moreover, with the "infiltration of models of non-standard employment from low-wage service sectors" into professional and creative occupations, they argue, a "multi-class precariat" may now span conventional class divisions as well (Ross 2008, 34–35). Just as C. Wright Mills (1951) saw the alienation of labor seeping upward into the middle-class occupations of mid-twentieth-century America, observers now see the plight of the low-wage precariat filtering into the professional lives of lawyers, university teachers, medical doctors, and others. By this logic, a part-time university instructor has more in common with the contract janitors that clean university buildings than she does with the few remaining tenured professors. Chapter 1 argued for a dialectical understanding of drift as both a longstanding phenomenon and a distinctly contemporary one; here we see a parallel. There have certainly existed prior historical periods in which all sorts of people lived profoundly precarious lives. Yet what may be different today is the extent to which such shared experiences of social insecurity hold the global potential for political engagement and resistance. As Kruglanski (2005) says, "Perhaps all this precarity is not new. What is new though is the use of this concept to create a common understanding for people to organize around" (see Neilson and Rossiter 2008; Kalleberg 2009).

If precarity is emerging as a node of shared resistance, a loose organizational net linking one drifter with another, then who else might be understood as holding at least provisional membership in the contemporary precariat? A social and cultural geography would include neohobos, wanderers, and nomads traversing North America, Europe, and beyond (Daniel 2008; Grant 2003); gypsy travelers moving across and against governmental boundaries (Shubin 2011; Ward 2000); economic and political refugees on the move from country to country in search of work, safety, or political renewal; migrant workers, regularly victimized by state and economic authorities but also carrying with them the potential to "evade state scrutiny and capitalist discipline" (Ross 2008, 37); sex workers and migratory prostitutes, who remain dislocated both from their home communities and their current communities of residence (O'Neill 2001; Oude Breuil 2008); those operating outside traditional work routines by way of urban scrounging and trash picking, or "homeworking, piecework, and freelancing" (Ferrell 2006; Gill and Pratt 2008, 3); millions of impoverished urban citizens, banished from one space after another and left to endlessly navigate "fractured fields of spatial discipline," from New York City to Phnom Penh (Beckett and Herbert 2009; Langegger and Koester 2016, 149; Springer 2010); and runaway and throwaway street kids made hypermobile by aggressive legal enforcement (Gibson 2011). To this we can add countless, unknown others whose day-to-day lives are shaped by spatial and ontological uncertainty—and more than a few of the activists and participants in Food Not Bombs, Critical Mass, PublicAdCampaign, and other progressive groups.

Within this eclectically precarious mélange, there are some commonalities. The first is the great likelihood that most all involved will continue to breach increasingly rigid spatial and legal boundaries as they drift across cities, countries, and occupations. As already seen, this spatio-legal transgression is all but assured, not only by the movement of the precarious themselves, but by the contemporary reconfiguration of public space as a series of closures, boundaries, and obstacles designed to catch and criminalize free movement. Second are the lines of gender, age, and identity that wrap around the globe. "The more insecure jobs are still and above all carried out by women" (Galetto et al. 2007, 106), for example, and "youth, women and immigrants are disproportionately represented in . . . the precariat" (Ross 2008, 41; see Aubenas 2011; Kalleberg 2009). These lines in turn intersect within particular groups or spatial situations—as in an illegal street blockade by Australian taxi drivers, many of whom were also international university students on limited visas. "The question thus arises," write Neilson and Rossitor (2008, 66), "as to whether the blockade should be read as taxi driver politics, migrant politics or student politics. We would suggest that one reason for the effectiveness of the strike . . . is the fact that it [was] all three of these at the same time." When we see French university students similarly working as part-time sales clerks, exiled Syrian health professionals driving buses in London, Los Angeles Uber drivers doubling as off-the-books bartenders, and Venezuelan nurses waiting in food lines with Venezuelan factory workers, we begin to see something else, too: the ways in which crisscrossing lines of precarious survival weave together odd coalitions and unexpected commonalities of experience, much of it crowding one margin or another. The cavernous factories of early industrial capitalism created a new hell on earth, an assembly line of human alienation, but they also created the spatial conditions that brought workers together and so produced the possibility of organized opposition to them. Now the enforced precarity of neoliberal late capitalism imposes a new kind of permeating pain, but with it come new global possibilities as well. In the mid-nineteenth century, Marx and Engels called for the workers of the world to unite; today a precariat manifesto puts it differently, and in so doing suggests something of the shared uncertainty now linking lives from Europe and the United States to North Africa and the Middle East: "We are all migrants looking for a better life" (quoted in Tari and Vanni 2005).

Those associated with precarity have begun to explore these broader cultural, political, and organizational possibilities. Echoing the experiential politics of the migrant drifter and the Situationist's *dérive*, Christina Morini argues that, while precarity denotes the negativity of instability, "it is at the same time also connected with the idea of re-questioning, of becoming, of the future, of possibility, concepts which together contribute to creating the idea of the nomadic subject without fixed roots. . . . The precarious subject has no fixed points and does not want any. He/she is always forced to seek a new sense of direction, to construct new narratives and not to take anything for granted" (quoted in Galetto et al. 2007, 106).

The new narratives of the precariat do indeed imagine alternative ways of collective living and being—and the potential for turning precariousness back on those whose economic and political policies promote it. Many of these alternatives point beyond traditional labor unions and political parties and toward forms of collective cultural activism that use "visual tools and images extensively" and employ "theatre, cinema, music and stunts to effect political change" (Gill and Pratt 2008, 10). This sort of interventionist cultural activism carries on the Situationist notion of *détournement*—the subversive undermining of dominant cultural narratives. It also develops from "an understanding that cultural production is not an adjunct or addition to the 'real work' of capitalist production but increasingly . . . *is* the work that is a key component of it" (Shukaitis 2009, 170; emphasis in original). Surfing through such cultural work as contract laborers and content providers, the precariat may not profit much from it—but they do understand it. Members of the Italian Chainworkers movement, for example, invented San Precario—the transgendered patron saint of disenfranchised workers and companion saint to Santa Graziella of the Milan Critical Mass—and paraded San Precario through the sorts of retail spaces that employ such workers. Subsequently, they employed their digital and media skills to invent the fictional Anglo-Japanese virtual fashion designer Serpica Naro (a remix of San Precario—an anagram of an imaginary saint), deploying her assumed legitimacy to infiltrate a fashion show at Milan Fashion Week 2005. In the course of the show, "it was announced that Serpica Naro does not exist, [and] the whole prank was revealed to the media, which duly reported the entire story, thus highlighting the issues of casualized work behind the glitter of Milan fashion week" (Tari and Vanni 2005; see Shukaitis 2009, 172–74). Since the show ended, Serpica Naro has continued to exist as both imaginary designer and actual artists' collective, staging events across Europe and Japan, blending "theory, practice, craftism and organization," and advocating on behalf of workers in the "creative industries" (www.serpicanaro.com/serpica-story).[4]

Recalling the nomadic politics that Christina Morini describes, while morphing the Situationist *dérive* into a sort of rolling research project, the feminist collective Precarias a la Deriva (2004, 157–58) has likewise undertaken to drift through "the metropolitan circuits of feminized precarious work" as a way of exploring the overrepresentation of women in such circuits, and of discovering some "common ground of precariousness." Initially staged in response to a Spanish general strike that failed to recognize this sort of "fragmented, informal, invisible work," Precarias a la Deriva, looking for the fraught connections between "a freelance designer and a sex worker," has engaged in an ongoing series of drifts through the spaces of female domestic workers, telemarketers, and food service workers. Through this sort of floating engagement, the members of Precarias a la Deriva have been able to discover nodes of common experience and to "find ways to turn mobility and uncertainty into strategic points of intervention" through the defamiliarization of taken-for-granted environments, collective gatherings, workshops, and other contagious techniques (Shukaitis 2009, 152–56; see Makeworlds 2003). They have also come to recognize the importance of confronting "the denied right to territorialize ourselves" (Precarias a la Deriva 2004, 159)—that is, the importance of constructing spaces in which those otherwise dispersed by part-time work, telecommuting, and insecure housing can come together.

The development and growth of groups like the Canadian Freelance Union and the Freelancers Union in the United States—the latter of which promotes itself as "a federation of the unaffiliated"—suggest that this model of loose affiliation and contingently shared space may in fact be emerging more broadly (www.freelancersunion.org/). Such groups work to legitimize the lives and labors of those caught up in a freelanced, flex-scheduled economy, in part by recalling older models of labor organizing and labor unions and reimagining them as parts of present circumstances. But there are more radical alternatives, too. As Precarias a al Deriva (2004, 160) say, "We can disobey, falsify, pirate, shelter and whatever else occurs to us." These alternative approaches advocate new terms of fluid, disobedient engagement with a world in which global capitalism has effectively annulled the social contract. This resistance and reengagement range from computer hacking and corporate shoplifting to urban/interurban train hopping and collective squatting, all of this a means of raiding what few amenities remain so as to create "a commons for people who do strange, illegal things" (Kruglanski 2005). Here is Kropotkin's (1902) anarchist mutual aid revisited, not as a permanent solution, but as a shared triage of contemporary troubles. And here are echoes of Marx and Engels again, too, their "workers of the world unite" slipping not only into "we are all migrants looking for a better life," but into something along the lines of The Smiths' (1987) "shoplifters of the world, unite and take over."

Collective squatting might at first glance seem an odd fit with a world awash in wandering uncertainty, and an odd strategy for confronting it. After all, squatters by definition hunker down in the domains they occupy, hold tight to their illicit homes, and defy attempts to be driven out with a sentiment regularly sprayed on walls and shouted out windows: "We will not leave." Yet as Lynn Owens (2013, 201) shows, squatting is every bit as much about mobility. A group of squatters may defiantly hold on to one illicit squat or another, but it's their ability to imagine and organize the next squat, and to move between squatted spatial environments, that makes squatting viable in the long term. As Owens says, a squat in this way exists mostly as "a resting place for transient populations," a bit of do-it-yourself spatial stability in support of, and in anticipation of, ongoing mobility. Over the past few decades the larger squatting movement has itself spread in this way, leap-frogging from one squat to another as squatters both defended local squats and traveled between them to share strategies and to assist in other local battles. The mutual aid afforded by squatting moves along with those in need of it, a series of temporary nodes in a shifting network of activism, survival, and free-form travel. For migrants, gutter punks, anarchists, and others, squatting forms another sort of federation of the unaffiliated. Decoded, "we will not leave" comes to mean that we will leave, eventually, but collectively and on our own terms (see CrimethInc. 2003; Mudu and Chattopadhyay 2016).

A similar sensibility has emerged among those activists who participated in Occupy Wall Street and the larger Occupy initiative in the years since this movement partially dissolved. Networks formed during Occupy Wall Street have expanded and dispersed into various forms of aid distribution and antigentrification housing defense, some of it formalized in groups like Occupy Homes and the New York City Antieviction Network, some occurring more episodically. As Laura Naegler (2016) has found, post-Occupy activists often situate their work in the context of precarity; their defense of affordable housing, for example, incorporates the understanding that "the insecurity caused by the precariousness of people's housing situation and their concerns with basic survival limits their abilities, space and time for political organizing." Much like the original Occupy movement, post-Occupy groups also mirror the progressive, nonhierarchical politics of precarity and drift that Critical Mass, Food Not Bombs, and others have developed. Naegler describes Occupy Homes as a "decentralized, loose-knit translocal association of homeowners, community organizers, activist groups, lawyers and unions" that embraces the sort of direct action and horizontal mutual aid offered by antieviction movements like Spain's Plataforma de Afectados por la Hipoteca. Post-Occupy activists in turn see their direct action as operating much like Carlsson's "assertive desertion"—as, that is, a conscious withdrawal from the conventional terms of engagement with authority, toward the goal of directly building do-it-yourself alternatives outside the orbit of traditional politics. One New York City Anti-eviction Network member characterizes this dynamic as shifting from "a logic of antagonism to a logic of subtraction" (quoted in Naegler 2016), not from fear of confronting those in power, but from a desire to undermine their legitimacy by ignoring their rules, withdrawing from their worlds, and crafting lived alternatives to their authority.[5]

Some evidence points to the "demise of [precarity] as a platform for radical political activity in Europe in the mid-2000s" and since (Arnold and Bongiovi 2013, 299); other evidence suggests that precarity continues to take hold as a key organizing concept linking, as Nyong'o (2013) says, the progressive possibilities of "street theorizing" and "straight theorizing." In reality it doesn't much matter. In a world adrift, concepts come and go—but so do millions of migrants, refugees, contingent workers, and homeless urbanites who are afflicted by the fragility of their circumstances. Whether we call this precarity or dislocation or drift, the problem remains—but so does the potential for confronting it and turning it on itself. As the Precarias a la Deriva (2004, 161) say,

"One thing leads to another. From the *dérives* to more *dérives*, from workshops to thousands more dialogues and debates, demonstrations, public spaces, the possibility of accumulation. Beyond the politics of the gesture: density, history, links, narration, territory . . . to be continued."

DRIFTING, DESERTING, SWARMING

Stevphen Shukaitis (2009, 166–68) notes that, among progressive groups in 1970s Italy, the phrase *precario bello* (beautiful precarity) was used to denote opposition to, and withdrawal from, the all too stable Fordist world of routinized industrial production. Now, he argues, an "inversion and transformation" has occurred, whereby neoliberal capitalism imposes precarity and flexibility as the conditions for new forms of degraded labor. Caught up in this awful inversion, our task seems clear: to explore the possibility that this imposed precarity might be remade into, or at least infused with, *precario bello*—and so be made a new sort of critical, progressive politics. If more and more people are forced adrift by emerging economic and spatial forces, how might we find in these circumstances hope of a *deriva bella* as well?

As with Precarias a la Deriva, Critical Mass, Food Not Bombs, and others, the key to realizing drift's progressive beauty may well lie in its parallel potential for creating shared, shape-shifting cultures and come-and-go communities. The work of Precarias a la Deriva suggests that drifters are particularly well placed—that is, displaced—to discover the marginal spaces of other drifters. If so, the pervasiveness of contemporary drift can lead to new forms of community and to new understandings of community itself—community that is uncertain, unsettled, and anarchic in nature, yet connected by the common experiences and perceptions of drift. Here drift also emerges as a potent form of dis-organization, a form that by its own dynamics guarantees loose alliances and evolving lines of direct action, along with forms of mutual aid defined by fluidities of collective self-help (Kropotkin 1902). At their best, these collectivities can preserve the progressive experiential politics of drift—the liberating sense of ongoing comparison, serial critique, and independent intentionality—while ameliorating the hurt, isolation, and victimization that so often accompany contemporary drift. They can honor the loneliness of the long-distance drifter while providing resting places along the way.

In this way drift can be turned back on itself; individual dispossession can become a collective commons of the dispossessed, a nonplace where young workers, homeless populations, migrants, and refugees can shape fluid commonalities of experience. Here in this collective commons we are indeed all migrants looking for a better life—but mostly looking for it among ourselves. Here Australian taxi drivers are migrants, and students as well, freelance writers are occasional carpenters and on-demand musicians, all of them an amalgam of occasional occupations and a hybrid of past and present identities. Here San Precario morphs into Serpica Naro, who lives on in the spirals of cyberspace and in the progressive politics of artist collectives. Here US activists infiltrate New York's Guggenheim Museum with *détourned* art, staging an action in solidarity with the exploited immigrant laborers building a new Guggenheim in Abu Dhabi— and they do so knowing that the contemporary ambiguity as to what constitutes "art" situates their action somewhere between protest and performance art, which in any case they see as part of a subversive "culture without permission" (Naegler 2016). Appropriately enough for those adrift, this collective commons is animated by muddled meaning and cross-cutting identities—and it is precisely the indeterminate, amalgamated nature of these drifter communities that grants their collective power. An ever-changing pack of mongrels and mutts, collectivities of drifters are as difficult to contain as they are to categorize, adept at flowing around and beyond barriers, accustomed to odd coalitions, and attuned to the potential of uncertain movement. Just as drifters transgress borders, ambiguity and confusion elude containment.

The politics of contemporary drift are such that it in turn forms the field of post-Fordist engagement—engendered by inequality, forced on vulnerable populations by law and economy, but in turn available to them as a weapon of assertive desertion and radical denial. Utilized in this way, drift constitutes the abandonment of a system that has abandoned all but its elites; it spawns a process by which the casual laborers and content providers of neoliberal capitalism turn their devalued skills back on the world that has devalued them. Graeber (2009, 213) notes that historically, anarchist and antiauthoritarian movements have drawn inspiration from theorists and activists, certainly, but also have "tended to draw inspiration from existing modes of practice, notably on the part of peasants, skilled artisans, or even, to some degree, outlaws, hobos, vagabonds and others who lived by their own wits—in other words, those who were to some degree in control of their own lives and conditions of work, who might be considered, at least to some degree, autonomous elements." Today those vagabonds and drifters proliferate in new forms, living by their collective wits amidst the ruins of globalized inequality—and as they do, new inspirations for autonomous living and moveable feasts of mutual aid emerge as well. In dialectical fashion, the same forces that sever security and unravel social ties spawn a growing population compelled to exist, as best it can, outside their orbits of control. To drift is to dream—the nightmare dream of home and family lost but the fantasy dream of otherwise unimaginable possibility too.

The dynamics of drift and of the communities that form around it create one final potential for progressive collective action: swarming. Swarms form in flight; their power is their intense ephemerality and unanticipated movement. Swarms are impermanent and unpredictable, intense and unsustainable—dangerous effervescences of collective energy, able to flow and mutate and accomplish on the fly what each individual alone cannot. Swarming is the collective action of those cut loose or, thought of in another way, a form of drifting direct action that is emergent in extremis. Chapter 1 argued that the social lives of drifters are often shaped by "intensities of ephemeral association"—moments of shared experience, whose innate brevity is balanced by their accelerated social bonding. Swarming writes this dynamic in larger letters; it is at its best the ephemeral democracy of the dispossessed. Recently, "swarm theory" models and notions of "swarm intelligence" have been applied with more or less success to ants, honey bees, robotic systems, and artificial intelligence—but whatever their limitations, they do seem to show that decentralized, leaderless systems somehow spawn collective intelligence in such a way that a self-organizing swarm of honey bees on the move comes to know strategies and solutions unavailable to any one member. Swarming in this way becomes a kind of alternative, collective epistemology; just as the flâneur evolves new visions of the city, and the participant in the *dérive* discovers the insights of disorientation, those caught up in a swarm are carried beyond the limits of their own knowledge. Swarming offers drifters both collective movement and a notion of how a social movement of drifters might emerge; it suggests ways to overwhelm obstacles of law and economy and to overcome the confines of individual imagination.

Chris Carlsson (2002, 78) invokes this sense of swarming in discussing the politics of Critical Mass rides, arguing that "in creating a moving event, celebrating and being a real alternative, Critical Mass simultaneously opens up the field of transit to new political contestation, and pushes it to another level by pioneering swarming mobility as a new tactic." Indeed, in the early days of Critical Mass, with San Francisco

Critical Mass rides drawing thousands of participants, then-San Francisco mayor Willie Brown and his administration sought to control the rides by negotiating designated routes and police escorts—except that they could find no Critical Mass leaders with whom to negotiate amidst its dis-organized, decentralized participants. As a result, San Francisco police were ordered to stop the next Critical Mass ride and arrest participants, and while many were arrested, the majority simply scattered and escaped along various spur-of-the-moment routes. "It was not possible for the mayor to engineer what would happen with Critical Mass," said Jennifer Granick, an attorney for some who were arrested. "How was he going to stop the ride? There just wasn't any way. There's no leadership. . . . And what were they going to do, arrest everybody? There's just too many people to arrest everybody. . . . And I think the bicyclists realized that" (quoted in White 1999). Or as another participant put it, "Arrest 5000 people and throw them in jail at once? It could be entertaining (quoted in Ferrell 2001, 109).[6]

Maybe this mélange of fluid collectivity, assertive abandonment, and swarming resistance can convert the enforced precarity and drifting predations of the contemporary world into a new sort of *precario bello* and *deriva bella*. Or maybe not—there aren't after all any maps and not much demand for them among drifters anyway. But if people do increasingly decide to abandon a social order that has abandoned them; to drift away from that which has set them adrift; to live on their own terms and by their own shared wiles in a "homeland of the uprooted," as Hunter S. Thompson ([1967] 1979, 110) put it long ago; and to swarm on occasion back into and against a sedentary social order for their own progressive purposes—well, as the next chapter shows, it won't be the first time.

PART TWO

American Drift

.

4

Hobo History

This chapter's title promises some history, and there will be some here—but it will be at best episodic and uneven. This isn't a generic disclaimer, nor a bit of false authorial modesty; it's more a statement about the subject matter and a manifestation of respect for it. As is perhaps already obvious by this point in the book, and as I'll argue explicitly in the final three chapters, a subject as slippery and uncertain as drift demands something other than static models and imposed certainty as we go about trying to understand it. Drift suggests instead an approach attuned to ambiguity and absence, and one comfortable enough with tangents, dead ends, and misdirection. Hobo history offers a case study in this. Discussing hidden hobo encampments ("jungles"), for example, Todd DePastino (2003, 71) notes, "Most jungle residents scattered when confronted by an investigator's camera, leaving behind nothing more than a bare and nondescript campground." Writing about hobos and ethnicity in the 1930s, John Lennon (2014, 25, 135) mentions similarly that, "numbers of non-white hobos (or any hobos for that matter) . . . are almost impossible to be verified; for the most part, black hobos avoided any official trying to 'count' them." He adds that female hobos were often ignored in public records altogether. Declining to be photographed, counted or accounted for, often excluded from the historical record, hobos and other drifters in this way don't lend themselves to precisions of analysis. When photo-documentarians like Robert Frank (1959) set out to photograph moments of drift, disequilibrium, and despair—to catch something of a shadow world hiding behind the obvious—they intentionally produced photographs that were themselves decentered and out of focus. You could call that visual homology, or maybe visual verstehen, and I'll try for a similar narrative homology here—try to keep things a bit out of focus, lest the subject matter be made to seem something it's not.

So if what follows is not an authoritative history of the hobo, is it at least an adequate one? I really couldn't say. It's probably more like the "secret history of the twentieth century" that Greil Marcus (1989) wrote, and wrote of. Marcus caught sight of that secret history bubbling up now and then in the pronouncement of the Situationists, in the stuttering wails of punks like Johnny Rotten, and in countless other little cultural interpolations and defilements. The secret history that I offer here hides in other places: around the edges of urban rail yards and inside the recesses of freight trains, in the dark dank of old flophouses, kicked out of town or locked away in the local jail. Like Marcus's, it's a history as irregular as it is rhizomatic, coming and going, losing its way—but with a certain sort of subterranean structure that's mostly invisible, or at least hidden away from the everyday citizen. Most remarkably, it's a history that on occasion coalesces, exploding into outright resistance to economic and legal authority, and doing so precisely because it's a history of drift, and of the quintessential American drifter, the hobo.

VAGRANCY

The prehistory of the American hobo might be traced in any number of directions. In 1961 Nels Anderson ([1923] 1961, xiv) wrote, "The hobo was American in the same way that the cowboy was. . . . The cowboy was a hobo type." In the early 1980s, a hobo named Carl located his lineage in early American explorers like Lewis and Clark and in "the mountain men, that's what I think this tramp is about. . . . Because we can make do and make things on our own. . . . And we ain't one bit afraid of work" (quoted in Harper 1982, 120). Richard Grant (2003) agrees about the mountain men and the cowboys and adds to the hobo's mutt-like lineage a mélange of other early American wanderers. "America is the motherland of bumdom," says Jack Kerouac ([1960] 1970, 178), taking a broader sweep still.

In another sense, though, the prehistory of the American hobo goes back a good bit further, to the early evolution of English law. In one of the foundational studies in the sociology of law, Bill Chambliss (1964,

67) set out to explore "the relationship between particular laws and the social setting in which these laws emerge, are interpreted, and take form," and to do so he undertook a historical analysis of the law of vagrancy. As regards the law of vagrancy, Chambliss found that this relationship took two forms. In their early English iterations, vagrancy laws were meant to control the flight of serfs from the manor—to "curtail the mobility of laborers"—and to compel the able-bodied to work, in this way forcing "laborers . . . to accept employment at a low wage in order to insure the landowner an adequate supply of labor at a price he could afford to pay" (69–70). Linked in this way to precapitalist economies of land ownership and production, the laws came to include language condemning beggars and questioning those who travel without purpose or invitation. With the decline of feudalism and the emergence of new economies that had their bases in commerce, trade, and industrial production, Chambliss found, the law remained in place but was now modified so as to protect this new political economy. Now vagrancy laws came to focus on "idle persons going about"; on "ruffians," who "wander, loiter, or idl[y] use themselves and play the vagabonds"; and on those "loitering or idl[y] wandering by the highway side" (quoted in Chambliss 1964, 71–73), because such populations were seen as a threat to the safe transportation of commercial goods. While the general notion of vagrancy as defined by idleness, begging, and illicit mobility remained in place, its meaning and application changed with changing historical circumstances.[1]

The statutes and historical circumstances that Chambliss (1964, 75) explored were English, but he also considered the importation of vagrancy laws to the United States, concluding some fifty years ago that "in America . . . the laws are now used principally as a mechanism for 'clearing the streets' of the derelicts who inhabit the 'skid rows' and 'Bowerys' of our large urban areas." Here Chambliss suggested a third relationship between vagrancy law and social setting, this one tied to the political economy of the contemporary city—and a half century later, as seen in chapter 2, the nature of this new political economy, and this new legal relationship, is increasingly clear.

The North American hobo has likewise evolved across changing historical circumstances—the American Civil War, the expansion of the railways west, the Great Depression of the 1930s—but across these circumstances, the hobo has consistently been caught within the legal definition of the vagrant. As Tim Cresswell (2011, 239) says, "The basic facts of this definition have remained constant for over 500 years. The vagrant is a person who has no established home and drifts from place to place without visible or lawful means of support. At least that is how vagrants have been legally defined. Key here are a lack of place to call home, constant but seemingly aimless motion, and poverty." For the last 150 of those 500 years, American hobos have been made the very embodiment of that definition—shaped by it, beaten and jailed because of it, forced into hiding from it.[2] In this sense they have been made to become that legal definition, to live their lives and move their bodies within and against it. "We were expected to 'keep moving,'" Ralph Chaplin (1948, 88) remembered of his days as an itinerant harvest worker, "yet we couldn't move at all without breaking the law. And, every time we broke the law, the law tried to break us."

Significantly, this definition in terms of vagrancy positions the hobo as a double danger to the sedentary and the successful, and, because of this, assigns to the hobo a debilitating double stigma. Bad enough that the hobo is seen to exemplify the undisciplined life of the underserving poor and is imagined to embrace a loitering sort of homelessness—but worse, the hobo is a stranger, who imports this shambling poverty from afar. In the view of the law, the hobo's mobility is as menacing as the hobo's homelessness and poverty are immoral; in combination, hobos' impoverished mobility positions them as both outside the law and outside the bounds of conventional community. Writing about a particular sort of stranger paranoia and its legal underpinnings, Zygmunt Bauman (2000, 93) notes that "public money has already been set aside in quantities that rise year after year for the purpose of tracing and chasing the stalkers, the prowlers and other updated editions of that modern scare, the *mobile vulgus*—the inferior kind of people on the move, dribbling or gushing into places where only the right kind of people should have the right to be" (see also Linnemann 2015). Hobos have long been America's essential *mobile vulgus,* amusing enough when sanitized for popular culture consumption but in everyday experience demonized for their illicit, uninvited intrusion into stable communities. As early as the 1870s, in fact, the first American "tramp laws" echoed early English law by criminalizing travel by the poor in search of work. And as part of a larger "tramp panic" (Hernandez 2014, 413), the *Chicago Tribune* called for the poisoning of tramps "so that the bloated dead bodies of the decaying corpses would serve as a warning sign for anyone looking for a handout" (quoted in Lennon 2014, 18).

Chapter 2 explored the potential that early sociologists like Robert Park and Georg Simmel saw in the migrant and the stranger: liberation from the conventions of custom, a cosmopolitan openness to new ideas, and an ability to think comparatively. In the view of many a past-or-present American judge, business owner, and newspaper editor, though, such traits when embodied in the hobo or the tramp signal mostly a dangerous sort of disruption to the everyday order of things. From their view, the hobo's mobility denotes a social and cultural distance from community life—even if the hobo is temporarily a part of it spatially— and the hobo's homeless poverty suggests a willingness to hustle and steal from more-established citizens. This perception is not entirely inaccurate, by the way, given that hobos often found themselves with few options but to wheedle their way through unknown, dangerous, or hungry situations. Having ridden thousands of train miles with tramps and hobos, Douglas Harper (1982, 153) reached a conclusion about them that entangled mobility, impoverishment, trickery, and law:

> The dominant theme in tramp tales is that of the tramp as trickster. The tramp invariably gets the last laugh, his free ride after the train crews and police grow weary of the chase, or his free food after the successful hustle. The tramp takes none but his own rules seriously and even those are negotiable. . . . The tramp remains free of and unrepentant to a society which he perceives as a set of pressures to conform, to take orders, and to be unadventuresome. . . . The tramp is a trickster both because he is colorful and arrogant, and because he has, compared to what most people naturally expect from the material world, little to lose. When jobs are intermittent and easily replaced, even a jail term for loitering, for a public drunk or for an illegal ride is a temporary stall along the road, and one with regular food.

In this way some tramps and hobos embrace "a life of amoral trickery on the road" (Cresswell 2011, 243) and come to resemble the itinerant peddlers of the nineteenth century. "Both Jewish and Yankee peddlers were stereotyped as tricksters and confidence men," Susan Strasser (1999, 77) writes. "Like other trickster figures, peddlers crossed and recrossed boundaries, in this case the threshold between the farm household or the rural village and the increasingly cosmopolitan outside world."

Strasser goes on to record the particular suspicion of Yankee or Jewish peddlers as they traveled the American South during this time, and here we see a further parallel with hobo life and its perils. As John Lennon (2014, 131–56) notes, the railroad boxcar that carried hobos across North American in the 1930s was an "interracial boxcar"; black and white hobos came together in the spaces of hobo life.[3] Pushed together by mutual economic desperation, they shared something else as they drifted through the American South: the likelihood of indentured victimization by the criminal justice system. Vagrancy laws were not only aggressively enforced against hobos but were enforced with the goal of stocking the pool of prison labor; for many convicted of vagrancy, the convict lease system and the chain gang awaited. The same vagrancy laws that criminalized the poor and the footloose were used to confine them within a system of brutal, unpaid labor. Those convicted of vagrancy were worked hard on farms, were worked hard on road building, sometimes were worked to death. But unsurprisingly, black hobos were the more harshly punished, serving longer terms than white hobos on chain gangs and, as Lennon (2014, 136–37) says, often "returned to the same fields that had forcibly held their family members during slavery." The illicit mobility of the hobo was not only to be halted; it was to be countered with a particularly brutal form of immobility. In this context, a Georgia roadside sign that Dorothea Lange photographed in 1936 offered both threat and invitation: ATTENTION VAGRANTS CONVICTION MEANS HARD LABOR ON GANG.

Mobility, poverty, ethnicity—all these and more were highlighted in the infamous case of the Scottsboro Boys. Involving nine black youth arrested in 1931 in Alabama, and later tried and convicted for the rape of two white women, the Scottsboro case is generally taught and remembered as an egregious miscarriage of justice rooted in Southern racialist myths about black manhood and its threat to white womanhood. The case is indeed well worth remembering on these terms but for another reason, too. The nine Scottsboro Boys were hobos, pulled off a westbound freight train when it stopped in Paint Rock, Alabama—and boys they were, their ages ranging from twelve to nineteen. In this they were not unusual; during the Great Depression, hundreds of thousands of young people of varying ethnicities hoboed around North America, many pushed onto the road by families who could not support them (Uys and Lovell 1997; Wellman 1933). The Scottsboro Boys came to the attention of the authorities after a fight on the train with white hobos, who having lost the fight and been booted off the train reported them to a local station master. When the local sheriff and his deputized white gunmen subsequently removed the Scottsboro Boys from the train in Paint Rock, they found two white women on the train as well, who then alleged that they had been raped by the group. These two women were also hobos, sporting soiled overalls and hiding in a box car. Young female hobos often attempted to pass as men for their own safety. Like the Scottsboro boys and the white hobos that reported them, like many other young women of the time, they were riding the rails and looking for work. In this they were no more embodiments of mythic Southern womanhood than the Scottsboro Boys were violent

Colored [*sic*] itinerants on oil tank cars passing through Kingsbury, California. (Photo by Dorothea Lange, 1938. Original caption.)

criminals guilty of the sexual assault with which they were charged. Mostly, they were all guilty of being hobos.

"Great sinister tax-paid police cars . . . are likely to bear down at any moment on the hobo," Jack Kerouac ([1960] 1970, 172, 174) wrote in his essay "The Vanishing American Hobo." "In America you spend a night in the calaboose if you're caught short without your vagrancy change." This was in 1960, yet as the next two chapters will show, sixty years on, the hobo has not so much vanished as been revivified in different form. And now as then, the police bear down, the vagrancy charges stick, and the hobo lives outside the law.[4]

WORKS AND WANDERS

The longtime criminalization of the hobo through vagrancy laws, with their twined illegalities of poverty and mobility, raises an obvious question: why and under what circumstances do hobos and others come to be both poor and on the move in the first place? The easy cultural answer, at least within American society and its mythologies, involves a potent intermingling of wanderlust and individuality: cut loose from bonds of career and property, hobos follow their own footsteps—independent individuals proudly chasing after the next horizon. A powerful and seductive notion, wanderlust—this irresistible desire to roam where one will—and certainly within hobo culture, such a notion is sometimes granted legitimacy and importance, as is a self-definition of autonomous individuality. Still, as with other vocabularies of motive (Mills 1940), it's difficult to know to what extent individualized wanderlust is an antecedent to hobo life and to what extent it emerges from the long-term practice of illicit mobility itself. One thing is not difficult to know, though: particular social circumstances have over time put the poor in motion more forcefully than their own motivations and desires. Or to put it as Nels Anderson ([1923] 1961, xvii) did, if we're to link wanderlust and hobo life, we should also acknowledge the particular historical situations in which such wanderlust became "a real asset for the hobo."

By most accounts, the hobo emerged from the profound social changes that animated the period after the American Civil War. Some of this was resultant from the war itself, and from its ongoing dislocations; war veterans often returned to find ruined homes and farms, alienated communities, or public vilification, and so resorted to the road once again, this time as transitory labor. The hobo was also born from the aggressive westward expansion of the railroads during this time. In reflexive fashion, the railroads both required a mobile workforce that they could import to each new work site and, with the completion of each new mile of track, created the machinery by which to import such a force.[5] The deep, ongoing connection between the itinerant hobo and the transcontinental American railroad was no accident; the two were born together. Moreover, this new population of mobile rail workers came to know the railroads and their workings intimately, to feel even their own sort of illicit ownership over that which they had built. To understand the origins of the hobo, then, is to understand "the ways in which the railroads created this disenfranchised class of itinerant workers who, consequently, empowered themselves by stealing rides from these same corporate entities" (Lennon 2014, 9)—and to know the ways in which hobos put all parts of the train to use, even the rods underneath the train cars, in accomplishing their illicit rides. The westward expansion of the railroads in turn opened huge swaths of western land to colonization and, with this conquest, created new industries founded in natural resource extraction and commercial agriculture. Here the hobo was born once again; these new industries themselves demanded—in many ways, created—a seasonal, migratory labor force traversing the vastness of the American West, moving by freight train between unreliable and low-wage jobs and remaining mostly disconnected from the relative stability of eastern North America. Not surprising, then, that by 1870s the *New York Times* was asking on its front page, "What Shall We Do with Tramps?"—and that, as already seen, the *Chicago Tribune* was answering with poison.

The social history of the hobo is at the same time a political economic and spatial history; the hobo emerged around the shadowy edges of a particular economic and geographic frontier, an impoverished worker drifting through an uncertain moment of western conquest and expansion. This distinctive intermingling of work, impoverishment, and mobility echoed earlier in Carl's claim that "We ain't one bit afraid of work." It can be glimpsed in the notion that the term *hobo* may have developed from *hoe boy,* a derogatory term for a seasonal farm laborer (Anderson [1923] 1961, 88; Kornbluh 1998, 67). It can be seen clearly in Nels Anderson's 1923 *The Hobo,* in which he takes pains to carefully define the hobo, in part by distinguishing between the hobo, the tramp, and the bum. Anderson ([1923] 1961, 87–88; emphasis in original) quotes Dr. Ben Reitman, the "hobo doctor," who argued that "there are three types of the genus vagrant: the hobo, the tramp, and the bum. The hobo works and wanders, the tramp dreams and wanders, and the bum drinks and wanders." He includes a variation from St. John Tucker: "A hobo is a migratory worker. A tramp is a migratory non-worker. A bum is a stationary non-worker. Upon the labor of the *migratory worker* all the basic industries depend."[6] And he quotes the hobo and writer M. Kuhn:

> The hobo is a seasonal, transient, migratory worker of either sex. Being a seasonal worker he is necessarily idle much of the time; being transient, he is necessarily homeless. He is detached from the soil and the fireside. By the nature of his work and not by his own will, he is precluded from establishing a home and rearing a family. Sex, poverty, habits and degree of skill have nothing whatever to do with classifying individuals as hobos; the character of his work does that.

The hobo is a made-in-America vagrant—a vagrant whose working impoverishment and idling inactivity, whose life as a perpetual and homeless stranger, are not so much the products of personal wanderlust as they are a social phenomenon, first engendered and then enforced by the emerging political economy of nineteenth-century America. In this way the hobo was also a member of the nineteenth-century proletariat—at first glance a dissolute member of the lumpenproletariat, those whom Marx (1935, 65) dismissed as "the scum, offal, refuse of all classes," including "vagabonds, discharged soldiers, discharged jail-birds . . . tricksters . . . rag-pickers . . . beggars"—but upon closer examination was part of a wandering frontier proletariat made to bear the brunt of capitalist development in the American West.[7]

A half century after the hobo emerged, the burden of this development had hardly eased, and in the summer of 1913, in and around the hop fields of California, the burden became unbearable. Camped in wagons and in tents—some of them no more than sacks thrown over fence lines—some twenty-eight hundred migrant workers had been brought in for the month-long hop-picking season at a ranch near the town of Wheatland. Perhaps half were recent immigrants, among them Mexicans, Syrians, Japanese, Italians, Greeks, Cubans, Puerto Ricans, and Swedes; seven or eight hundred were distinctly "of the 'hobo' class" (Parker 1920, 189). Soon enough this polyglot labor force had coalesced around their discontent with work and living conditions, and when around a thousand of them gathered—speakers were said to have addressed the crowd in seven languages—an armed sheriff's posse intervened. Two hop pickers, the local district attorney, and a deputy sheriff died in the subsequent "Wheatland Hop Fields' Riot," which quickly came to be constructed as emblematic of "the state's great migratory labor problem" (Parker 1920, 172). In response, Carleton Parker, the executive secretary for the State Immigration and Housing Commission of California, was enlisted by the governor to produce a report on the riot and its causes. Parker (1920, 177) found that the ranch owner over-recruited workers, adopted artificially stringent picking standards that reduced earnings to around a dollar a day, and then held back wages and used the uncertainty of payment as "a whip to force pickers to stay out the season." In temperatures ranging from 106 to 110 degrees Fahrenheit, the owner provided little or no water for the pickers while they worked—though they could buy "lemonade" (mostly water and citric acid) for five cents a glass from the ranch owner's cousin. When not working, the pickers slept on piles of straw in the tents, shared nine toilets among twenty-eight hundred people, walked amidst their own garbage—and because of this suffered from malaria, typhoid, dysentery, and diarrhea. Parker (1920, 88–89, 194–99) concluded that legal changes were needed, as well as better working and living conditions, if such riots were to be avoided in the future. But elsewhere he reached a more general conclusion:

> As a class the migratory laborers are nothing more nor less than the finished products of their environment. They should therefore never be studied as isolated revolutionaries, but rather as, on the whole, tragic symptoms of a sick social order. Fortunately the psychologists have made it unnecessary to explain that there is nothing willful or personally reprehensible in the vagrancy of these vagrants. Their histories show that, starting with the long hours and dreary winters of farms they ran away from, through their character-debasing experience with irregular industrial labor, on to the vicious economic life of the winter unemployed, their training predetermined but one outcome.

Two decades later, with the onset of the Great Depression, the hobo's "eternal chase for the elusive job" (Ashleigh 1914, 35) continued—but it was now a chase with considerably less chance of success. As glimpsed in the Scottsboro Boys case, adults and young people, women and men, and members of many ethnic groups took to the trains and the highways in desperate, usually futile quests for work, food, and housing. The Great Depression in North America was defined by systemic economic and ecological failure, and horrific economic hardship; it was lived out by many as a time of profound drift. The failure of crops and farm economies meant dislocation from one's land and a wandering search for something better. Joblessness spawned not only the loss of career identity but the necessity of drifting away from the social networks that had once supported it. One survivor of the Great Depression recalled that, "a man had to be on the road. Had to leave his wife, had to leave his mother, leave his family just to try to get money to live on. . . . The shame I was feelin'. I walked out because I didn't have a job" (quoted in Terkel 1970, 58). In *Waiting for Nothing*, his haunting account of hoboing through the Great Depression, Tom Kromer (1933, 52) confirms this. "When a guy loses his job in his hometown, he has to go on the fritz," says Kromer. "He has to grab himself a drag out of town. A guy can't be dinging back doors for hand-outs and flopping behind signboards when his girl lives in the next block." Once out of town and on the road, the dislocation redoubled. As millions hoboed their way across the continent, even the small stabilities of a trackside hobo camp were subject to the brutal disruptions of the "bulls," or railroad police. Hobos "huddle around their fires in the night," Kromer

(1933, 114) reported. "Tomorrow they will huddle around their fires, and the next night, and the next. It will not be here. The bulls will not let a stiff stay in one place long." Others wandered in rickety automobiles or trucks, most famously in the lyrics of Woody Guthrie songs like "Hard Travelin'" and "I Ain't Got No Home," and in the pages of John Steinbeck's *Grapes of Wrath*. As Dorothea Lange and Paul Taylor ([1939] 1969, 108) documented in their pioneering photo-ethnography of these wanderers, their experience of perpetual drift mirrored that of the hobos. "People has got to stop somewhere. Even a bird has got to rest," reported one of those interviewed in the book. "What bothers us travellin' people the most is we cain't got no place to stay still." Cut loose from any certain trajectory, they and millions others had become what Kromer (1933, 115) said of himself: a "restless ghost."

With the Great Depression, the political economy of capitalism and its crises once again put the proletariat in motion. Such was the awful sweep of the Great Depression that it served in some ways to democratize hoboing, to leave it a last-ditch option for many groups other than the western migratory laborers more accustomed to it. In this way former farmers and factory workers were now made vagrants, too, vulnerable to the railroad bull, the deputy sheriff, and the chain gang. This dispersal of drifting hard times and existential hopelessness resonates in the literature of the Great Depression. Kromer's *Waiting for Nothing* catches something of it, as does the "abiding dispossession" that Kenneth Rexroth (1968, 50–51) described, whereby "there is nothing for these men and women to do but wander, drifting like garbage on a polluted stream, from nowhere to nowhere, for nothing." This confluence of spatial and social drift shaped a sort of hoboing that Nelson Algren ([1935] 1966, 320–1) called, in his 1935 *Somebody in Boots*, "the big trouble":

> By the winter of 1931 Cass knew that disaster had come to the world above him. For all through the South that winter, East and West, the trains gathered people like flies. Whole families piled into cattle-cars, women rode on reefers; old men rode the brakebeams, holding steel rods above the wheels with fingers palsied by age. Several times Cass saw pregnant women riding in empties. "It's the big trouble everywhere," a girl told him. Wherever he went men spoke of "the big trouble."

Writers and hobos themselves have been announcing the "death of the hobo" off and on for a century now; yet while hoboing may have reached a sad sort of apogee with the Great Depression, it didn't die with that era's end. The next two chapters will document a style of hoboing that goes on today, some of it in perfect parallel to that of earlier hoboing, some of it a distinct response to contemporary conditions. But of course hoboing also continued in the intervening years, and so to suggest something of that we'll end here with Kerouac. Author of "The Vanishing American Hobo," he was also author of *The Dharma Bums,* whose opening lines suggest otherwise. "Hopping a freight out of Los Angeles at high noon one day in late September 1955, I got on a gondola and lay down with my duffel bag under my head and my knees crossed and contemplated the clouds as we rolled north to Santa Barbara," Kerouac says. "Somewhere near Camarillo . . . a thin old little bum climbed into my gondola as we headed into a siding to give a train right away and looked surprised to see me there."[8]

HALLELUJAH ON THE BUM

In 1914 Charles Ashleigh (1914, 34–38) set out to explain the hobo to folks back East, who thought that western itinerants—"floaters," in Ashleigh's term—must be shiftless bums "because we beat the trains." He noted that in the East the "the industries are territorially stationary" and staffed by sedentary workers, while out West work was periodic and widely dispersed. Consequently, he continued, the western hobo must continually ride the freights to the next job, along the way living in hobo jungles, outsmarting local authorities, and confronting "the unceasing, gnawing fear of arrest for vagrancy or of a beating up by the railroad police in the yards of the town or destination." Once at the work site, he added, the hobo must then endure strenuous outdoor labor and further encampment in primitive conditions. As a result, Ashleigh argued, the hobo was distinguishable from the eastern worker in another way—and in a way that left the hobo anything but an unmotivated bum: "The constant matching of wits and the daring needed for the long trips across country have developed a species of rough self-reliance in the wandering proletariat of the West." A half century later Nels Anderson agreed. Looking back on his own history of hoboing and his subsequent scholarly study of the hobo, Anderson ([1923] 1 1961, xiv) concluded that, "apparently the hobo life was severely selective. Continuation in it called for a capacity to move from one type of work to another and from one place to another. Adapting to the strange and new in tools, work, machines, and scenes was for him a normal consequence of moving. Such resourcefulness was expected of all who went out into the wide areas."[9]

Rugged self-reliance, adaptiveness, resourcefulness, all honed and deployed while wandering 'the wide areas'—these would seem essential attributes for today's drifters as well, as chapter 1 suggested and as following chapters will confirm. But as regards the historical politics of hoboing, these attributes and the conditions under which they were acquired presented a significant contradiction. On the one hand, such attributes, attitudes, and conditions would seem to inhibit any type of progressive collective action among hobos aimed at addressing working conditions or other issues. The sort of rough individuality and rugged pride in lone survival necessary to ongoing migratory labor in the West hardly promoted a sense of collective engagement or common good—and there were many hobos who harbored this individualistic ethos, most famously the young Jack London (1907). The hobos who embraced this sense of self were moreover endlessly scattered about and on the move through the very environment that had shaped them: the wide areas of the American West. Such people and places didn't lend themselves to conventional organization and shared political practices; in fact, they would seem the perfect prescription for undermining them. On the other hand, if such hobos could somehow come together in some alternative form of collective progressive action, they would bring to the battle an oddly powerful set of skills. Their toughness and hard-earned self-reliance would allow them to bear forms of brutalization and exclusion under which others might wither. Their comfort with adapting to dislocation would be exceeded only by their considerable skills at engineering their own illicit mobility. Perhaps most importantly, countless episodes of matching wits with deputy sheriffs and enduring beatings from railway bulls would provide both a comparative study of authority and a healthy disregard for its logic and legitimacy.

This particular potential for progressive hobo action was certainly seen in the 1930s. In 1932, unemployed veterans of World War I set out on a "Bonus March" to Washington, DC, where they demanded payment of their delayed war bonuses. Described as "latter-day hoboes," whose camps looked like "an immense hobo jungle," the Bonus Marchers incorporated both progressive and reactionary political factions among their ranks (DePastino 2003, 195, 197). Taking over freight trains and gathering recruits as they went, the marchers numbered twenty-five thousand by the time they reached Washington, where they constituted the largest protest the city had encountered up to that time. With federal and military officials fearful that the assembled Bonus Marchers might spark a revolution (or a coup d'état), their Washington campsite was condemned, and police and the US Army utilized tear gas and tanks to drive them from the city. As the Great Depression dragged on, this sort of drifting discontent coalesced into more general collective protest as well. The people that Rexroth (1968, 51) earlier described as "drifting like garbage on a polluted stream, from nowhere to nowhere, for nothing" later formed "the vast masses of men and women who eventually stirred, marched in hunger marches and demonstrations, and were the bottom foundation stones of the radical movements of the latter thirties."

One of the more significant radical movements of the latter 1930s emerged with the volunteer International Brigades who traveled to Spain to fight Franco and the Fascists during the Spanish Civil War of 1936–39. Among these international brigades, Canada's MacKenzie-Papineau Battalion most strikingly embodied the political potential of hobos and others left adrift. Unlike some of the other international units, the Mac-Kenzie-Papineau Battalion was predominantly working class—and beyond this, was made up of many recent immigrants to Canada, along with young people and adults who had spent the early 1930s hoboing across Canada. Members of the battalion in fact argued that it was their rough wandering that eventually led them to—and prepared them for—the physical pain and radical politics of participation in Spain's civil war (Kish 1975). Michael Petrou (2008, 27) notes that "the vast majority were immigrants. . . . Almost all were leftists of one degree or another. Most suffered grievously during the Great Depression. They were overwhelmingly single and frequently unemployed. Hundreds were transient, with no homes other than temporary ones in lumber camps and mining shanties or, more often, relief camps." Some five hundred members of the MacKenzie-Papineau had also been part of a 1935 "On to Ottawa Trek," in which Western Canada relief camp workers and the skid row unemployed boarded eastbound freight trains, intent on delivering their grievances to the prime minister, before being stopped by the clubs and guns of the Royal Canadian Mounted Police. In this and other ways the MacKenzie-Papineau volunteers were made criminals—and not only because many had been charged in Canada with fighting the police, illegally boarding freight trains, or vagrancy. Canada's 1937 Foreign Enlistment Act outlawed participation in foreign wars like the Spanish Civil War; investigated by the Royal Canadian Mounted Police both before their departure for Spain and after their return to Canada, the volunteers were forced to violate the act in order to engage the fight against Fascism. But for them, of course, evasion, dislocation, and illegality were nothing new; such experiences constituted the curriculum they had learned long before their departure for Spain.

Yet the epic economic and political conflicts of the 1930s were not the first instances in which the hobo's collective politics of illegality and dislocation had come into play. The 1932 Bonus March, for example, was anticipated by the mobile Industrial Armies that emerged during the economic depression of the 1890s. Like the Bonus Marchers, members of the Industrial Armies hopped boxcars and commandeered entire freight trains—some fifty in all—in their attempt to reach Washington, DC, there to protest and petition for unemployment relief. Like the Bonus Marchers, the Industrial Armies also embodied a contradictory sort of class politics. Though they included hobos and other transient workers, their leaders at times took care to distinguish the armies' more craft-oriented and law-abiding working-class members from wandering laborers, and they sometimes attempted to exclude hobos from the armies' ranks. Consequently, John Lennon (2014, 64) sees the Industrial Armies of the 1890s as a "collective working class political movement" that existed in tension with the individualism and rugged autonomy of the hobo. Todd DePastino (2003, 61, 70) finds that the "improvised responses to rootlessness" of the Industrial Armies "heralded the birth of a radically new subculture of western hobo labor."

That radically new subculture and politics of the hobo would come to full fruition a decade later, with the founding in 1905 of the Industrial Workers of the World (IWW, also known as the Wobblies)—and this time there would be few concerns about conventional legitimacy or legal obedience. Established by a collection of socialists, anarchists, and radical unionists that included Mother Jones and Eugene Debs, the IWW was meant to operate both as a union and more broadly as an anticapitalist, working-class social movement. Rejecting the divisiveness and relative elitism of craft unionism and the moderately reformist aims of many craft unions and socialist organizations, the IWW set out to organize the working class into "One Big Union" toward the goal of overthrowing capitalism and establishing an industrial democracy. In this effort, the IWW embraced the least-paid and most stigmatized sectors of the working class, including recent immigrants, unskilled workers, and itinerant workers. "We are going down into the gutter to get at the mass of workers," said IWW leader Big Bill Haywood, "and bring them up to a decent plane of living" (quoted in Kornbluh 1998, 2). Through this strategy, the IWW quickly gained membership and momentum and began to fight for its brand of revolutionary unionism on any number of fronts. Over the next ten years, the IWW was in fact a force nationwide, orchestrating the first sit-down strike in America against the General

Electric Company in Schenectady, New York; staging a strike of twenty-five thousand textile workers, many of them women and children, in Lawrence, Massachusetts; leading a strike of silk workers in Paterson, New Jersey, which included the production of the Paterson Strike Pageant at New York's Madison Square Garden; and, with its affiliate the Brotherhood of Timber Workers, organizing a racially integrated battle against the Southern lumber trust in eastern Texas and Louisiana.

It was in the American West, and among itinerant western workers—the "bindle stiffs," who carried their few belongings bundled into a small bindle—that the IWW took on a distinctively fluid shape while adopting a particularly militant approach. Central among the groups that founded the IWW was the Western Federation of Miners; with leaders like Big Bill Haywood—"a powerful and aggressive embodiment of the frontier spirit" (historian Foster Dulles, quoted in Kornbluh 1998, 2)—the Western Federation of Miners had in 1897 split from the more conservative American Federation of Labor and now sought to push union radicalism further still. As Haywood said, "To understand the class struggle, you must ride on top of the box-cars or underneath the box-cars" (quoted in Foner 1965, 120). Other Wobbly leaders and organizers likewise embodied the West's "frontier spirit" and its hobo heritage as well. IWW writer and organizer Joe Hill was "the hobo-martyr," a worker who "drifted from job to job like most single migrants" before joining the IWW and who was ultimately executed by firing squad at the Utah State Penitentiary (DePastino 2003, 105; Kornbluh 1998, 127). Ben Reitman, the "hobo doctor" already seen, was also an "agitator . . . anarchist . . . confidant of Emma Goldman" (Lennon 2014, 13) and IWW sympathizer and supporter. Legendary IWW organizer Frank Little "was the 'hobo agitator.' More than any other individual he personified the IWW's rebelliousness and its strange compound of violent rhetoric, pride in physical courage (the *machismo* element), and its seemingly contradictory resort to nonviolent resistance. Part American Indian, part hard-rock miner, part hobo, he was all Wobbly. . . . This one-eyed rebel never occupied a comfortable union office, or kept books . . . instead he always went where the action was" (Dubofsky 1969, 186; emphasis in original). Worn down by repeated beatings and imprisonment, Frank Little nonetheless went where the action was one last time—to Butte, Montana, in 1917, to support the local copper miners—where he was lynched and left to die by corporate vigilantes.

Few western Wobblies came to be as (in)famous as Frank Little or Joe Hill—but many personified the same sort of freewheeling mobility

Napa Valley, California. More than twenty-five years a bindle-stiff. Walks from the mines to the lumber camps to the farms. The type that formed the backbone of the Industrial Workers of the World in California before the war. (Photo by Dorothea Lange, 1938. Original caption.)

and courageous disregard of authority. In an uncanny echo of Ashleigh's and Anderson's evaluations of the hoboing western worker, the IWW newspaper *Solidarity* published in 1914 a laudatory essay on "the nomadic worker of the West," who

> embodies the very spirit of the IWW. His cheerful cynicism, his frank and outspoken contempt of bourgeois society . . . make him an admirable exemplar of the iconoclastic doctrine of revolutionary unionism. . . . His anomalous position, half industrial slave, half vagabond adventurer, leaves him infinitely less servile than his fellow worker in the East. Unlike the factory slave of the Atlantic Seaboard and the Central States, he is most emphatically not

"afraid of his job." His mobility is amazing. Buoyantly confidant of his ability to "get by" somehow, he promptly shakes the dust of a locality from his feet whenever the board is bad, or the boss is too exacting, or the work unduly tiresome, departing for the next job even if it be 500 miles away. Cost of transportation does not daunt him. "Freight trains run every day" and his ingenuity is a match for the vigilance of trainmen and special police. No wife or family encumber him. . . . Nowhere else can a section of the working class be found so admirably fitted to serve as the scouts and advance guards of the labor army. Rather they may become the guerillas of the revolution—the francs-tireurs of the class struggle (quoted in Kornbluh 1998, 66–67).

Summarizing his official investigation of the 1913 Wheatland Hop Fields' Riot, Carleton Parker (1920, 123) offered a socioeconomic explanation for this easy cynicism and general contempt for respectable society. "The casual migratory laborers," he argued, "are the finished product of an economic environment which seems cruelly efficient in turning out human beings modeled after all the standards which society abhors." A second IWW newspaper, the western-based *Industrial Worker* (1912, 2), confirmed Parker's analysis. "We are not 'undesirable citizens,'" the paper editorialized. "We are not citizens at all. We are rebellious slaves, scorning the morals, ethics and institutions of the Plunderbund. Therefore we are not respectable. We admit it and we are proud of it."[10]

An episode early in the IWW's history confirmed the essential role that these disreputable western rebels played. In 1908, with the IWW's fourth convention in Chicago looming as a battle between those who advocated engagement with politicians and political action versus those who favored a more militant strategy of direct action in the workplace, James W. Walsh and some twenty direct action Wobblies assembled in the Portland, Oregon, rail yards to set out for the convention. Hopping freight cars as they went, camping in hobo jungles, the group dressed in denim overalls, black shirts, and red bandanas, with an IWW button on the coat. Along the way they were confronted by armed railroad officials, jailed, forced to walk miles between trains, and regularly made to wait hours before catching their next ride—but they used such times to hold rallies, make speeches, and sell IWW literature to crowds that gathered. Once in Chicago, they slept on lakefront benches, survived on a few cents a day, and most significantly succeeded at the convention in moving the IWW away from political accommodation and into a long-term strategy of radical direct action. Appropriately enough for the hobos who made up this "Overall Brigade," their medium of transportation was also their message. "The outstanding thing about the fourth convention," an IWW publication noted soon afterward, "is the spirit that actuated to an unusual degree those delegates who, lacking the means of transportation, had to cover hundreds of miles on foot, travel by freight and in boxcars in order to participate in the convention" (quoted in Foner 1965, 112).

In reality, though, Walsh and the Overall Brigade didn't just happen to come together in the Portland rail yards; most of them were also members of the Industrial Union Singing Club, a group of musicians and singers that Walsh had put together to provide music for IWW rallies and to counter the street proselytizing of the hymn-singing Salvation Army. At the meetings they held on the way to Chicago, the Overall Brigade sang IWW songs and sold "song cards," on which were printed the song lyrics. Walsh reported from Missoula, Montana, that their meetings were out-drawing those of the Salvation Army, and that enthusiasm was high. "We put the 'Starvation Army' on the bum, and packed the streets from one side to the other. The literature sales were good, the collections good, and the red cards containing the songs sold like hotcakes" (quoted in Kornbluh 1998, 42). The most popular of the Wobbly anthems was "Hallelujah on the Bum" (alternately "Hallelujah I'm a Bum"); like many Wobbly songs, the melody for "Hallelujah on the Bum" was borrowed from a well-known hymn that the Salvation Army sang, in this case the hymn "Revive Us Again." The new Wobbly lyrics were hardly sacred:

> I can't buy a job,
> For I ain't got the dough,
> So I ride in a box-car,
> For I'm a hobo.
>
> Hallelujah, I'm a bum!
> Hallelujah, bum again!
> Hallelujah, give us a handout
> To revive us again.[11]

So popular was "Hallelujah On the Bum" that, over time, the Salvation Army was forced to quit singing the original "Revive Us Again" at its street revivals (DePastino 2003, 62). The Overall Brigade's singing of "Hallelujah On the Bum" at the 1908 convention had a different effect; offended, the more respectable eastern socialists at the convention took to calling the western workers "the bummery."

The following year the red song cards were expanded into a pocket-size IWW songbook, popularly known as the *Little Red Songbook*. Soon enough the songbook came to include direct attacks on the

Salvation Army, as in Joe Hill's "The Preacher and the Slave." Sung to the tune of the hymn "In the Sweet Bye and Bye," the song ridiculed "long-haired preachers" of the "starvation army" who promise a better life in the hereafter but condemn those who fight for one in the present. More than a few songs described the hoboing western worker—songs like "My Wandering Boy," already printed on the 1908 song cards, which recounted a tatterdemalion arrested for vagrancy ("pulled for a vag") and sent to the chain gang.

> Where is my wandering boy tonight,
> The boy of his mother's pride?
> He's counting the ties with his bed on his back,
> Or else he's bumming a ride . . .
>
> His heart may be pure as the morning dew,
> But his clothes are a sight to see.
> He's pulled for a vag, his excuse won't do.
> "Thirty days," says the judge, you see. . . .
>
> "I was looking for work, Oh Judge," he said.
> Says the judge, "I have heard that before."
> So to join the chain gang far off he is led
> To hammer the rocks some more. . . .
>
> Don't search for your wandering boy tonight,
> Let him play the old game if he will—
> A worker, a bum, he'll ne'er be right,
> So long's he's wage slave still.[12]

It was not only the content of the *Little Red Songbook* that resonated with hobo's lives; it was the book itself, its size, and its portability. Slipped into a pocket, the songbook went with the wanderer, arriving at the next hobo jungle or work camp unnoticed by camp boss or police officer. With its arrival, the IWW arrived, too, even with no union organizer or union hall nearby; for a mobile and widely dispersed population of workers, the songbook kept the seeds of rebellion in circulation. The songs that the songbook recorded in turn became the soundtrack of hobo jungles, strikes, and jail cells. Mostly taken from hymns or popular songs, the melodies were already widely known; once the lyrics were learned, and sung collectively amidst gatherings of hobos, a living culture of organized resistance began to emerge among a come-and-go population seemingly ill-suited for it.[13] And a living culture it was; while the songbook provided a set of lyrics for each song, Wobblies and other hobos regularly added or amended lyrics as they saw fit, or as the labor situation demanded, so the songs continued to emerge.

The pervasiveness and the power of the songbooks, and of the songs they taught, were well understood at the time. Noting the "phenomenal spread of the propaganda of the IWW," Ashleigh's (1914, 37) 1914 report emphasized that while "the size of the local membership is an uncertain gauge in that territory of ever-moving fluid labor . . . certain it is that around nearly every 'jungle' fire and during the evening hours on many a job in the great westland, the IWW songbook is in evidence, and the rude rebel chants are lustily sung and discontent expressed more and more defiantly and impatiently." In 1916 the *Industrial Worker* (quoted in Kornbluh 1998, 84) published the poem "The Migratory IWW," by "J. H. B. the Rambler," which lamented the plight of the transient worker and noted that

> At night he wanders beneath the stars
> With the mien of an ancient seer,
> And often he's humming a few sweet bars,
> Of a Rebel song soft and clear.

Carleton Parker's (1920, 189–90) careful investigation of the 1913 Wheatland Hop Fields' Riot confirmed this. As already seen, he found that "some 700 or 800" of the hop pickers "were of the 'hobo' class"—and he added that, because of this, they were "in every sense potential I.W.W. strikers." He also provided an explanation of this tendency. "Where a group of hoboes sit around a fire under a railroad bridge," he said, "many of the group can sing I.W.W. songs without the book."

Parker's investigation uncovered yet another dimension of Wobbly songs, and of the Wheatland "riot" itself. At the hop pickers' rally, speeches had been made, and an IWW organizer, Blackie Ford, had held up a sick baby before the crowd, shouting, "It's for the life of the kids we're doing this" (quoted in Parker 1920, 192). But at the rally's close, as the sheriff's posse arrived, and with gunfire soon enough leaving four dead, the assembled crowd of two thousand hop pickers wasn't listening to a speech. They were together singing a song—"Mr. Block," written by the drifter and Wobbly Joe Hill. Mr. Block was a long-standing IWW character, a nonradicalized, obedient, patriotic blockhead who came to life in Wobbly songs, stories, and cartoons. In Hill's song "Mr. Block," he's joined the migratory workforce and paid an employment agency—an employment "shark"—to secure him a faraway job:

> Yes, Mr. Block is lucky; he found a job, by gee!
> The shark got seven dollars, for job and fare and fee.
> They shipped him to a desert and dumped him with his truck,

Mr. Block

He Goes Harvesting

Originally published in the *Industrial Worker*, 21 August 1913. (Public domain.)

But when he tried to find his job, he sure was out of luck.
He shouted, "That's too raw,
I'll fix them with the law."[14]

Bad enough that Mr. Block would trustfully pay the employment "shark" to secure him a job or, as in the cartoon above, gullibly accept stories about plentiful jobs and high wages on down the line; worse yet was his patriotic belief in the justness of American law, by which he would "fix them" for shortchanging him. The Wobblies knew better. In response to the Wheatland "riot," the California governor sent five companies of the National Guard to put down the unrest and protect property. Ranch owners deployed their own private police force, with private detectives systematically detaining and torturing alleged IWW members. Two years later governors of the western states petitioned President Wilson for a federal investigation of the IWW; by then Blackie Ford and another IWW organizer, Herman Suhr, had been convicted and sentenced to life in prison for the killings at Wheatland. As Parker (1920, 193) reported, "We have talked hours with the IWW leaders and they are absolutely conscious of their position in the eyes of the law."

Migratory workers of many nationalities, made IWW rebels by the serial brutality of their work conditions; Wobbly organizers floating between labor camps and harvest fields; incendiary songs secreted away in coat pockets and sung at shadowy gatherings beneath railroad bridges and in hobo jungles—the western IWW was everywhere and nowhere. IWW organizer Frank Little, it will be recalled, had no office and kept no books; and in any case, the recorded size of an IWW local's membership wasn't really much of a measure, Ashleigh (1914, 37) reported, in a world of "ever-moving fluid labor." Beyond this, any IWW member of any nationality was welcome to work as an informal organizer by acquiring membership cards and some IWW literature and taking these along to the next job, thereby becoming "an official whose headquarters was where he hung his hat" (quoted in Foner 1965, 118). Along the way, a migratory worker might or might not encounter an IWW "Flying Squadron"—a group of two or three IWW members, working autonomously while traveling the rails, confronting robbers, violent railroad detectives, and others who posed a threat to migratory workers (Higbie 2003, 153, 186–67). Certainly the national IWW had officers, a constitution, committees, even an elaborate organizational diagram ("Father Hagerty's Wheel of Fortune," it was called) by which the IWW hoped to structure a new industrial democracy. But by intention and necessity, among western migratory workers the IWW's organizational structure unwound—and sometimes became as liquid as the lives of its adherents, drifting along with their changing circumstances.[15] In his report, Parker (1920, 114–15, 190–91) noted that "the dues-paying membership of the IWW is an uncertain and volatile thing," and he alleged that "its treasury is merely the momentary accumulation of strike funds." He offered an elaboration and a warning:

> The IWW in California is not a closely organized body with a steady membership. The rank and file know little of the technical organization of industrial life which their written constitution demands. . . . It is in their methods of warfare, not in their abstract philosophy or even hatred of law and judges, that danger lies for organized society. . . . The IWW is teaching a method of action which will give this class [migratory workers] expression in violent flare-ups such as that at Wheatland. The dying away of the organization after the outburst is, therefore, to be expected. Their social condition is a miserable one.

As Parker's comments suggest, the western IWW's organizational elasticity may have been necessitated by the uncertain circumstances of its member's work and movement—but it also constituted a particularly potent method of collective action and class warfare. It was a method of action that the Wobblies would perfect in one particular set of battles that they launched against those predatory "employment sharks," who had charged poor Mr. Block seven dollars for a job he never got. It was a method that Blackie Ford and Herman Suhr knew before they arrived at Wheatland; by then they had already used it to fight the employment sharks in Fresno, and San Diego, California. In fact, by the time they got to Wheatland, Ford and Suhr knew what the IWW knew, what Frank Little and the Flying Squadrons knew: that drift could be made the dynamite by which to explode an everyday order of legal and social injustice.

FELLOW WORKERS AND FRIENDS

Migratory workers endlessly came and went between job sites, which were themselves little more than temporary assemblages of machinery and housing; IWW organizers in the West were equally transitory, generally working without benefit of office or union hall. While organizing did go on at work camps and along the rails, this collective fluidity meant that the skid rows and mean streets of western American cities became essential venues for IWW organizing—not only because this was where transient workers washed up and waited between jobs but because this was the location of the hated employment sharks through whom the next job might or might not be secured.[16] In this way, western towns and cities were the nodes of the western worker, the junctions of labor, travel, and potential recruitment into the IWW. Because of this, IWW organizers held regular, well-attended meetings on the street corners of western towns and cities, making speeches, countering antiunion reports in the commercial press, singing songs from the *Little Red Songbook*, handing out literature—and, as always, competing with the Salvation Army for the hearts and minds of the workers. "Soapboxing," this practice came to be called—a Wobbly mounting the platform provided by an overturned soapbox to deliver an organizing speech on the street, and often a condemnation of the employment sharks and their practices.

In city after city, the official response was the same: a legal clampdown on street speaking, with an exception often provided for the Salvation Army. Working with employers and employment agencies, probusiness city councils across the West devised a variety of legal strategies to shut down IWW public gatherings and the speeches that animated them. In Missoula, Montana, IWW success in open-air recruiting led to an ordinance outlawing street-speaking. In Spokane, Washington, the city council passed a prohibition on public meetings on streets, sidewalks, or alleys (except for those of the Salvation Army), ostensibly in the interest of traffic safety. In Fresno, California, the police chief revoked the IWW's permit to speak on the streets—though the Salvation Army was allowed to continue—and threatened to jail all involved for vagrancy. In San Diego, California, an ordinance banning street-speaking was supplemented by a second "move on" ordinance and by a general roundup of vagrants. In Aberdeen, Washington, the city council was straightforward; its amended ordinance allowed any organization to assemble and speak in the city's main streets *except* the IWW. In cities throughout the America West, the decade of 1907–16 saw the same cycle: the increased militancy and organizational success of the IWW matched by increasing legal prohibition of urban street gatherings and speaking.

Anyone who knew the Wobblies knew that they weren't likely to abide by these new legal constraints—but it was the particular manner in which they violated them that defined the thirty or so IWW "free speech fights" that erupted during this time. The IWW decided to break these new laws en masse, sending one speaker after another up onto the soapbox to court arrest and jailing. The IWW's intention was to turn each new ordinance back on itself by filling the jails with Wobblies who had violated it—Wobblies who would then each demand an individual jury trial, thereby overloading the criminal justice system, straining city finances, and forcing repeal of the ordinance. Notably, and despite the IWW's often aggressive rhetoric, their strategy also emphasized passive, nonviolent resistance to police and jailers; the goal was not physical confrontation with individual authorities, but collective confrontation with a rigged legal system. Notable also was the IWW's larger goal in engaging these free speech fights. Though the fights came to constitute "some of the most spectacular attempts to put the Bill of Rights into practice the country has ever seen" (Foner 1965, 172), the Wobblies were less interested in defending the Constitution than they were in defending their ability to battle employment sharks and to organize itinerant workers as they paused, if temporarily, in places like Fresno, Missoula, and Spokane. The free speech fights weren't abstract arguments over freedom of expression; like the itinerant workers themselves, the fights were spatially and historically situated, on the skid rows and the street corners of the cities, and across the wider spaces of the American West.

And as it turned out, it was the very itinerancy of these workers—their practiced mobility, their gritty durability and on-the-fly self-reliance, their serial disregard for locality and law—that provided the IWW its strategic advantage. When a free speech fight erupted in a particular city, the IWW couldn't simply rely on however many members and sympathizers might currently be present if they were to effectively challenge the law by overloading the jails. Instead, the IWW each time sent out a call to members and "fellow workers" throughout the West, urging them to flood the city and so provide the necessary numbers for clogging the criminal justice system. Western workers and Wobblies responded by the hundreds and thousands, as well they might. Often they were themselves between jobs, and so free to come when called. Other times they quit jobs in lumber camps to come—sometimes whole camps emptied out—since they had little long-term commitment to any one job anyway and could always track down another. They certainly knew how to get there, having spent years hopping freights and traveling light. And they were no more intimidated by the police or jails in one city than in another; many of them had seen as many jails as they had cities, had been arrested time and again on charges of vagrancy or public disorder. The labor historian Philip Foner (1965, 174) concludes that "the IWW worked out a pattern of free-speech fighting which enabled it to make the most spectacular use of its scattered members and created the impression that ten men existed where there was only one," and he includes a song verse, taken from a 1914 issue of the IWW newspaper *Solidarity:*

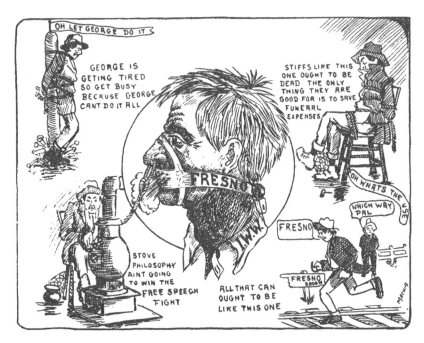

Fresno Free Speech Fight. Originally published in the *Industrial Worker*, 2 February 1911. (Public domain.)

There is one thing I can tell you,
And it makes the bosses sore.
As fast as they can pinch us,
We can always get some more.

Getting some more Wobblies to a free speech fight sometimes became a battle in itself—but one the Wobblies were well prepared to fight. Attempting to get from Seattle to Portland and on to the 1911 Fresno free speech fight, over a hundred Wobblies and sympathizers banded together, designating duties (secretary-treasurer, medical director, cook) and electing a train committee charged with identifying hoppable freight trains. Eventually exhausting their train options, the group set out by foot, walking 244 miles through snow and rain with many of its members "lightly dressed" and "nearly barefoot," with "blistered and bleeding" feet. In towns along the way, the group was interrogated by railway police, but the police "always found the more questions they asked the less they knew about us" (Clyde [1911] 1988, 101–2). Two years later, another group set out from San Francisco for Denver in support of the free speech fight there, "travelling light" on the freight trains and embracing "speed by all means" (Nolan 1913a, 1). Organized like the Fresno group around various duties and committees, the group also carried two signs: "On to Denver, Free Speech Denied the Right to Organize One Big Union" and "We Are in Your Town and Must Eat." Arrested and jailed repeatedly en route, other times successfully dodging police and vigilantes, the travelers handed out IWW literature, staged a mock free speech fight in Elko, Nevada, and passed the time singing "Mr. Block" and other Wobbly songs while stranded in the Utah desert. Eventually covering sixteen hundred miles in fourteen days, and growing from an initial membership of twenty to ninety by the time they reached Denver, the group reported that "their sole wish is to be taken from a soapbox, not from a boxcar" (Nolan 1913b, 4).

As Wobblies surged into a city, public speaking on behalf of the union became radically, sometimes absurdly, democratic; one after another an often inexperienced Wobbly mounted the soapbox, getting out only the salutation "fellow workers" or "fellow workers and friends" before being pulled down and arrested by the police and replaced by the next speaker. But this serial soapboxing, and its effects on city government, was a success; over and over again the Wobblies won the fight and forced repeal of the targeted ordinance. In Missoula the work of Frank Little and countless others led to the ordinance being rescinded and all cases against IWW members dropped. Frank Little showed up in Fresno as well, where the IWW's success in organizing Mexican American rail workers and farm migrants had steeled the local authorities against the Wobblies—but the local authorities nonetheless eventually buckled to IWW demands, revoking the ordinance, paroling convicted prisoners, and releasing the others. The Washington governor's denunciation of the IWW as "illiterate hoboes" (quoted in Foner 1965, 179) notwithstanding, Spokane city authorities likewise finally agreed to allow the resumption of street speaking and to release all IWW prisoners.

In the same way that the free speech fights were rooted in immediate, practical issues of union organizing and opposition to employment sharks, though, the Wobblies' success in these fights was grounded in something more practical, more sensual, than the eventual revocation of a local legal ordinance. Put bluntly, it was grounded in the Wobblies' ability to endure tortuous brutality. Ultimately the arrested free speech fighters may have been released from jail—but while they were confined they were made to suffer. Men and women alike were jailed; pregnant

IWW organizer Elizabeth Gurley Flynn was arrested, jailed, and charged with criminal conspiracy in Spokane. Prisoners were confined in fetid cellars and unheated school buildings, jammed into claustrophobic jail cells (twenty-eight prisoners in a seven-by-eight foot cell), hosed with cold water and scalded with hot, beaten by their jailers, and put on diets of bread and water. Often working in concert with the police, local vigilante groups made up of business owners and their allies, and at times deputized by the local mayor, in turn attacked and beat IWW members with axe handles, raided and burned down local IWW headquarters, and violently deported IWW members from within city limits. In San Diego, police released prisoners into the hands of vigilantes, who drove them into the desert, where they were beaten, made to run a gauntlet of attackers, and forced to kiss the American flag. When the anarchist Emma Goldman and her companion, the "hobo doctor" Ben Reitman, arrived in San Diego, they were met by a vigilante mob; Reitman was later abducted and taken to the desert, where he was beaten and branded with the letters "IWW," burned into his back by a lit cigar. More than a few Wobblies died of illness, beatings, and gunshot wounds.[17]

Meant to warn the IWW away from the free speech fights, this official, organized violence carried some other meanings as well. Historians generally interpret it as evidence of militant antiunion hostility among business elites, and as confirmation of their collusion with the criminal justice system in suppressing labor organizing. This is certainly the case; during the free speech fights, mayors, police chiefs, business owners, commercial newspapers, and local merchants' associations worked in concert to suppress the IWW, to brutalize Wobblies in the streets and in the jails, and to maintain their structural dominance over labor. But in addition, the pervasive top-down violence of the free speech fights tells again the story of vagrancy, and of the double stigma of poverty and mobility that the vagrant carries. From the view of local and regional business elites, it was not only that the free speech fighters were rebellious workers, intent on overthrowing the law; worse, they were *itinerant* workers—dislocated, disinclined to spatial or occupational permanency, swarming into cities and towns, daring to organize and fight back, and using their impoverished mobility to do so. "The freewheeling insolence of the revolutionary–minded hoboes" (Rosemont 1988, 431–32) must have stung indeed; local newspapers echoed the violence against them, calling for the whipping post, the cat-o'-nine tails, and hanging. In fact, "hanging is none too good for them and they would be much better dead," argued the 1912 San Diego *Tribune*, "for they are absolutely useless in the human economy; they are waste material of creation and should be drained off in the sewer of oblivion there to rot in cold obstruction like any other excrement" (quoted in Foner 1965, 196).

But of course the Wobblies and other itinerant workers weren't absolutely useless in the economy of the West; they were absolutely essential to it and well-hardened by their circulation amidst its undercurrents. And here is the second lesson of all that violent brutality: toughened and turned self-reliant by their lives on the rails and in the migrant labor camps, the Wobblies survived it. They survived it and found ways to thrive amidst it. To the amazement and consternation of jailers and local business people, the imprisoned Wobblies sang night and day from the *Little Red Songbook*. Accustomed to waiting out periods of unemployment, they waited out jail, too, organizing their own affairs inside the jail and setting their own rules. They held recruitment and propaganda meetings in the cells—meetings that succeeded in pulling new members into the IWW. They launched hunger strikes against their bread and water diets, and when released from jail while a free speech fight was still under way, they went back to the streets to face the vigilantes and be arrested again. "These people do not belong to any country, no flag, no laws, no Supreme Being," complained the San Diego police chief. "I do not know what to do. I cannot punish them. Listen to them singing. They are singing all the time, and yelling and hollering, and telling the jailers to quit work and join the union" (quoted in Foner 1965, 200). Accustomed to adaptation, inured to discomfort, and unimpressed by legal authority, the Wobblies turned the jail into a union hall.

Wandering the American West, the hobo and the Wobbly embodied a complicated politics of drift. The conditions of their working lives kept them on the move, hopping trains and chasing jobs—and the corruptions of the employment sharks and the employers meant that this movement might be toward only the briefest of jobs, or toward no job at all. A way of life defined by drift and its demands in turn produced itinerant workers who carried with them particular strengths, attitudes, and adaptabilities—characteristics that made them a challenge to organize but a hellacious force for social justice once they were. Their organization, the western IWW, itself embodied a sort of liquid defiance that washed up in great waves here and there—waves that rolled in from afar as Wobblies rode the rails or walked their way to the next free speech fight, picking up supporters as they went.[18] Once there, the old notion of the hobo trickster—beholden to no rules and no town, adept at outsmarting one authority or another—now reemerged collectively in the form of the Wobbly free speech fighter, who defied a law that would soon enough be turned back on itself and so terminated. Concluding his 1914 report on the Western "floater," Charles Ashleigh (1914, 37–38) argued,

> The free speech fights of San Diego, Fresno, Aberdeen and Spokane, the occasional strike outbursts in the lumber country, the great railroad construction strike in British Columbia and the recent tragedy of Wheatland are all indications that the [floater] is awakening. It was indeed an unpleasant surprise to the masters of the bread in the booster-ridden West when the much-despised tramp worker actually began to assert himself. . . . Suddenly, lo and behold, the scorned floater evolved his own movement, far more revolutionary and scientific than his skilled brother had ever dreamed of! From the lumber camps, from the harvest fields, water tanks, jails and hobo campfires came the cry, ever more insistent, of the creator of western wealth.

Forced mobility had become a force for social change; if the problem was drift, so was the solution.

5

Catching Out

It's late May, Memorial Day in the USA—Fort Worth, Texas, USA, to be exact—and I'm celebrating the same way I celebrate most every day: out on a bicycle ride, hitting trash bins and Dumpsters as I roll along, scrounging for clothes, tools, food, or whatever else might be of use to somebody (Ferrell 2006). Heading back toward home, I decide I'm enjoying the ride and the late spring Texas heat too much to want to end the ride just yet, so I wander away from my usual semiplanned trash circuit and simply ride where my wheels take me. After another forty minutes or so I end up along Vickery Blvd., the busy street that parallels the equally busy Davidson rail yards of the Union Pacific railway. From there I cut in behind the Whataburger and the Shell station, then onto a freeway access road, so I can hit the Montgomery Street Bridge over the freeway and head back home. Now on the access road, I notice ahead at the Montgomery Street intersection a young guy with a cardboard sign, panhandling money from cars stopped at the light. That's where I'm headed anyway, so it's not like I decide to roll up on him, but I do figure I'll say hello when I get there.

As I slow down and offer my greetings, he asks me if he can ask me something: Where do you catch a bus around here? He explains that he has to be downtown for an 8 a.m. appointment tomorrow morning, and he doesn't want to have to walk it like he did last time. We get to talking about the shitty bus service and the inadequate bus routes, and about the time that I'm noticing the railroad crossing tattoo on his right arm and the railroad tracks image on his "Cash Needed, Even Pennies Help" panhandling sign, he confirms what I'm beginning to suspect: he's a train hopper. I mention my own experience with trains and train graffiti (Ferrell 1998, 2001), and after a while he feels comfortable enough to tell me that his name is Zeke and that the reason he has to be downtown tomorrow morning is a probation hearing. Seems that back in February, having just joined up with two guys and a girl who were also train hopping, he was riding a freight train though Arlington, about ten miles east of where we now stand. Tragically, the train hit and killed a young woman lying on the tracks, and so while police and railroad officials investigated, the train stayed stopped. After a while, the train-hopper girl got off to take a piss, at which point some guy along the tracks tried to assault her, so Zeke and her boyfriend jumped off and came to her defense. Punches were thrown, and with all the police in the area, Zeke ended up arrested for assault.[1] Worse, he'd left his belongings back in the boxcar, and his beloved dog Hannah, with whom he'd freight hopped to some forty states. Asking the arresting officer "What about my dog?" Zeke was told, "I don't give a fuck about your dog." The officer wrestled Zeke to the ground when he resisted.

Back in 1923, when Nels Anderson researched and published *The Hobo: The Sociology of the Homeless Man,* he had a sense of just such encounters. "The hobo's suspicious attitude toward all organizations and persons in power is not altogether without ground," he noted. Anderson ([1923] 1961, 248, 166) also concluded that "the experiences of the tramp or hobo in the police court do not increase his respect for the law and the administration of justice," and Zeke would no doubt agree. Convicted of the assault, offered two years in prison or five years' probation, Zeke took the probation, even though friends advised him to go ahead and do the time, since the probation system was rigged for failure and so an eventual trip to prison anyway. And indeed, as we talk, Zeke is panhandling—"flying a sign," as he calls it—not only for food money and bus fare to his probation hearing but for the seventeen dollars he'll need tomorrow to pay for the mandatory drug test that his probation requires. Now this is nothing on the order of some of the legal abuses seen in the previous chapter, or that Anderson ([1923] 1961, 165–66) documented back in the day—like the young hobo, convicted of vagrancy and sent as convict labor to a lumber camp, there to be whipped to death by company officials—but it's certainly an example of what Pepinsky and Jesilow (1984, 10) call the "state protection racket," with Zeke and countless others forced to pay for their own urinary surveillance in order to stay out of jail. Not to mention, as he tells me later, "probation fees, payments to the courts—and I got to go to anger management."

At this point I decide to lend a hand—that is, to bike back to my place, grab some cash and cold water, and bike it back to Zeke. Returning, I find him resting in the shade near the Shell station. "Hot one today," I say—not a complaint really, since I actually like the heat, actually like being outdoors under almost any circumstances—but just to reopen the conversation and to account for his having temporarily abandoned his panhandling and repaired to the shade. "Yeah, but anything's better than being inside," he says. As I find out later, he means it: since being released from jail a while back, he's been Dumpster diving for food, panhandling for change, cleaning up in a nearby creek, and sleeping rough in and around the rail yards. He knows the area well from years of passing through Fort Worth as a train hopper—and as he tells me later, even if he can't currently hop a train because of the probation problems, he still enjoys being around them. Still, this situation creates yet another set of probation problems—problems that have echoed throughout the vagrant's life for generations. "You wake up breaking the law drinking in public, you go to sleep breaking the law sleeping in public, how are you going to do that probation time?" Zeke says. "'I don't want to violate and I don't want to pick up a different charge, to get more time." I give him the cash and the water, we talk a while longer about our shared love of trains and the outdoors, and then I head home—but not before giving him my phone number and telling him to stay in touch. Maybe, I suggest, I could even talk with him for this book on drift that I'm writing?

A few days later, I hear from Zeke and the conversation comes off— we sit for a couple of hours and talk on the curb of a parking lot behind a little business near the rail yards. Turns out Zeke left home eight years ago, at the age of seventeen, to ride trains. He tried to go back to school but "couldn't stick"—the road "whispers in your ear the whole time," he says.[2] Also in those early days, he remembers, "I didn't know what I was doing, I'd occasionally get off [a train] and just, you know I'd be, my family's in New Mexico and out in California, and I wouldn't have a way to get ahold of them, I'd just sit down and start crying, you know I'm tired, it's raining outside, I just want to go home and have a place to sleep, and somewhere to call home." But he learned the skills of hoboing, made friends among fellow train riders, and "now, I've been doing it for so long, that nah, I don't get disoriented anymore. . . . You know what, I got air in my lungs and blue skies over my head, and that's what makes me happy. As long as I'm not behind bars, rock solid."

Much of that learning and many of those friends came from the world of punk and its core philosophy of DIY—do it yourself. "DIY for sure," says Zeke. "I've been DIY since I was, man, birth really. I grew up in a household my dad cooked meth and my mom was a heroin addict. My two older sisters raised me, and I was taught how to cook rice by the time I could stand on a stool and see up onto the stove. Do it yourself was definitely in my book. And then growing up in the punk age, and stitching your pants up a little tighter so that they fit right, or your t-shirts, and puttin' studs and sewing up your own patches on your clothes, you know that was just the way I was raised. But again in the punk scene I was what 14, 15 when I was just solid into it, but I really got into it when I was about ten. And since then on, older kids, twenty years old, they're like here's a CD, here's an album, check this band out." Specifically, Zeke considers himself a gutter punk—the sort of "street punk kid" who "grew up riding trains and going from show to show to show by way of freight trains." For gutter punks, the game is street-level autonomy, do-it-yourself survival, and drifting perpetual motion—as distinct from the well-groomed, stay-at-home "housy punks" with whom they sometimes come into conflict. "More power to them, I'm not doggin' anybody out," says Zeke. "But that's the difference between us. I'm a gutter punk."[3]

I've known such kids—I hung out with a few gutter punks fifteen years ago while I was writing a book on battles over urban public space (Ferrell 2001), and in my experience Sarah Ferguson's (1994, 70) description of their world from those days still generally holds: a "subculture of run-aways, misfits, self-proclaimed freaks, anarchists, and unrepentantly dirty crusties who roam the highways and freight lines of America." I even dedicated that book to Brian Deneke, a young punk murdered in Amarillo, Texas—and in fact Zeke says of Deneke, "I've almost lived my life *for* him this entire time, because I was a kid when he died." But what talking with Zeke now helps me understand is the particular constellation of actions and attitudes that defines gutter punks as modern-day hobos. As practiced by Zeke and others, day-to-day survival as a gutter punk draws on three seemingly distinct activities: train hopping, flying a sign, and Dumpster diving. On one level, these three endeavors do indeed fulfill different needs: train hopping provides mobility, flying a sign generates cash for food or legal fees, and Dumpster diving dredges up practical necessities like food, clothes, and water containers. At a deeper level, though—that is, at the level of shared meaning and lived politics—these practices coalesce within the lives of gutter punks. If hopping a freight train defines the classic sense of hobo-ing, then Dumpster diving or flying a sign can be thought of as commod-ity hoboing—practices that replicate hoboing's mobility, uncertainty, and independent survival. In each case, the dynamic is one of making do with what's available, and doing so outside the bounds of legality and consumerism, on one's own do-it-yourself terms. "Running trash cans," as Zeke calls Dumpster diving; flying a sign; hopping a train—notice that in each instance the language suggests autonomous agency, ongoing motion, and uncertain results. Train hoppers hop trains, but first they wait for trains that may or may not arrive, and may or may not depart once boarded; Dumpster divers take action to scrounge for goods that, on any given occasion and in any given trash can, are not likely to be available; panhandlers seek money that may or may not be proffered.

In this sense gutter punks are defined by drift, even when they are not aboard a moving freight train bound for wherever. All of their essential endeavors are shaped by the dynamics of drift, by a mercurial mix of self-determination and abandon amidst situations beyond their control. Theirs is a sort of survival surfing; the ocean of straight society generates the wave, but they figure out how to surf it—and upon wiping out, as they always do, they figure out how to catch the next one. Hopping a freight, diving a Dumpster, or hustling for a dollar are all ways of riding the rhythms of contemporary commerce while withdrawing from those rhythms as well.[4] Remembering his own early life drifting down the road from job to job, Nels Anderson ([1923] 1961, ix) recalled that, "I did find myself penniless a number of times. I used these occasions for get-ting another kind of hobo experience, begging from passers-by on the streets ('panhandling') or begging at back doors for food"—and indeed, all of these are equally uncertain hobo experiences. Then or now, hobo-ing is clearly desertion from the standard valences of sedentary work and money but at the same time it's the kind of "assertive desertion" (Carls-son 2002) discussed in chapter 3, a form of survival that is both do-it-yourself and derivative. Dumpster diving constitutes a series of drifting encounters with the regulated and commodified products of contempo-rary life, not only by the peripatetic nature of movement to and from Dumpsters, but by the haphazard nature of what is found and how it is reused (Ferrell 2006).[5] Flying a sign involves episodic dips into the pock-ets of the more settled, a series of beseeching raids on the budgets of the more affluent. And hopping trains—well, as I was to find out, that is itself an uncertain, glancing encounter with a massive system dedicated to the orchestrated movement of commodities.[6]

For his classic study of youth subcultures, Dick Hebdige (1979, 113) drew on the work of Claude Levi-Strauss and Paul Willis to suggest that practices such as those just described can be understood in terms of homology—that is, "the symbolic fit between the values and lifestyles of a group." For gutter punks, the values of street-level survival and DIY autonomy, and the practices of train hopping, Dumpster diving, and flying a sign, exist in just such a fitted relationship. Each embodies and amplifies the other within the dynamics of day-to-day living; within these dynamics, practical necessities at the same time become symbolic statements. Zeke, for example, relishes telling me how, when Fort Worth city workers came early one morning to clear out a hobo jungle campsite that he and other young gutter punks had established, the punks asked if they could at least have their breakfast first. The workers agreed—and were then frustrated and astonished to see the punks take the time to start a fire and cook a big breakfast of eggs, Spam, and tortillas on a piece of plate metal they had scrounged from the yards. Likewise, explaining why he's continued to sleep rough near the rail yards since getting out of jail, Zeke tells me, "The shelters to me, they're off limits to me, they're full of junkies, and people who actually need it. I can get by on my own . . . there might be family that if I take a night bed that night maybe they won't be able to get in."

And then there are Zeke's tattoos—by their design and by the circumstances of their acquisition an epidermic catalogue of do-it-yourself dedication, geographic drift, and general gutter-punk living. He got his first tattoo—the one that's "supposed to say anarchy"—when he was twelve, a do-it-yourself job "with a guitar string, a motor from a Walkman, a spoon, a Bic pen, and some electrical tape." The black dots tattooed on his face stand for "my crazy life"—and speaking of which, "I got this tattoo driving down interstate 95, I was doing about 85 miles an hour, and my girlfriend was picking me with a safety pin, under my eye." His (ex-)girlfriend did most of his other tattoos as well, and along with various train images, he sports a dog paw tattoo, a "vagabond" tattoo, a tattooed image of "kill your television," and a tattoo of a trash can. "Man, I've almost got a decade of eating out of a trash can," he says, explaining the idea behind this one. "I better just go ahead and put one there." He also has "1987," the year of his birth, tattooed on his hand. He doesn't often possess any sort of official identification—and so as he tells me, laughing, this tattoo is especially useful for buying beer. His only concern has been that some of his tattoos might be mis-interpreted as gang tattoos when he's in jail, and thereby force him to affiliate with one ethnic jail gang or another—since as he says, he's "half Mexican, half Anglo," and uninterested in any sort of enforced ethnic categorization.

While we're sitting and talking about Zeke's tattoos, he mentions one of mine—a big bicycle sprocket that I have inked on my right arm. "Whenever I seen you come riding up, I seen that right there and I'm like man, this guy is like old school bike punk," he tells me. Turns out, I wasn't just reading his tattoos when we met; he was reading mine, too. Thinking about this, about drift and homology, and about other situa-tions in which strangers and I have first known each other by our tat-toos (Ferrell 2001, 118), I realize something. While tattoos can serve as markers of membership or memory in any number of subcultural worlds, they seem to serve a special purpose in worlds defined by dis-jointed relations and spatial drift. In these worlds, tattoos often become a person's street passport, portable proof of subcultural citizenship inked onto an arm or ankle. Zeke's "1987" tattoo may buy him a beer—but more important to his social and practical survival are the tattoos that buy him hard-earned status among other train hoppers and entry into the next jungle campsite or shared boxcar. Now of course government-issued passports can be faked, and so can the street pass-ports that are tattoos—but to the extent that either stands up to scru-tiny, the holder is granted both social recognition and entry into alter-native worlds. Like a well-used passport, a drifter's body illustrated with tattoos also becomes a personal travelogue, a bodily repository of places, people, and experiences encountered along the way. If for some, tattoos operate as little more than trendy (if mostly permanent) decora-tion, for the hard traveler they function as essential travel documents. Don't leave home without them? Hell, you couldn't if you wanted to.[7]

Wrapping up our interview, Zeke takes me to see another sort of travel document. We walk a mile or so down Vickery to a little Quick-Way convenience store across from the rail yards, and easing into the alley behind it, Zeke points out some graffiti on the power boxes attached to the store's back wall. Now I've been writing graffiti, and writing about various forms of graffiti, for a long time (Ferrell 1996), but this is something different. As Zeke explains to me, these markings are "sign-ins"—a form of graffiti that train hoppers use to encode their travels and to communicate with other train hoppers. Like contempo-rary urban graffiti writers and their crews, train hoppers often sign in

Sign-ins, Fort Worth, Texas. (Photo by author.)

using the name of the train-hopping crew to which they belong and
their own nicknames within the subculture. But in addition, they also
use sign-ins to provide local information, and to denote the direction
they're traveling, for the benefit of other train hoppers who may arrive
after they do. As Zeke decodes the sign-ins for me, I can begin to see it:
the wall parallels the rail yards, and sure enough, some of the stylized
train tracks written, along with crew and individual names, point west
out of the rail yards, some east. Zeke explains, "My sign-in is SDK, it
stands for Slow Drunk Krew, and my [nickname] is Get Bent. A sign-in
is you put your logo and then you put your name and then you put the
date that you were there and the direction you were headed . . . anywhere around the train yards, on the train too . . . say some kids had
never jumped into Ft. Worth before, they'll find a light pole with a train
riding sign on it and there'll be an arrow pointing, store half a mile that
way, or cheap beer that way."

As Zeke is well aware, these contemporary sign-ins recall and reinvent long-standing traditions of coded and dated hobo graffiti (Daniel
2008; Rogers 2016), black ink bread crumbs scattered along the way to
confirm a hobo's fleeting presence at a particular time and place, and to
commemorate the many little moments along an unwinding journey.
Like this earlier hobo graffiti, sign-ins serve as shared travel documents

as well. As they accumulate in a particular spot, sign-ins become a collective archive of arrivals and departures—until they're painted over, as the QuickWay sign-ins eventually were. More importantly, sign-ins serve to encode and communicate important knowledge amidst an inherently dispersed community. Written near rail yards or at the rail-yard "catch out" spots, where train hoppers surreptitiously board trains, sign-ins point new arrivals toward safety or food or beer. Written on the trains themselves, sign-ins move about as a form of subcultural knowledge and communication—a form of communication riding in precisely the right place for other train hoppers to encounter it. Stationary or on the move, sign-ins operate as an alternative network of communication that links the lonely autonomy of drifting adventure to the possibility of shared community. Zeke adds that, after any big punk music gathering, sign-ins proliferate around nearby rail yards, as participants disperse by freight train and leave last-minute notes as to their intended next destinations. "Without the ever-present crutch of the Internet," Aaron Dactyl (2012, 3) writes in the preface to *Railroad Semantics* #1, his account of a two-week train hop through the American Northwest, "every train car is a web page in its own right and every marking a log-in date and blog post of a life lived well beyond what any web posting can convey."[8]

All of which is true enough, except that as Zeke had laughingly admitted earlier, he and his friends do sometimes use the crutch of the Internet, or the digital convenience of the cell phone, to keep in touch. If enough money accumulates from flying a sign or scrapping scrounged metal, a cheap laptop or a prepaid cell phone can sometimes be acquired, and with it at least temporary access to Facebook pages, online information, train-hopping forums, or friends' phones—though as I later learn from Zeke, finding a place to plug in and recharge can itself be a challenge. Just as this occasional digital technology supplements the communicative web of subcultural sign-ins, it also sometimes provides practical assistance with the ongoing work of train hopping. Zeke and others have come to know certain informational phone numbers utilized by the various railways—and by calling these numbers and entering the identification number of any particular rail car, one can often find out that car's destination. While train hoppers generally rely on their accumulated knowledge of rail yards and train patterns to discover which trains are departing when and for which destinations, this digital information can be especially useful—and in fact, Aaron Dactyl (2012, 8) uses this technique himself, noting that "after calling in some cars, I found them to be headed north of Pocatello, to Blackfoot." Of course digital access can occur in the other direction as well, with railroad officials sometimes monitoring websites on which train hopping information is exchanged (O'Connell 1998).

The continent-wide web of stationary and mobile sign-ins, and its supplemental assemblage of cell phones and computers, suggests something about the nature of gutter-punk community. Talking about the girl he defended from assault, Zeke tells me that he had met her long ago, lost track of her for years, saw her again while train hopping, fell out of touch once more, and met and traveled with her again just before the assault. More generally, and despite his membership in the Slow Drunk Krew, Zeke allows that he sometimes chooses to ride alone and sometimes with others—and that he has been known to leave someone behind if that person is being a "knucklehead." Learning her way around the world of train hoppers in her documentary *Train on the Brain*, Alison Murray (2000) comes to realize that, "friendships are made, you travel with someone for a while, then you go your separate ways—that's the way it seems to work." Indeed during the course of the film, Murray and her companions meet a young runaway in a truck stop restroom and begin traveling with her—and two train hoppers reunite for the first time in years when they spot each other riding the same freight train across western Canada. Others record similar experiences. Sarah Ferguson (1994, 74) watches her on-the-fly contingent of train hoppers fall apart as some exit the train early and two others are arrested, but she also sees little reason for concern. "Our road family was gone like a bend in the tracks," she says, "but we had escaped—no time to miss anything." And as recorded in chapter 1, Ted Conover's (1981) long-term adventure with hobos and train hoppers was permeated by groups coming together, going bad, falling apart, and sometimes reuniting. As also seen in that first chapter, this seems to be the nature of community among gutter punks and other drifters—intensely shared experiences separated by transient ephemerality—and under such circumstances, sign-ins and cell phones form an important if porous exoskeleton for otherwise fragile associations.

While Zeke and I have been talking about sign-ins and cell phones, though, a more immediate issue than community has come up: Zeke has a meeting with his probation officer tomorrow, this one to decide whether he'll have to serve his probation here in Fort Worth, or will be allowed to have it transferred to his hometown in eastern New Mexico. This is a meeting of no small consequence. As Zeke and I discuss, he knows no one other than me here in Fort Worth, and has no prospects for housing or work—whereas back in New Mexico he has relatives, a place to stay, and a good chance of finding work in the oil fields. Worse still, we agree, he doesn't stand much chance of impressing his probation officer with his upright attitude, and thereby persuading her to move his probation to New Mexico, given that he's only creek-clean and is wearing, as he has been for days, the one set of clothes and raggedy shoes he had on him when he went to jail. A plan emerges: we'll walk the mile or so back to my house, where Zeke can shower, get some fresh clothes, and spend the night in preparation for the meeting.

After a shower, I outfit Zeke in a pair of Dumpster-dived boxer shorts; pants and a shirt that were handed down to me a while back; and a serious pair of black, high-lace army boots. A couple of years ago, I had discovered the detritus of a returning Iraq war veteran tossed into a Dumpster: desert camouflage uniforms, flashlights, guidebooks, maps of Al Fallujah, and four pair of like-new military boots. Two pair I passed on to the homeless shelter, two I kept to wear myself—and now one of those pair is on Zeke's feet, courtesy of the US Army. After dinner and a few beers, Zeke beds down in the backyard—anything's better than being inside, you know—and the next morning we're up early so I can drive Zeke downtown for the meeting. A couple of hours later, he calls; she has granted the probation transfer to New Mexico, he tells me, in part because she was impressed that he'd made the effort to get cleaned up and to acquire some new clothes. He also tells me that, given the approved transfer, he now plans to hop the next train out for West Texas—Pecos, Texas, to be precise; from there he'll hitchhike to his hometown in New Mexico.[9] First, though, he wants to come by to thank me in person for all the help. I offer to pick him up, but he says he has too much good energy from the successful meeting and wants to walk. When he hasn't shown up a couple of hours later, I call him back; turns out he's made it all the way back to the rail yards, almost to my house, but has run into some novice train-hopping kids he's having to deal with. He's appreciative when I arrive to pick him up there, since it creates a pretext for ditching the knucklehead kids; Zeke doesn't trust their novice skills and so doesn't want to catch out for West Texas with them. In response, I propose one more on-the-fly plan: well, speaking of novices, how about I catch out with you instead?

Zeke thinks this is a fine idea, and so now back at my house, I quickly stuff one of my Dumpster-dived backpacks with a couple of shirts, a bandana, spare socks, matches, a water bottle, two cans of beans, a sleeve of saltine crackers, some packages of nuts I scrounged from a liquor store Dumpster, and an old paperback copy of Kerouac's *The Dharma Bums*. To the bottom I tie a bedroll—actually, a big old woolen poncho that I'd scrounged a few months before. In my pocket I have a scrounged Swiss Army Knife, my driver's license, and a few dollars. And we're off. We catch a ride down to the QuickWay, stopping there to buy two gallon jugs of water. Nels Anderson ([1923] 1961, 17) said of the old hobo jungles that "if there is a general store nearby where bread, meat and vegetables may be had, so much the better," and indeed Zeke and other train hoppers have utilized the QuickWay many times while camped nearby—though these days the purchases tend to be more along the lines of Raman noodles and beer. Today, starting out in the Texas heat and heading into more, our primary interest is water.

Back outside the store, hoisting our packs and water jugs and getting ready to walk the two miles down Vickery to one of Zeke's preferred catch-out spots, a big guy in cowboy garb eases up, a bit unsteadily.[10] "You guys need any help?" he asks. Zeke tells him, "Nah, we're good," but when he offers to give us a ride to the spot, we agree—it is indeed hot as hell, and in addition this saves starting the trip with a long walk along a busy and distinctly pedestrian unfriendly, police-patrolled street. "You been drinkin' today, man?" Zeke asks him before we get under way. The guy admits he has but says his girlfriend, currently in the QuickWay, will be doing the driving. Turns out she does, but while doing so she spends most of her time facing backward, telling the two of us in the backseat how cool it is we're hopping a train. We're thinking that maybe she's had a few herself—and then she volunteers that she just got out of four years in prison, that she lost everything while imprisoned, and that she's now trying to put her life back together. Later, Zeke tells me that this made him suspicious—too much information, too quickly. Still later, he offers me some parallel advice regarding train travel: the more eager someone is to share a campsite with you, the more cautious you should be about doing so.

After they drop us off at a small city park across Vickery from the catch-out spot, we walk down a little creek that runs through the park and under Vickery to the rail yards, hopscotching pools of water and using the creek underpass to cross unseen to a deep, high-banked, paved drainage ditch that channels the creek next to and below the yards. This long ditch seems to be some sort of hidden third rail to the transportation systems of West Fort Worth. Up above and behind, I can see a chain-link fence and hear Vickery traffic humming and clattering by, though I can't see the cars from down here fifteen feet below street level. Up ahead I can hear the train yards—but, like the street, can't see them. Down here there's just this long cement corridor, steep walls on each side angling out to the top, and all of it more or less overgrown along the tops of the walls and out over the ditch with trash trees and weeds and vines. A hundred yards to the left, the ditch disappears into a big corrugated steel culvert, wide enough for two automobiles and cut deep under a city street; beside it is a smaller drainage culvert. Here's a place to hide out or get out of the weather, and along with little jumping frogs, raccoon tracks, and some sort of small dead animal, there are sign-ins: "TOPH3P," with vertically drawn train tracks; a group of sign-ins that includes "C" and "R" in a crossed track circle, "C R A B" (each letter underlined), "W D D ?," and what appears to be "Canadian . . . fuck"; "M!tch! G"; and "Nort Texas Grupo N1, Agosto—Fiedel, Ramon, Raul, Joel, Ivan, Tomas." It strikes me that, if the cops weren't looking for you, and if a big rain didn't wash you out, you could hang out down in here a long time, waiting for a train or for nothing in particular.

Zeke has already warned me that we could indeed be in this spot for a long time—that we could well wait hours or days for a suitable train to depart—and I've told him, only half-kiddingly, that if I get too bored or impatient, I'll just walk home. As I'll come to find out, this is a distinctly inappropriate response. It's not just, as seen in the previous chapter, that Wobblies and hobos of the early twentieth century waited interminably for trains to take them to jobs, free speech fights, and other trouble; or that, as Nels Anderson ([1923] 1961, 215) wrote in the 1920s, "'killing time' is a problem of the homeless man"; or that, as Dorothea Lange documented, waiting afflicted itinerant populations in the 1930s. It's that killing time remains the perpetual problem and the necessarily accepted fate of the freight hopper today. Experienced train hoppers can read rail yards and rail cars for signs of departure or destination, and can sometimes glean specifically useful information from sympathetic train workers or informational phone numbers. Yet this expertise is cut with big doses of ambiguity and imprecision as to when trains will be made up and sent out, and which directions they will travel and for how long. Access to trains is in turn sometimes blocked by high fences, deep ditches, surveillance cameras, or the sudden appearance of rail workers or railroad police. The results are generally false starts, revised plans, and long, unpredictable periods of waiting.

Ted Conover (1981, 3, 26–27), for example, began his adventures as a train hopper not with a rambunctious train ride but with a three-day

A hitchhiking family waiting along the highway in Macon, Georgia. The father repairs sewing machines, lawn mowers, etc. He is leaving Macon, where a license is required for such work (twenty-five dollars) and heading back for Alabama. (Photo by Dorothea Lange, 1937. Original caption.)

wait—and a realization that his impatience with this and other delays was a product of his inexperience. "Here on the rails," he concluded, "it seemed that dispensing with the poisonous hurry habit was the key to embracing a new way of life." Likewise, upon resuming train hopping, Douglas Harper (1982, 23, 96–97) realized that, "it was up to me to still my impatience and learn again the pace of tramp traveling"; later, stranded after a long ride, he acknowledged that "the wait was as much a part of the tramp life as had been the two-thousand-mile road before." Once I came to understand this, the result for me, as for Conover and Harper, was an insight: working the boundaries between autonomy and uncertainty, lost within a vast railroad transportation system that runs on any schedule but your own, you don't have the privilege of being in a hurry. In fact, you're just as much adrift standing still as you are on the move; as Milton (1655) might have said, they also drift who only stand and wait.

In the months after Zeke's initial warning about waiting, I would learn this insight both observationally and, as they say, the hard way. The observation came first. Out on yet another scrounging bike ride, I come upon three train hoppers, two guys and a girl, just in from Austin, and now resting outside the Shell station, after thirteen hours of riding and waiting on a train. They're heading to a Rainbow Family gathering in Montana with eight or so other train hoppers—except that the others somehow caught out from Austin ahead of them, so now they figure they'll just catch up to them in Montana.[11] They hope to go by way of Colorado, and so they ask me how to get to another rail yard across town, from which trains are more likely to head north; they say they may or may not stay the night in Fort Worth, depending on how long it takes to walk to those yards and catch a train. Most of this conversation occurs with Goddamn It Dale, the clear leader of the group, who sports Carhart-style overalls, no shirt, and tattoos across face and body. Like Zeke, and like other young male and female train hoppers I've met, Goddamn It Dale offers an interesting mix of friendly engagement and ready menace, a necessary stance for those whose lives are mostly first encounters. Readying an inexperienced rider for the trains, Ted Conover (1984, 250) "explained that in most situations, it was important to strike a tough pose when meeting new tramps. The toughness could be softened once the other tramp was sized up and his trustworthiness assessed, but if he was a bad character, it would help keep him from taking advantage of you." Accompanying Dale is his new girlfriend, First—who's adopted this as her road name because this is her first freight-hopping trip—and a big, strapping kid whose name I don't catch. We talk about the usual—Dumpster-diving locations, techniques for flying a sign, ways to ride a freight, how to get to that other rail yard—and I wish them well before riding off.

Four days later I'm bicycling up to the QuickWay, where Zeke and I bought water, when I see two people sitting on a ledge and waving at me; it's First and Goddam It Dale. They tell me that they just spent eighteen hours aboard a freight train that never departed; changing their plans, they have decided to catch out west from the Davidson yards, rather than the other yards across town, so as to get to Montana by way of California. First tells me that they're almost out of money and smokes, but excitedly reports that they found fruit and steaks in the Trader Joe's Dumpster I recommended and that a little taqueria that I directed them to (having learned of it from Zeke) did give them some free meals. About this time the QuickWay manager comes out and runs us off, so we move down the alley and continue talking. Mentioning that I don't see the big kid from the other day, Dale says that "he took off as soon as the money ran out" and if he finds him he's "gonna beat his ass." Must've been a knucklehead.

Riding near the Davidson yards three days later, I run into Dale and First yet again; they've now been stuck in town a full week. The night before they thought they had a train out of town but missed its departure; in desperation they tried to hitchhike out of town earlier today, but no one would pick them up. They're now walking to a big intersection to fly a sign.

All of which brings me to learning about waiting the hard way—or maybe the hardheaded way. That third time I encountered Goddamn It Dale and First down by the Davidson yards, it wasn't because I was looking for them; it was because I was looking to catch out myself, solo. So just a few days later, thinking maybe I'll have better luck than First and Dale, I'm back at that long ditch I shared with Zeke, hunkering in a tangle of underbrush along the ditch's top edge and waiting for a train. After a while a Union Pacific truck passes near me in the yards, and worrying that I might have been spotted, I cleverly take a tangle of small leafy limbs and shoots and fashion it around some branches, creating a little blind in which to hide. The hours roll by and the trains don't—it's only lines of railroad cars being moved back and forth within the yards. Wait as I might, I never do catch out that day, finally giving up and heading home at dark, reminded that the wide open exhilaration of open country fast freight train riding is available only at the price of sneaking around gritty rail yards and waiting in confined spaces—and that sometimes you pay the price but don't get the product. But actually, I do catch one thing. Those leafy little limbs and shoots? That, I come to find out, was poison ivy.[12]

From that painfully itchy experience, from the experiences of Ted Conover and Douglas Harper, First and Goddamn It Dale, it would seem that in train hopping—to paraphrase Lou Reed and the Velvet Underground—the first thing you learn is you always got to wait.[13] But for me, oddly enough, this doesn't turn out to be the first lesson. Back in that long ditch with Zeke, clambering up the steep vine-covered embankment ahead of us, risking a quick peek over the top, we find ourselves with only a line of scraggly trees and maybe ten yards of open gravel between us and the very sort of train Zeke hopes to catch—a train that experience tells him will depart sooner or later for points west and on to Pecos. Experience also tells him that this train is designed to carry global-shipping containers. In fact, the train car directly in front of us, and each of the hundreds of other cars that make up this mile-long train, hold two such containers, one stacked on top of the other. This accounts for one of the nicknames given to such a train: a "double-stack." The train's other nickname—a "hotshot"—accounts for our intended presence on it.

Along intercity rail routes, short stretches of parallel track—"sidings"—are located every few miles, so that trains can when needed "side out" on these parallel tracks and allow other trains to move past them. Which train sides out for another is determined by the priority assigned to each train and its load—and as their name implies, fast-moving, double-stack "hotshots" have priority over "general manifest" loads or "junk trains" made up of a mix of car types.[14] If a train hopper is in no hurry and doesn't mind siding out, or prefers to ride other sorts of rail cars than double stacks, then a junk train is suitable; in fact, the "stay punk, ride junk" graffiti that one sometimes sees stands as a subcultural endorsement of this choice. When, on the other hand, a rider wishes to get somewhere more quickly or directly—as with Zeke today, eager to get back to New Mexico—then a hotshot is sought. In this sense the pace of a train hopper's movement, the elapsed time to the next stop and the next, is subject not only to the happenstance of rail-yard security or missed connections but to the particulars of trade agreements and shipping contracts. To catch a hotshot is to catch the dispersed currents of global capitalism and to ride along with the priority given its products. Think a prioritized hotshot isn't built from and for the global supply chain? Among the shipping containers you can see double stacked on a hotshot most any day in the Fort Worth yards are Hapag-Lloyd (Germany, 6,900 employees in 114 countries), Hanjin (South Korean conglomerate), OOCL (Orient Overseas Container Line, wholly owned subsidiary of Orient Overseas International Ltd., Hong Kong), APL (subsidiary of Neptune Orient Lines, Singapore), Evergreen (Taiwan), China Shipping, and Italia (Italy).

Sitting now at the top of the embankment I notice some "Team Enemy" graffiti, paired with an anarchy symbol, on the train car just to the right. A hundred yards farther to the right is a group of track workers, so we're careful to stay out of their sight; we quickly arrange some discarded black plastic wrap in front of us as a supplement to the cover of the tree line. I'm noodling around in my backpack when suddenly, amazingly, after just thirty minutes or so, Zeke hears the train brakes airing up and says the train is about to go. We grab our stuff, scramble over the top of the embankment and past the trees, and run in a crouch across the open gravel toward the train.[15]

And, well, this is it—the moment of catching out. "Most hobo autobiographies . . . refer to this moment of 'catching out' as the location of their subcultural power," John Lennon (2007, 214; emphasis in original) writes. "By using their physical and mental skills in life-threatening situations, they *proactively* become invisible on the moving train." Catching out is freight hopping's essential moment of exposure, risk, and subcultural skill; at a minimum it involves surreptitiously boarding a train not designed for passengers, and then successfully hiding one's newfound passenger ship until the train clears the yards. Catching out also rests on a defining decision: try to hop a moving train (catching out "on the fly") or a stationary one? Many freight hoppers travel with big dogs, and, as Zeke explains, those who do so prefer to hop a stationary train; running over rough gravel while lifting a large dog onto a moving train is generally not good for the health of the person or the dog. In fact, a train hopper I later befriended—while she was traveling with a group of six people and five dogs—assured me that she had not once caught out on the fly since she started hopping trains with her dog. Those fond of their appendages often prefer stationary trains as well. "I was greatly relieved we were climbing aboard a stationary train," Richard Grant (2003, 266) recalls of an adventure with train hoppers. "There are so many amputation and decapitation stories about people trying to 'catch out on the fly,' or swing themselves up into moving boxcars; so many tramps with names like One Wing, Lefty and Stumpy." Even an experienced train hopper like Aaron Dactyl (2012, 5) confirms it; he begins *Railroad Semantics #1* with a bad fall, swollen knees, a bleeding hand, and an introductory conclusion: "Do not try to catch a train on the fly." Zeke explains the danger, and the skill required to beat it:

> When you're runnin' for a train you're not just runnin', you got to run and you put your hands on the ladder and you keep runnin' and it kind of picks you up all together when you're catchin' on the fly. And you catch it with your strong foot back and your weak foot forward, your weak foot will catch the rung and then the train will pull you on and then you put it on with your strong foot. But when you're getting off the train you get off the train with your strong foot so that all that momentum pushes straight to your weak foot and then you take off running.

Knowing this, remembering a time years ago when the momentum of a slow-moving train all but pulled me under it as I grabbed a passing ladder, and these days sporting a wrecked right ankle and aging knees to boot, I've promised myself and others: only stationary trains on this trip. It's like what Douglas Harper (1982, 101) said about an "old man" he watched trying to hop a moving freight. "He seemed poised to make the jump and then backed off and I was relieved," said Harper, "for I was certain that if he had jumped he would have gone onto the rocks, or under the wheels."

Freedom in the Form
of a Boxcar

The train is indeed still stationary as Zeke, younger and quicker, gets to the car first and clambers up the ladder at the car's end. By the time I and my bad ankle arrive, though, the train has started rolling forward, heavy and slow but picking up speed. Had I time to think about it, this would be another nice example of drifting uncertainty: at the moment of catching out, a commitment to hopping only standing trains rolls right away. But all I have time to do is toss my backpack and water up and onto the train, reach for Zeke's hand, and pull myself up the ladder and on. Safely aboard, we immediately drop down into a little sunken space at the back of the car, a three-by-eight-foot rectangle three-feet deep, so as to avoid being seen by rail-yard workers. This space is the "well" or "mini-well" or "bucket," formed by the gap between the car's fifty-three-foot length and the two forty-eight-foot global-shipping containers that it holds.

As the train lumbers and rolls and picks up speed, the residual exhilaration of the successful catch out and the intensely sensual experience of the big train's bumps, grinds, and sheer moving mass carry us along. After a while we risk little heads-up glances over the sides to see if we're clear of the yards, and soon enough we are, though we stay low to avoid being seen by the city traffic backed up at rail crossings. Twenty minutes later, we're out of town, comfortable with sitting up or standing on a corrugated metal walkway (sometimes called a "cheese grater") to see the countryside, and settling in for the trip. Though we may not know

In the well. (Photo by author.)

what's in all those shipping containers stacked ahead of and behind us, we do know we've caught a good ride—a ride on the type of car that Alison Murray (2000), in her train-hopping documentary *Train on the Brain,* refers to as the "Cadillac of train cars." Unlike some other types of train cars, the double-stack's well has afforded us sufficient protection to make it out of the yards and out of town undetected. Having caught the tail end of the car, we're also riding "clean face"—that is, with the car and its big load sheltering us from the blasting wind generated by the train's forward momentum. On this hot summer day, I'm enjoying the face full of wind I get from now and again sticking my head out around the edge of the car—it reminds me of my old days riding a motorcycle—but if we were riding "dirty face" at the front of the car, that same wind would soon enough wear us out. Best of all, we have a heavy metal floor under us. Though they try to avoid it, train hoppers are sometimes forced to ride "suicide wells" or "suicide porches." Floorless compartments at the ends of train cars, with only crossbeams beneath them, they leave riders hunkering down and holding on, exposed to the track passing beneath and to the train's flashing wheels. Zeke tells me of a kid he knew who nodded off while riding suicide. He didn't wake up.[1]

Clattering across the countryside, the hotshot is living up to its promise: the train's making steady time, and every so often we duck down, so

Well sign-ins. (Photo by author.)

as not to be seen as we pass other trains that have sided out for us. Sometimes Zeke whistles loudly when we pass open boxcars, just to see if any other train hoppers are riding inside; blasting past lines of sided-out boxcars covered in multicolor graffiti murals creates a blurring fast-forward graffiti movie (Ferrell 1998). Now and then I pluck a smoke from a scrounged half pack of Parliaments I brought along; Zeke is rolling his own. We're snacking on those scrounged nuts, which have gotten a little greasy with age; at one point Zeke uses one to grease some graffiti on the floor of the well, then pops the nut into his mouth. A little later we decide to do it right, using a fat-tip marker to sign in on the well walkway. Below one of his sign-ins Zeke adds a note about his lost dog. "I went to jail, lost my dog," he writes. "She was last seen with a girl named Answer. Dog's name, Hannah." I decide to resurrect my old graffiti tag but with a forward-pointing arrow, out of respect for sign-in conventions.

More than anything I'm struck by the overwhelming, embodied sensuality of the train, its mass, and its rolling rhythms. The ride bounces my body and bounces inside my body, a rhythm that is both powerfully and industrially steady and ever changing with variations in track, grade, and terrain. As subtle and complex as a salsa, it's a rhythm that keeps the train swaying and switching like a mile-long conga line: buck, glide, clack, creak, twist, buck, glide, bounce, screech, chirp, buck, glide. The physical and the auditory flow together in the loping, forward motion of the train, the wheels visible and audible just ahead of us, the tracks themselves producing sharp bumps and little sonic complaints as we move from better sections of track to worse. In a chapter on "hobo songs and ballads," Nels Anderson ([1923] 1961, 203) includes Henry A. White's "The Hobo Knows." If you listen to the first verse you can hear it:

> He knows the whirr of the rolling wheels,
> And their click on the time-worn joints;
> His ear is attuned to the snap and snarl
> Of the train, at the rickety points.

You can hear it too in "The Song of the Rail," a poem by the old Wobbly poet Ralph Chaplin:

> Say, ain't you ready to beat it, by crickity –
> Jump on a freight and be off on the trail,
> Hearin' the noise of the wheels that go clickity,
> Clickity, click on the glimmerin' rail.[2]

All of these sensations flow over and around us, our experience of them defined by a distinct sort of disproportion. On the one hand, we're not in a padded passenger car but out in the open, hurtling through the backcountry, two small bodies riding a massive machine, whose tons of weight and power stretch out from us half a mile in either direction. On the other hand we're confined to a little metal box barely big enough for the two of us—and more to the point, we'll stay confined there for as many hours as it takes until this train decides to stop. We've caught the ultimate free ride, and yet we're trapped in a sort of claustrophobia of fast motion. There's no jumping off at this speed, and this being a hotshot, the speed isn't likely to abate anytime soon. The only thing to do is to kill your ego and roll with the ride. The only thing to do is drift.

Rocking along through the afternoon, I spot a cow's carcass near a watering hole off to the left, a mass of black skin poked through with white ribs.[3] A few miles later and to the right, a small deer kneels under a tree close to the tracks; deer blinds and deer feeders dot the nearby fields. We pass a beautiful old milky-tan water tower, maybe thirty feet tall, a metal ladder up its side. We coast through Strawn, Texas, and then Ranger, Texas, past the old train depot and behind the rodeo arena. To paraphrase Gram Parsons (Parsons and Brown 1974), all these things and more pass by the two grievous angels—but it's not billboards and truck stops and twenty thousand roads rolling by, as in his hymn to the open highway, but instead railroad sidings and rusty equipment, open

Rolling with the ride. (Photo by author.)

fields and cattle pens, and gullies clogged with defrocked furniture and discarded machinery. That's the thing about freight trains. They generally keep to the urban backstage, to the industrial areas and the depressed property values—and when out of town, their tracks often wander well away from the main highway. Lee, an anarchist, environmental activist train hopper and author of the zine *There's Something about a Train*, sums it up nicely. "I love riding freight," he says. "You're seeing the backside of America" (quoted in Irwin 1998). Being on this backside, storefronts and advertisements tend to point the other way. Hopping her first freight train, heading out from Canada's west coast, Alison Murray noticed the same thing. "My first ride is on a grain car, through the Rocky Mountains," she says. "Not exactly comfortable, but no billboards, no road kill, no litter—breathtaking—I didn't want to blink in case I missed anything." We're traversing West Texas, not the Canadian Rockies, so I'm not sure I'd say "breathtaking"—but still, the little towns, long vistas, and distant buttes aren't bad. In fact, by late afternoon I'm singing to myself "Waiting for a Train," Jimmie Rodgers's 1928 hobo song, with that verse about Texas and the wide open spaces all around.

About this time I notice something: I'm filthy. I've only been on the train a few hours, but my hands are already a ground-in grey from the pervasive grime of the train, and my blue jeans and brown shirt are streaked with black. If you watch *Train on the Brain,* you'll see a similar transformation. Alison Murray starts out on that grain car fresh-faced and clean, but a few frames later she's already painted with grime—and by the end of the film you'd swear she's in some sort of hobo blackface.[4] Zeke's filthy too. He's still wearing the black army boots I gave him, but otherwise he's changed back into the train-hopper clothes he was wearing when he went to jail. And they're not only grey-grime filthy, they're all black to begin with: black t-shirt, black bandanna, heavy canvas black pants. In this regard Zeke impresses on me the importance of wearing dark colors, so as not to be seen, and affirms that my brown t-shirt was a good choice—though actually it was no choice at all, just what I happened to be wearing when we decided to go. Zeke's sartorial sensibility is historical and subcultural as well. Nels Anderson ([1923] 1961, 157–58) records an early train hopper's account of two young men who were apprehended by a railroad bull, while he and his traveling partner were not. "They had been jumping on and off and having a good time generally," he says. "Both of them had on white shirts and could be easily recognized by the train men." Today the preference for dark clothes is widely discussed among train hoppers—and gutter punk train hoppers are seldom seen dressed in anything other than all black.

But that dirty train grime—there's something distinctly social and historical about that, too. In Jack Black's 1926 account of his life as a freight hopper and road criminal, he recalls riding in a freight car when another rider jumped in. "I saw he was ragged and frightfully dirty, road dirt—coal smoke, cinders, ashes, grease," says Black ([1926] 2000, 61). "His coat, too large for his thin frame, was full of holes and its lining hung in tatters. His trousers were greasy and full of hot-cinder holes." Almost a century later, Zeke and others have turned this sort of episode into an affirmation. "We call ourselves the dirty kids," he'd said back when I had interviewed him in Fort Worth, certainly more proud than ashamed, and to emphasize his point he'd added, "My best friend is 45 and he's been ridin' trains forever, and he goes by 'a dirty kid,' and if you call him an old man you're probably going to get punched in the face by him." The grease and grime that were for Jack Black's companion a consequence of impoverished train hopping have become for contemporary gutter punk freight hoppers a subcultural identity and identifying aesthetic.

Ironically, this "dirty kid" identity has been so thoroughly embraced that it sometimes serves to distance today's gutter punk freight riders from the earlier generation of which Black's filthy companion was a part—or at least from the sanitized image of that generation. In an essay tellingly entitled "Too Dirty to Be a Hobo?," John Lennon (2007, 219) reports on the annual National Hobo Convention in the small town of Britt, Iowa. Begun, as legend has it, in 1900, the convention is a town-supported event that includes many older hobos and celebrates the history and culture of the train-hopping hobo, complete with a permanent town boxcar and an annual King and Queen Hobo. When gutter punks began train hopping in for the convention a decade or two ago, many older hobos and some townspeople welcomed them—but some worried about their dirty appearances, to the point of suggesting wristbands to distinguish "real" hobos (older, cleaner) from "fake" hobos (younger, dirtier).

Indeed, when in *Train on the Brain* Alison Murray and her friends arrive in Britt for the convention, a friendly but concerned townswoman can be seen quizzing one young woman on the limits of on-the-fly cleanliness and hygiene. "I like being dirty," the young train hopper replies sweetly. "It feels earthy. Kinda sexy." In this way the issue of young women's gender presentation can be glimpsed in the grime as well. One of the young female authors of *Off the Map* says, while reflecting on being made the object stares and surveillance, "I know it happens because I'm dirty, because I carry my life on my back and have no apparent home or gender" (CrimethInc. 2003, 107). I've noticed this lack of apparent gender myself; more than once I've come upon a group of gutter punks near the railyards or in the QuickWay, all of them adorned in dirty, disheveled black clothes and matted hair, and found myself unable to tell girl from boy until well into a subsequent conversation. This gender ambiguity strikes me as yet another important subcultural accomplishment. Built from the black clothes and boxcar grime that form a burqa-like barrier to easy identification, it serves the purposes of both gender equality and gender protection.[5]

Amidst all that smudge and grime, it turns out that the dirty kids have pulled off some magical cultural inversions. Just as their Dumpster diving converts the negative connotations of "trash" and "waste" into the proud possibilities of independent survival, their dirty kid aesthetic transforms the inevitability of their own filth into a visual affirmation of independent identity (see Ferrell 2006). Along the way this transformation inverts—and subverts—the usual cultural hierarchy that privileges cleanliness over filth. It likewise undermines the cleanliness by which young women are conventionally made presentable, allowing instead for a sort of grimy hobo-erotic sexuality in which gender is allowed to drift a bit. As the freight train she's riding coasts by a suburban golf course in *Train on the Brain,* Alison Murray adds in a voiceover, "I wonder if the people on the golf course are looking at the dirty kids on the train, thinking, 'There but for the grace of God go I,'" she says. "Little do they know that the dirty kids on the train are looking at them, thinking the same thing." For her, for Zeke, and for others, their shared "veil of darkened railroad skin," in Allen Ginsberg's (1956, 29) lovely phrase, has become a faithful stigmata, a dark mantle of honor, and, like their tattoos, a skin-tight record of hard miles traveled. To live as a freight hopper is to live dirty—not only because the train gives its rider nothing but grime but because indigent freight hopping carries the rider far from a privileged middle-class aesthetic that rests on regularities of soap, shampoo, showers, and fresh clothes. Living this way, Jack Black's "ragged and frightfully dirty" hobo becomes a contemporary gutter punk who is, in Riley Puckett's (1929/1934) phrasing, "Ragged but Right." As recorded by the great old-timey string band the Skillet Lickers, the song "Ragged but Right" assures the listener that the singer may be ragged and dirty but is nonetheless all right, since as the song says,

> I go everywhere,
> I don't pay no fare,
> I can ride a freight train just anywhere.

Gutter punks' cultural inversion of cleanliness and filth, their conversion of ragged and dirty into ragged and right, is no abstract exercise. Instead, they construct this transformation from what's available and not available, from the day-to-day interplay of necessity, creativity, and symbolic display. Like their tattoos, like the intertwined endeavors of train hopping, Dumpster diving, and flying a sign, dark clothes and dirt form a homologous relationship. Black clothes display subcultural identity while helping to hide members of the subculture from those who would apprehend them. The dark railroad grime that inevitably accumulates on the clothes and bodies of impoverished train hoppers is both an unfortunate consequence of train hopping and a fortunate form of added camouflage for those illicitly hopping trains. As such, black clothes and ground-in railroad dirt form a dark complementarity, and along with Dumpster diving and flying a sign, come to embody practical necessity and proud declaration—and both an interruption and continuation of long-standing hobo traditions.[6]

That black bandanna Zeke is wearing around his neck—his "rag" as he calls it—carries those same complexities of meaningful practicality.

Neck bandannas have long been symbolically associated with railroads, railroad workers, and rail hoppers and have long served a variety of everyday purposes, including protecting their wearer from sun, wind, fumes, or sweat. They have also served as markers of status or honor among various hobo groups. Richard Grant (2003, 267, 274), for example, writes of learning hobo history from Pappy, an elderly retired hobo. "He started wearing a bandanna and silver conch in 1938," Grant says. "The Hole in the Wall gang wore them, but so did a lot of other committed, full-time hoboes. It was a way for them to recognize each other, an outside sign that someone was pledged to the code of the rails." Grant also notes the more recent use of bandannas as markers of membership and status among the Freight Train Riders of America, a loosely organized "gang" of freight riders, and Zeke confirms bandannas' contemporary currency among gutter-punk train hoppers, too. Ideally, he tells me, a freight hopper's first rag should come from an experienced rider; a white rag should denote those who've ridden only ten thousand miles; and a black rag like his should be reserved for those who've managed a million miles by freight train.[7] As he suggests, these mileage counts and shared meanings aren't ironclad—and yet the rags and their meanings do matter, serving an important practical purpose beyond keeping dangerous fumes from one's mouth and nose when a train is caught in a long tunnel. Like tattoos and sign-ins, that practical purpose is one of informal policing, of checking freight hoppers and their passports, in the interest of subcultural survival. Zeke explains, "This bandana that I'm wearing right now was taken off of a kid's neck, because he was talking shit about shit that he didn't know, and I told him, I said, 'rag check or ass check' . . . if I don't believe that you are who you are, I'm going to call you out on it, and if you make yourself look like an ass I'm going to make you feel like an ass, cause out here we don't need idiots getting their legs cut off and making it hot for everyone else." A freight train is after all a mechanized wave of mutilation, and it's in the interest of train hoppers and railroad workers alike that those frequenting the trains know their way around them.

Dark and dirty as we may be, Zeke and I are now coming to a clean stop for the first time since we caught out in Fort Worth, as the train grinds to a halt in the Abilene rail yards. It's great to have gotten this far, and we can't help but notice that the train and the yards are bathed in a warm late-day West Texas light. But we're a little nervous. There's a two-story apartment complex backed up to the south side of the yards; behind its tall wooden fence we can hear but not see kids playing and riding bicycles, and a mom yelling, "Slow down Michael! Listen!" More importantly, we can see folks sitting out on second-floor balconies or looking out over the rail yards from second-floor doors, and we're worried they may see us and call the cops.

We sit and wait, and now it's gotten dark and we sit and wait some more. Looking now and then around the side of the car and up toward the front of the train, we notice in the far distance lights jiggling along each side of the long train. Zeke confirms my fear—those must be the flashlights of railroad workers or railroad police, checking around and under each car of the train—and he guesses that indeed someone in the apartments must've called us in. As the lights get closer we hunker down, pull our gear in around ourselves, work on flattening ourselves out in the bottom of the well, and occasionally steal glances around the side of the car to confirm that . . . yeah, dammit, they're still coming, working their way down each side of the train. Now they're almost on us, and we're pressed hard against the floor of the well. As I turn just a bit to screw my shoulders and hips down into the bottom of the well as far as I can, I feel some change in my pocket start to trickle out. I carefully reach my hand to staunch it; at the same moment I feel Zeke's hand on my foot, and I know what he's saying: stay still, stay quiet. By this time we can hear them, the slow crunch, crunch of their boots on the railbed gravel, and then that crunch is right beside us.

As viscerally immediate as this moment may be, it's not without historical context. To begin with, this isn't the first time I've run or hidden from the police, not always successfully, in the course of conducting research (Ferrell 1997). More to the point, as you might guess, this isn't the first time freight hoppers have endeavored to avoid detection; this moment of hunkered-down hiding affiliates us with the history of train hopping as surely as Zeke's black clothes and bandanna. Remember that early train hopper's account that Nels Anderson recorded, in which the train hopper and his buddy dodged the railroad bull while the other two train hoppers got caught? It wasn't only because the other two were foolish enough to wear white shirts; it was also because, when the bull got to the rail car, the first two "were lying flat on one corner" of the railcar and so went unseen. And then there's Nels Anderson himself. Recalling a youth spent as an itinerant laborer, working and traveling with other "hobo workers" long before the research that would lead to the publication of *The Hobo* in 1923, Anderson (viii–ix, 158) recalls also what he learned. "Like the student who learns the 'theory' of his occupation in school," he says, "I learned how the hobo behaved, or should not behave,

Inspecting a freight train from Mexico for smuggled immigrants. El Paso, Texas. (Photo by Dorothea Lange, 1938. Original caption.)

in town, how he went about from place to place on freight trains, how he evaded train crews and railroad police, and how he found work." That learning continues to be passed along today—and a train hopper named Milenko's account of successfully hoboing through the well-patrolled Yuma, Arizona, rail yards confirms its importance. "'Passing through Yuma AZ, watch out folks,' he says. 'Stay on the south side of your car and don't fuckin move.' Wise words from some drunk hobo in Colton [California]. We listened. It was weird having your 48 car lit up by spotlights, hearing the footsteps and voices of train yard workers and your body squeezed against cold train metal" (quoted in Daniel 2008, 53).[8]

So like I say, those two flashlights are only the latest of countless attempts by the authorities to interrupt the progress of train-hopping drifters—or maybe they're part of drift itself. Just as long waits and uncertain departures seem inherently a part of drifting, in that one can be soundly adrift while forced to stand still, it seems to me that being pulled off a train is as much a part of train hopping as riding one. In both cases it is not only uncertain movement that defines drift but uncertainty itself—even uncertainty as to whether the movement will begin or continue. Likewise, it's not just drifters' uncertain movements that shape them as drifters but their willingness to embrace uncertainty on its own terms. Back in Fort Worth, Zeke had told me of a punk/folk band that I really must check out: This Bike Is a Pipe Bomb. So I did, and what I heard was this very ethos, played out in songs like "Trains and Cops":

> I live down by the railroad tracks
> One of these days I wanna hop on board a train rolling down the line
> I won't care where it takes me because as long as I'm moving fast
> Call it easy riding, call it hard traveling; I won't mind
> I won't mind at all where I'm going
>
> It can take me east or west I don't care
> By that time I'll be glad to be most anywhere
> Don't that sound quite alright by me
> I won't mind at all where I'm going
>
> There's a police station just down the street from here
> I imagine one day there's gonna be a good ol' boy
> Trying to pick me up for something I didn't do
> I won't care where he takes me
>
> As long as I'm still alive, as long as I'm still breathing
> and my fingers are picking out songs I won't mind
> I won't mind at all where I'm going
> he can haul my ass to jail I don't care.[9]

There're some other serious uncertainties attending to these probing flashlights and crunching boots, too. These might be railroad bulls, or they might be city cops. They might, on the other hand, be rail-yard workers, and if that's the case, they might be looking at the train itself for defects or needed repairs, looking to apprehend us or kick us off the train, or even looking to lend us a hand. Zeke and I had talked about this before we departed Fort Worth, and it's confirmed throughout various accounts of contemporary train hopping: sometimes train workers are a problem, and sometimes they're a much-appreciated source of information or assistance. Zeke and others emphasize that this is mostly a matter of a shared railroad culture; the more fluently train hoppers can converse in railroad language with a worker, and the more train hoppers already know about trains and train yards, the more likely they are to be shown respect and provided further information by rail workers. As a brakeman told Douglas Harper (1982, 5) when he found Harper holed up in a boxcar, he was always happy to help out a freight hopper "as long as they looked like they knew what they were doing." At the moment, though, I'm not particularly interested in risking a clarification as to whether these are bulls or cops or sympathetic workers. It's like a twenty-two-year-old freight hopper told a *Los Angeles Times* reporter, "You don't need money out there. You don't need anything. You have the greatest time in the world. But when it gets down there, it's really down there" (Goffard 2009).

Turns out it doesn't get down there; the crunching boots and flashlights, whoever they were, don't catch us. They crunch on past, and after waiting many long minutes, we ease up on our elbows to check. We see only one light moving away from us, and not knowing the whereabouts of the other, we hunker down and wait some more. Finally we sit up, stand up, stretch, and with no one in sight and the train still parked, we decide to climb off and try for a beer run. Grabbing our packs, but leaving our water jugs, we slip off the side and skulk over and up from the tracks to the shadows in the north edge of the yard. Zeke offers to go looking for beer if I'll stay with the gear; as he walks away, I realize that the top of my head is caught in a security light and casting a shadow, so I grab our gear, move ten feet to the west, and sit back down in the shadows. I'm settled in, sitting and digging the yards and the dark and the West Texas night air, but before I know it, I make out Zeke's silhouette as he's easing his way back along the edge of the yards; damned if there wasn't a beer-stocked convenience store just up the road. First thing he asks me, while looking over at the train, is if I moved while he was gone; I now realize that I was the marker by which he'd know which of those hundreds of identical, in-the-dark double-stacks was ours—that is, the one that still held our water jugs. We get that settled, and now it seems to me it can't get much better—we're sitting and sipping our first cold tallboys and there're four more close beside us. I'm lost in some sort of train-hopping, open road, cold beer bliss, but before we can finish those first ones, Zeke jumps up. "Hey, this train's pullin' out!" he says, once again alert, in a way I'm only learning, to the sounds of a train readying itself to get under way.

We grab our packs and beer, run and stumble back across the dark yard, and hop into our well just as the train is getting under way, headed for Sweetwater. Now I have to tell you, the forty miles of arid West Texas wasteland from Abilene to Sweetwater is nobody's idea of a scenic ride or preferred route. Nobody's . . . unless, that is, you just spent hours stalled in the Abilene rail yard. Unless you recently found yourself pressed to the floor of a railcar's back well, figuring you might be about to be kicked off the train or handed a criminal trespass citation or worse. Unless you thought to yourself, man, just let those boots crunch on by— and they did. Unless you now find yourself with four, still-cold tallboys, snug back in your well, and picking up speed. Unless, while you're downing those boys and barreling through the night, you notice that lightning is beginning to filigree the sky, jumping from cloud to cloud, lighting up the route ahead of the train on all sides, and that big drops of rain are shooting up over the top of the car in front of you and swirling in the back draft behind you, and that the sweet rich smell of that rain hitting the weeds and fields of the countryside is all around you, and that the cool cloud-charged air is sweeping by, and you find yourself whooping and hollering into the night, all the way into the Sweetwater yards.

At which point the train rolls to a stop—and we're out of beer.

After waiting awhile and hearing no indications of the train's imminent departure, we decide on a modified reenactment of our earlier beer run: this time I'll wait on the train with our water and gear while Zeke goes in search of a convenience store. Zeke disappears to the north, toward what appears by the lights to be the main drag through town. Twenty minutes later I'm hanging out in the well, waiting for Zeke, when I hear a sound I've already heard twice on this trip and am learning to recognize: the hiss, moan, and creak of the train getting ready to roll. Yelling out to see if Zeke's nearby isn't really an option, and in any case I realize I have just a few seconds to make a decision, given that the train is already beginning to ease forward. Forsaking the water jugs, I grab our two packs, toss them from the train, and jump off after them—and just as I'm gathering myself after the jump, and the train is beginning to pull away, I see Zeke closing on me at a fast run from across the yards. The clean-up crew at a little restaurant had told him about the only convenience store still open, and working his way in that direction down through the edge of the yards he'd seen and heard the same thing I had and had sprinted for the train, figuring he could catch it, and catch up to me, on the fly. And you know, he probably could have—except that just as he was catching up to the train, I and our gear were getting off. So by a matter of seconds our water's gone, we're stuck in the Sweetwater yards in the middle of the night, the lightning show's been replaced by a light rain—and we're still out of beer.[10]

Hoisting our gear we set out walking for the convenience store, find it a ways down the drag, and buy a tallboy six pack and some spicy tortilla chips. Disappearing back into the darkness, we find a low brushy draw between the rail tracks to our south and the backside of the main drag to our north. Zeke has a small ground tarp he spreads out as I take the beer out of the convenience store plastic bag, and we each pop open a fresh one. Laying the plastic bag on the ground, we open our two cans of beans and plop the beans down on the bag; Zeke crumbles the spicy tortilla chips over the top. With the sleeve of saltine crackers as a side, it's dinner. Afterward, we settle in to finish the beers and get some sleep, but now the rain's coming down heavier, so we gather up the ground tarp and our gear and set out looking for a dry spot. We wander around behind various stores and storage areas, all of them long closed for the night, looking for a shed or an overhang, but find nothing dry; an old wrecked motel looks promising, but the rats run us off.

Finally we find a little metal overhang beside some sort of store and ease ourselves down on the concrete beneath it. My wool poncho bed-roll is working well enough as a blanket, except that gusts of wind keep blowing the rain in on us, so we remain more groggy drunk than ever really asleep. And it's right about here, stuck and drunk in the rain in the middle of the night on the edge of the Sweetwater rail yards, that I begin to understand some things. First, I begin to understand why it is that Zeke and his group of train-hopping comrades call themselves the Slow Drunk Krew. If we hadn't been slowed by our hours-long stop in Abilene, we'd be hours nearer our destination, and we wouldn't have had time for that first beer run. If we hadn't launched the second beer run, hadn't consequently missed connections by a few seconds, we'd likely be making good time—fast time—westward right now, toward Big Spring and Odessa and on to Pecos. And if we hadn't launched that second beer run, we'd be sobering up on the way to Big Spring and Odessa, too. But we did launch it, and because of that our general progress west could now be described as, well, slow drunk. A hundred years ago, management consultant Frederick W. Taylor developed the time-motion study as a method of "scientific management"—that is, a method of measuring worker productivity, enforcing efficiency, de-skill-ing labor, and increasing employer profits. The Slow Drunk Krew, and tonight the two of us hunkered down under this overhang, are a sort of time-motion study as well—a study of unabashed inefficiency and inebriated uncertainty that undermines everything Taylor and his corporate allies sought to enforce. Likewise, back in Taylor's day, the itinerant hobo worker was essential to the western expansion of the railroads, and of capitalism—but I like to think that tonight the two of us, like many an "old hobo lost out in the rain" before us (Bonus 1969) have slowed our own westward trajectory to a drunk wet crawl.

"I was drinking beer with some tramps one night in the fall of 1973." That's the first line in Douglas Harper's (1982, 1, 98) participatory ethnography of tramps and train hoppers. Later in the book he considers that, while skid rows include hobos and others suffering from "alcohol dependence," they also harbor those for whom a bout of heavy drinking is "an episode on the way to other, very different experiences." There may be something to this. Drunk is not necessarily adrift, but drinking while drifting does seem to accelerate the disorientation. Thinking about his own inebriated immersion among hobos and train hoppers, Ted Conover (1981, 209; emphasis in original) wonders, "Did we drink too much? Did *I* drink too much? I had the same concern about cigarettes. . . . The way I used to dislike the company of smokers, and look down on heavy drinkers, was a dissonant memory." Revisiting a box of field notebooks that he accumulated in ten years of wandering with hobos and drifters across the American West, Richard Grant (2003, 257–85) realized, "It would be all too easy to hold up these notebooks, in the manner of a prosecutor or a preacher, and declare that the American road is tawdry and depraved, the last refuge of scoundrels, wastrels, mountebanks and lunatics, and that the American rails are even worse. . . . There has been so much drinking, justified in the name of immersion reporting, and it shows up in my handwriting from time to time." Now here we are, two grimy, trespassing train hoppers full of cold beans and beer, ducking the rain in the middle of the night—it's the next notebook. And my beer drinking? Let's call that accelerated disorientation, or immersion reporting. Yeah—immersion reporting.

There's something else I'm also beginning to understand at some deeper level that I might call experiential immersion, or maybe existential disorientation. Colossus of Roads, for almost half a century a prolific and poetic freight car graffiti artist, suggested something of this understanding when years ago he began to haphazardly affix phrases and quotations to the standard image he painted over and over on rail cars, so as "to avoid the redundant commonness" of his own art. This chaotic linking of image and word, he said, was a matter of "adding to the idea of chance, as the randomness of freight car selection, destination, etc., was already inherent to the system" on which he painted. Or, as he put it more pointedly, "Practice Noncertainty" (quoted in Daniel 2008, 101,

113). Jack Kerouac (1958, 96) caught something of this understanding too, back in his own train-hopping days. "The only alternative to sleeping out, hopping freights, and doing what I wanted," he wrote in *The Dharma Bums,* "would be to just sit with a hundred other patients in front of a nice television set in a madhouse, where we could be 'supervised.'"[11] As Colossus of Roads and Kerouac imply, this understanding has to do with the randomness of the road and the way in which this radical, moving uncertainty undermines exterior supervision while mixing with the autonomous intentionality of those caught up in it. This understanding makes room both for decision making and for the inevitability of disorientation. Perhaps most importantly, it suggests that being lost doesn't mean you're looking for a map—and that missteps, failures, and slow drunk detours may be fleeting signs of success.

Interestingly enough, contemporary train hoppers have their own term for this phenomenon: *the drift.* Interviewed for a newspaper article on train hopping, fifty-year-old train hopper Todd Waters proposed that "the appeal of freight-hopping is due to what he calls 'the drift.'" Waters explained, "For me, the drift occurs when I migrate from the linear world, neat with its processes and models, to the road, where everything happens at once. You've got a general direction, but it doesn't have much glue on it. The plan has equal weight to every new direction that comes along" (quoted in O'Connell 1998). For Waters, the drift is not a state devoid of plans or decision making; it's a state in which planning and decision making lose their linearity and efficiency as they collide with immediate contingencies and the inevitability that new possibilities will emerge on the move. For someone in such a state, a plan or a decision serves less as a detailed map of the terrain than as a vague compass direction, itself vulnerable to the volatility of emerging situations. After all, Zeke and I weren't without an initial plan—hop the next available hotshot out of Fort Worth and ride it to Pecos—but we had no idea whether that next hotshot would be two hours or two days away, and no way of knowing it would stall out in Abilene and stop all too briefly in Sweetwater. So new decisions were made, and by necessity made quickly—and this series of decisions left us a couple of hundred miles west of where we started, true enough, but also laid up now in the Sweetwater rain. The immediacy of experience and of changes in experience, the compressed interim between decisions and their execution, the necessary openness to contingency and revision— all of these make up the drift and ensure that, as Waters says, even a "general direction . . . doesn't have much glue on it."

After a while, Ted Conover (1981, 167) came to understand this dynamic. "The tramps understood plans in a way I did not," he realized. "Plans, to me, were something you made and then carried out. But to tramps, plans were simply possibilities." In the previous chapter, God-damn It Dale and First lived this dynamic, when initially they intended to catch out north to Colorado, then decided to catch out west to California, then didn't catch out at all. A train hopper named Bugs told me about it. When I hung out with Bugs, her boyfriend, and their two dogs under the shed roof of an abandoned lumber yard, she described how they had holed up at a church the previous night so as to stay out of a storm, only to have a cop run them off, telling them "if you're not gone in twenty seconds you're going to jail." Now they're looking to visit their families in the northeastern United States and hoping to catch out to the north or east—as to which, "it doesn't really matter," Bugs assures me. And by the way, Todd Waters experienced it himself; traveling with his daughter on his final freight-hopping run, he was arrested for trespassing on railroad property.[12]

In the course of her own train-hopping travels Alison Murray hap-pened to meet another train hopper, Wendy, when they discovered that they were riding a car apart on a freight train rolling across Western Canada. One of "the many women who, according to longtime tramps, are taking to the rails in unprecedented numbers" (Tudor 2001), Wendy had herself begun riding when she met yet another train-hopping woman in the West Coast punk scene. "I'm totally blown away by Wendy," Murray says. "She's the first woman I've met who's ridden trains alone. She started three years ago; she's addicted to the rush of the rails." Like-wise, Zeke tells me that "my ex-girlfriend that did all my tattoos, she's riding with four girls right now, four girls and four dogs, they're all out together. . . . I wouldn't want to cross any one of them women in a dark alley." In this context Alison, Wendy, and others with whom they're traveling come up with a plan to hop their way to the Britt, Iowa, National Hobo Convention. As already seen, they do get there eventually—but that doesn't mean the initial plan has much adhesion. Intending to hop a westbound freight out of Chicago to Iowa, they discover a few hundred miles later that they've in fact hopped a southbound and are now outside Nashville, Tennessee. "We're way off course," Murray says, "but some-how don't mind." Along with teaching Murray about female independ-ence on the road, Wendy has taught her a certain mindset, too. "Wendy's told me about 'the drift,'" Murray recalls, "a carefree state of mind that overtakes you on the train. I'm losing all sense of time and place."

A reporter for *Esquire* lost it, too, the longer she rode with train hoppers. The "magic of the freights," their "sudden rush of movement," left her with "an incredible feeling of lightness." As she said, "On the freights, time flows around you—there is no goal other than movement" (Ferguson 1994, 74). When a *San Francisco Weekly* reporter set out to hop trains with Lee of *There's Something about a Train* and some of his friends, she found herself lost in the same state of mind. "I have no idea what time it is," she says as they rest in a track-side jungle between rides. "Welcome," replied Ballast, one of the group. "Time doesn't matter after a while" (quoted in Tudor 2001). It doesn't matter somewhere in the middle of a Sweetwater night, either; up under the overhang I've lost track entirely. I'm pretty sure Zeke has as well, but as usual he has nonetheless remained more alert than I to the nearby yards. At some point he hears a train pull in, so we gather our gear and go over to check it out. It's a westbound, all right, but it's a junk train, not a hotshot, and it's rolled to a stop in the yards so that only the very rear of the train is located where we can reach it. "Looks like we're riding a unit," Zeke says, motioning to the locomotive unit attached to the rear end of the train. A modern freight train, especially a long and heavy one, often has auxiliary locomotive units placed in the middle or at the rear, so as to augment the lead locomotive's power and to distribute power more evenly throughout the train. Train hoppers generally refer to these as "units," or "DPUs," for "distributed power units." I was aware of this configuration before catching out with Zeke, but I'm still a bit hesitant. We're going to climb into a unit? Zeke assures me that train hoppers do so all the time and guarantees that we'll find the unit unlocked when we get to it. Turns out he's right, so we climb up and into the unit, careful to stay below the unit's windows, and decide to sit on the floor rather than in the engineers' chairs, so that we can't be seen.

We may be out of the rain, but I'm still not comfortable. The quarters are cramped, we're shut inside them with few avenues for escape should we need them—and to my mind it seems that we've just upped our legal liability significantly. Back in the 1980s, about to board his first unit, Ted Conover (1984, 35) had the same sense. "I had never heard of hoboes doing this," he recalls, "and had assumed it was so grave a trespass in the eyes of the railroads as not to be contemplated, much less committed." Milenko may have blown through the Yuma yards smoothly enough, but later in his trip he shared my trepidation upon climbing into a unit. "I'd never been in one before and it has an eerie feelin'," he says. "Like you're definitely doing something bad (illegal) but also 100% rush" (quoted in Daniel 2008, 58). In my present condition, there's not so much of a rush—just that eerie feeling of illegality. Then again, Conover came through well enough, even encountering a helpful trainman, who discovered him asleep in the unit. Milenko and his traveling buddy likewise survived with no problems from the authorities—and were eventually joined in the unit by eleven undocumented Mexican migrants, who survived just fine as well. And then again, well, we are out of the rain and closer to continuing west than we were up under the overhang. And for that matter, Aaron Dactyl (2012, 14–15) recorded many a ride in a DPU, including some similarly friendly encounters with train workers, even recalling one cold time when he traded his desired direction of travel for the warmth of a DPU. I realize that part of the eeriness is the sheer number of valuable technological devices that the unit holds. We're surrounded by buttons, levers, gauges, and switches. In fact, though Zeke seems entirely at home here, he does warn me to be careful as I move around not to bump into any buttons or switches, lest we set off an alarm. I address the potential problem of unintended movement by falling asleep on the floor.[13]

I'm awakened by the swaying and bouncing of the train. At some point while I slept—time doesn't matter after a while—the train pulled out, and now we're rolling west. At least I guess we are. The drift is carrying me along: I have no idea what time we got under way, no idea what time it is now, no idea where we are, and no particular eagerness to find out. "I must have spent the night on a siding just south of Albany," Aaron Dactyl (2012, 37) says at one point, "but I did not care to know exactly where." I can hear rain spitting against the unit's windows, and looking up through them I can just make out low crepuscular clouds; it must be getting near dawn. Standing up to get a better view, I can see that we're rolling through some sort of eroded, mined-out moonscape, and I glimpse a highway now and then off to the north. From this, I guess that we are indeed paralleling the westbound interstate, and Zeke, who's been sleeping off and on in the unit's cramped stairwell, knows this section of track and confirms it.

Inside the unit I can hear coded instructions and directions coming over the radio, evidence that the engineer, somewhere far ahead of us in the front locomotive, is conversing with other train workers. A tiny toilet off to the side of the stairwell and a small refrigerator full of bottled water are also evidence that we're temporarily occupying a rolling workplace. On the wall behind me is another sort of evidence. A round, yellow-and-red sticker, it includes the phrase "Fix the Hazards, Don't Blame the

Victims" and a locomotive with the letters "RWU" superimposed over a map of North America. This I later discover is a sticker from Railroad Workers United, an organization founded in 2007 with the intention of uniting North American rail workers across the many crafts and unions that separate them. The RWU argues that the railways have successfully pitted crafts against crafts and points out that the various rail workers' unions continue to fight internecine battles among themselves, with the result being a weakening of workers' collective rights and collective bargaining power. To overcome this, the RWU advocates cooperation across the various rail crafts and unions, "rank-and-file democracy," direct action by rank-and-file union members, and a general resurrection of the labor solidarity of earlier years. As the RWU's statement of principles says, "It's time we returned to the labor standard of 'An Injury to One Is an Injury to All!'" Notably, this phrase is not only a labor standard but the longstanding motto of the Industrial Workers of the World (IWW). Though much diminished from the peak of its powers in the early 1900s (as seen in chapter 4), the IWW continues to organize today—mostly fast-food workers and others precariously employed. Indeed, the RWU includes a link to the IWW and its current activities on its website (railroadworkersunited.org), and the IWW includes news of the RWU in its *Industrial Worker* newspaper (Wright and Michael 2013). The RWU's website also "proudly presents" a page dedicated to socialist and labor leader Eugene Debs, who helped found the pan-craft American Railway Union in 1893 and the IWW in 1905.

With that Railroad Workers United sticker, the ghosts of old-time rail workers and rail battles have found us here in the unit. Lipstick traces on a locomotive (Marcus 1989), they've drifted out of the past with the RWU and into present-day dynamics of corporate power and workplace resistance. The RWU's list of grievances situate the past in the present, too, echoing complaints laid out by labor a century ago against Frederick Taylor and scientific management and confirming the degree to which his management principles remain in play: "The carriers are degrading and deskilling our crafts, implementing new technologies that threaten our jobs, our safety and livelihoods, propose the dismantling of FELA, demand drastic health care concessions, and more." The railroads' opposition to FELA, or the Federal Employers Liability Act, in particular suggests the degree to which the ghosts of old conflicts are still around; passed in 1908 in response to the growing dangers of railroad work, the act was intended to compensate railroad workers for on-the-job injuries incurred as a result of corporate negligence. Or as Supreme

Court justice and former hobo William O. Douglas put it, FELA "was designed to put on the railroad industry some of the cost for the legs, eyes, arms and lives which it consumed in its operations" (quoted in DeParcq and Wright 1956, 430). Likewise, the RWU conducts a campaign against an initiative by the railroads for "single-employee operating crews"—that is, the running of freight trains staffed only by a single engineer. For the public, and for freight hoppers like Zeke and me, this initiative portends a nightmare action movie scenario: mile-long freight trains, barreling through road crossings and cutting through urban neighborhoods, with only a single rail worker aboard. For rail workers, this initiative means not only greater danger—as the RWU says, "no conditions exist where one-person operations are safe"—but vulnerability to the very sorts of corporate downsizing that has cast so many others adrift. Who knows? If the railroads can defeat the RWU and implement full-scale, single-employee crews, maybe today's railroad employee will become tomorrow's train hopper.[14]

Come to think of it, with their intimate knowledge of trains and train operations, Zeke and other freight hoppers already constitute a kind of free-form auxiliary train crew for the railroads. Ever since we left Fort Worth, I've noticed how Zeke has kept alert to the train, checking out train cars and stretches of track, anticipating the next railroad crossing or side out, evaluating sight lines and situations. Now I notice that occasionally Zeke steps out of the unit onto the catwalk that surrounds it. When he invites me to come out with him, I'm struck again by the sheer length of the train, visible as it bends through a long left-hand curve. Then I understand what Zeke's up to. Sensing when the train is entering a curve, he's going out on the unit's catwalk—the catwalk on the side to the inside of the curve—so that he can see and search the line of cars ahead. And what he's searching for is an open boxcar—one to replace our current conveyance in the unit. He asks me if I'm willing to risk the move, and I'm all for it, ready to escape the close quarters of the unit and to get back to fresh air. Zeke eventually spots an open boxcar some twenty-five cars ahead, and we retreat into the unit to wait. Unlike the hotshot we rode yesterday, this junk train is all but sure to side out soon enough, and when it does we'll make for the boxcar. After another half hour or so, our train does side out, and we hop off and begin the walk forward through the railbed gravel. Where there are two sets of tracks like this, Zeke had schooled me earlier, you always want to throw any trash away from the second set of tracks so as to avoid possible detection; by the same logic he's made sure that we're now walking down the

Freight moving east near Odessa, Texas. (Photo by Dorothea Lange, 1937. Original caption.)

side of the train facing away from the passing hotshot. Still, we're both aware of another gamble—of getting left out here in the middle of West Texas nowhere should the hotshot complete the pas de deux and our train get back under way before we reach the boxcar—and so we fast walk as best we can through the deep gravel. Because of this I'm a little surprised when Zeke slows down to look for and pick up a couple of railroad spikes; seems like an odd time to grab a souvenir.

We do make it to the boxcar and pull ourselves up and in through the big open door. As I'm stowing my pack, Zeke turns back to the open door, jams one of the spikes into the heavy metal bottom track on which the door slides and stomps the spike in with his boot. Ah, so that's it: not

Boy riding freight. West Texas. (Photo by Dorothea Lange, 1937. Original caption).

a souvenir but a door stop—and an important one at that. Reporting on a boxcar ride with a group of freight hoppers, Grant (2003, 266) remembers, "Bones jammed a spike under the door to stop it slamming shut and trapping us inside—another of the myriad forms of accidental death that await the unwary or unlucky freight-train rider." Likewise, Sarah Ferguson (1994, 71) records the preferences of a veteran gutter punk and train hopper named Dumpster. "Most people think of tramps riding in rusty boxcars, but Dumpster steered clear. He'd come across too many old-timers who'd lost their feet and hands in the boxcars' sliding metal doors. Even if you pegged the door securely with iron spikes from the yards, you never knew who might be lurking inside a boxcar." No one lurking here; just the two of us rattling around the cavernous, off-white insides of the boxcar as the train pulls back onto the mainline and picks up speed. Two weeks earlier, though, and we'd have had company. Just inside the door someone has signed in—"Toronto, Canada, 05–24 (ELP)"—and included beside it a little stick figure drawing.[15]

Zeke signs in on the boxcar's front wall with another message about his lost dog, Hannah, and we settle in to sit against the side wall opposite the open door. The space we're now occupying couldn't be more different from the stale intimacy of the unit. Fifty-feet long and thirteen-feet high, the boxcar's vaulted emptiness isn't cluttered with switches, gauges, seats, or cargo. It's filled only with a soft shadowy glare, shafts of West Texas sunlight shifting in through the open door, and the rattling cacophony of the tracks as amplified in the car's echo chamber. Off-white and open, with an oddly syncopated soundtrack of sharp creaks and booming clanks, the interior reminds me of some minimalist art installation, or maybe a hobo's mobile mausoleum. As the day goes on, the car also fills with West Texas heat, so we take turns sitting at the rear edge of the open door, catching the wind and watching the land close on us. When the train slows for crossings or sides out, we ease away from the door or the opposite wall and press ourselves back into the shadows. More than once, I'm rocked to sleep by the boxcar's floating rhythms—and more than once I'm jolted awake by the concussive pop of the car hitting a section of bad track, its lack of cargo offering no weight to dampen the blow. At one point, lying on my right side, I half-wake from a drowsy sleep to see that a particularly sharp jolt has thrown my left arm and left leg high up in the air like some levitating marionette. "I try to sit and my body leaps off the floor," says Douglas Harper (1982, 6) of a long ride in an empty boxcar. "The car, sprung for hundreds of tons, carries me as a tiny piece of flotsam bouncing, banging, swaying." "Better to sleep in an uncomfortable bed free, than sleep in a comfortable bed unfree," says Kerouac (1958, 97–98) of his freight-hopping days. That might be too neat a dichotomy, but one thing this trip has taught me: it's not just a metaphor.

As the hours slide by, our junk train sides out over and over again, the last time only a few miles short of Pecos. Zeke assures me that this isn't owing to any sort of karmic lesson that freight hopping means to teach me once again about patience but to the fact that the small Pecos yard has only a single track. As a result, trains must side out and pass just before or after Pecos. Finally arriving in Pecos, we don't actually arrive. Having started out in the train's rear unit and then walked to a

Zeke signs in. (Photo by author.)

boxcar twenty-five cars forward, we're still near the back end of a long train. So when the train's front end rolls to a stop in the small Pecos yard, it leaves us a mile or so out of the town itself. Walking the tracks into town we notice the remnants of other train hoppers and their camps: bits of torn clothing, broken down shoes, beer cans, and bean cans—this last not unlike what we left behind in Sweetwater. Once in Pecos, we head for a little convenience store a few blocks from the tracks. I buy a soda, and Zeke buys a beer, which he pours into a paper cup that he retrieves from the trash can so as to avoid harassment by the local cops. Likewise, looking to stay out of sight, we ease around in search of a secluded spot and some shade from the afternoon sun—scarce commodities in a little West Texas town. We finally find both in a park adjacent to a small downtown museum across from the old train station. As a bonus, the museum offers outdoor restrooms, where we're able to inconspicuously wash up a bit and replenish our meager water supplies.

Sitting in that little Pecos park, talking about trains and hoboing and the like, I figure I now know Zeke well enough to ask him a question: Ever heard of Woody Guthrie? In answer, he begins singing "Hard Travelin'," Woody's 1930s hymn of hopping freights and doing time for vagrancy, and we sing a couple of verses together. Now that's not a bad ending to our freight-hopping journey—a few hours later, Zeke heads out to hitchhike his way on to New Mexico, and awhile after that I catch a Greyhound back home—but for me the better ending had already occurred about forty miles back down the line. Riding along, I noticed that Zeke was writing something on the inside front wall of the box car. A little later I moved toward the front of the car and was able to make it out.

"Freedom," it said.

"Freedom in the form of a boxcar."

PART THREE

Uncertain Knowledge

7

Beneath the Slab

At some point in most any book that claims to be even marginally academic, the discussion turns to "method." This generally occurs somewhere near the beginning of the book, and generally involves the author's careful rehearsal of the various techniques and procedures used in generating the information on which the book is based: historical research, online surveys, statistical analysis, field research, maybe content analysis of media forms. Here the discussion arrives near the book's end—and that's not the only difference, nor the most important one. To be honest, I have little interest in a conventional discussion of method—mine or others'—if by this we mean parsing the predetermined technical procedures deployed in the generation of "data." Such discussions tend to be tedious in the extreme, and in any case most always miss the deeper significance of method itself. At this deeper level, method is not a set of procedures but the way we orient ourselves to the world around us—our way of noticing and ignoring, selecting and making sense amidst the welter of phenomena that surrounds us. Because of this, the methods we choose inevitably reflect and affect who we are and shape the possibilities for what we'll come to understand. Methods in this way unavoidably embody particular sorts of politics and morality; they create distinctive ways of knowing what we know and come to life or death within particular historical circumstances. So if the historical circumstances in which we're caught are those of drift, the question becomes how we might usefully attune ourselves to it and make sense of it. That is, the methodological question becomes how to navigate without a map, how to find one's way forward when no destination awaits—how to orient oneself to disorientation.

METHOD AND DRIFT

Thinking about this sociologically, we can imagine a double connection between drift and method. For researchers or writers or filmmakers seeking to understand the drifters who increasingly populate the contemporary world—migrants, refugees, gutter punks, the perpetually unemployed, the college educated sans career—methods will be needed that are as fluid and episodic as are the lives of those they study. Researchers may need to approach their drifting subjects of study not as groups or communities but more as loose federations or temporary assemblages. Writers may well need narratives that are distinctly nonlinear, sentences that fall apart into fragments, chapters that float free of enumeration and headings. Filmmakers may need to be concerned less with scouting locations than with embracing dislocation, may need to abandon establishing shots altogether, may need to imagine movies sans central characters and fixed plots. Here we and they might even consider what film producer Bernd Eichinger (n.d.) calls *fetzendramaturgie*—a "shredded dramaturgy" or "dramaturgy of fragments"—by which a film unfolds nonlinearly, as a series "of puzzle pieces, which the audience has to piece together themselves in order to get the overall picture," a film ultimately designed "to ask questions without providing any answers." In all of this, it is not only the medium that's the message but the method that's the message as well; if drift is the subject, it demands methods that avoid boxing it in and stopping it cold, lest it be made into something it's not.

That's one sort of connection between method and drift, and here's another: what if those researchers and writers and filmmakers are themselves increasingly adrift? The world of academic researchers is falling apart, with universities increasingly reliant on part-time faculty who piece together a course here and a course there while being excluded from any meaningful investment in their universities, their research, or their careers. Hollywood film studios are shrinking just as digital technology now makes most everyone—at least most everyone who can afford it—a potential filmmaker, if one without salary or health benefits. Old-line media institutions continue to conglomerate, hiring fewer writers and photographers and paying those they do hire less, while digital media runs on the work of poorly paid, or unpaid, "content providers." In such a world, artists and writers of all sorts will need new methods, not only to attune themselves to their subjects of inquiry, but to attune themselves to themselves—that is, to make their way through a world in which their circumstances may well be as fragile and uncertain as those of the subjects of their films or photographs or books. This double connection between drift and method suggests a particular sort of potential relationship: if the appropriate methods can be found, these methods can perhaps open up new sorts of shifting commonality between those who employ them and those who are their subjects. Maybe the better we understand drifters, the better we understand our own lives within a world adrift.

At issue here is what the great nineteenth-century sociologist Max Weber called "verstehen." For Weber, an objective description of an event or a group wasn't sufficient for making sense of the social world; a researcher or writer also needed to establish verstehen—empathic understanding, a sort of informed subjectivity—with those who occupied the group or event, a sense of how it felt to be a group member, of what it meant to be a part of the event. You can describe the inside of a long-haul trucker's cab, for example, cataloguing the entries in the log book and noting the various knobs and switches—but Weber would argue you'll not know long-haul truckers until you're able to understand what it feels like to drive ten hours straight, to be away from family and friends for weeks on end, to catch a night's sleep in a truck-stop parking lot. Reaching that understanding probably means riding along for days or months, hanging out at truck stops and weigh stations, sitting and talking with truckers over bad food or hot coffee—that is, making the kinds of choices and living a kind of life, so that, to at least some extent, truckers' emotions become your emotions. Here again is that double methodological connection: verstehen demands not only understanding those you photograph or write about but understanding yourself as well and your relationship to them. Now maybe long-haul truckers constitute one sort of drifter or maybe they don't, but in any case Weber's ghost would these days have some other questions: How do you approach a migrant labor camp, or a group of kids squatting an abandoned house? Who do you need to be in the world, how do you need to be oriented to it, to understand what these folks understand? I mean, you don't . . . have . . . to live like a refugee. Or do you?

There's a good bit at stake in how we answer that question. Toward the end of *American Nomads,* for example, Richard Grant (2003, 269) recalls his experiences with the FTRA, or Freight Train Riders of

America, an alleged hobo gang or "hobo mafia" that showed up in the mass media some years ago. He also describes reports on the FTRA prepared by the Union Pacific Railroad Police and the Spokane Police Department. "Very impressive they are, too," says Grant, "complete with flow charts and diagrams, detailing the FTRA's command structure, seniority rankings, its various chapters and subsets." Grant suspects that these reports are indeed impressively descriptive of something—just not the FTRA. For him, "these diagrams and ranking systems reveal more about the mind-set of the men who made them, because they describe something that operates like a police department—organized, disciplined, hierarchical, rigid in structure, with specialist units that carry out orders and report back to a central command." We might call this a form of organizational projection, the mistake of attributing to outside groups the characteristics of the organization from within which they are viewed. We might call it failed verstehen. Whatever we call it, and whether our goal is to understand groups like the FTRA, or stop them or support them, the error is a dangerous and debilitating one, akin to mistaking a wild river for a ribbon of concrete.

So instead, having himself hopped freights with self-proclaimed FTRAers, having gotten drunk and swapped drunken stories with them—that is, having drifted into some form of verstehen—Grant (2003, 269, 270–71, 273) wonders "if it was even possible to distinguish truth from rumor about the FTRA." He tends to agree with a different investigation that found "no organized pattern" to FTRA crimes and a "random, disorganized quality" to the killings attributed to the FTRA. He notes that, where police investigations imagine a hierarchical organization, he finds "a general breakdown of hobo society, the kind of anarchy that gives anarchy a bad name." And as evidence, or maybe as lack of evidence, he includes the FTRA's origin story:

> It was founded by Daniel Boone under a bridge in Libby, Montana, or maybe Whitefish, Montana, in 1981, or 1983, or 1985. Daniel Boone can't remember because he was drunk and high at the time, and has done his best to stay drunk and high ever since. Fixing the precise date and location in his mind has not been a priority. But let's say Libby in 1985. A group of Vietnam veteran train tramps were drinking under a bridge when a freight train came rolling by with the letters X-TRA on the side. "We should call ourselves FTRA," quipped Daniel Boone. "Fuck The Reagan Administration." Later they altered the acronym's meaning to Freight Train Riders of America or Free to Tramp and Ride Alone. Mississippi Bones swore up and down that the FTRA, meaning Freight Train Riders of America, was founded in the 1940s by a black hobo called Coal Train. Bones had heard the whole

story from Coal Train himself as he lay drinking wine on his deathbed in . . . the Mojave Desert. . . . Some of the older hobos dated the origins of the FTRA back to the 1930s.

Just in case Coal Train was indeed in on it at some point, we might consider the solidity of evidence about him as well. Through a decade riding the rails and interviewing countless hobos young and old, Bill Daniel (2012, 118) collected the following hobo accounts of Coal Train—or maybe that's spelled Coaltrain:

> "Josh Easley is young Coaltrain. Old man Coaltrain is dead, gone, buried."

> "Well, I run up on an old boy said that John Easley had stole his name Coaltrain from an old black dude about 80 years old."

> "There was an old guy named Coaltrain. He was an old black guy, he lived in Spokane on the train tracks."

> "But at least we do have a sketch of Mister Coaltrain. Some people call him the U.S. Scout. Some people call him a pot head."

By conventional standards of solid investigative reporting or sound academic research, the work of Grant and Daniel is easily enough evaluated: inadequate and inconclusive. Clearly, more thorough accountings are needed, more sorting through competing claims and historical ambiguities to arrive at the truth of the matter. From the perspective of drift and drifters, though, "clearly" really doesn't have much to do with it. In this world, identities and origin myths are as fluid as the social relations that spawn them; here, epistemic certainty is as foreign as spatial stability. "What do the initials FTRA really stand for? Who is Coal Train, really?"—these are the sorts of questions asked by settlers and the sedentary. These are questions that, like the organizational models noted above, mostly just project the perspectives of those who would think to ask them, imposing their sensibilities, their methods, and their desired certainties onto worlds that generally operate without them. They're questions meant to establish a truth that never was. For drifters, they're nonsense, or worse—because to answer them in any definitive way is to distort the subject of study, to arrive not at the truth of the matter but at a false destination to which no drifter was ever delivered.

Simon Hallsworth would agree, and with a vengeance. As one of Britain's leading scholars on street violence, gangs, and the politics of local crime, he has for some years been confronting the issue of British street gangs—but more so he's been confronting the claims of street gang "experts." As Hallsworth (2013, 3, 4, 6) argues, these "experts" collectively constitute a "burgeoning anti-gang industry" that makes good money hiring its members out as professors, policy advisors, and public speakers. The industry's methods are "positivistic and numbers-driven," designed to measure at a distance the amount of gang activity, the number of gangs and gang members, and the overall magnitude of the gang problem. Unsurprisingly, the findings that these methods produce are in many ways artifacts of the methods themselves, and of the antigang industry's desire to confirm the need for its own existence. According to the research of these gang experts, gangs are growing in number, in their power over neighborhoods, and in the danger they pose to society itself. This spreading power and influence in turn derives from the nature of the gangs, with their "elaborate corporate structures with complex divisions of labour" and their dedication to maintaining rigid boundaries and vertical hierarchies of authority. A growing and virulent form of youthful organized crime, street gangs therefore demand a firm, punitive response—a response that gang "experts" in the antigang industry of course consider themselves well placed to provide.

As Hallsworth shows, and as contemporary research by on-the-ground gang researchers confirms, such antigang industry findings are not only baldly self-serving—they're also profound distortions of street gangs as they exist in everyday life. These are findings produced, as Hallsworth says, by those who are themselves "products of sedentary regimes"; who "inhabit sedentary organizations"; and who, like the police departments trying to understand the FTRA, project the rigidly hierarchical framework of such organizations onto those they study. Within such organizations, positivistic assumptions and quantitative methods seem a matter of rational common sense, and so those defined by these organizations utilize them to study gangs—with the effect of reducing street gangs to "denaturalized and decontextualized clusters of risk factors from which the truth of gangs is then discerned." For Hallsworth, then, the contemporary gang "problem" is in many ways a problem of improper method. It's a problem spawned by the mismatch between the static, formalized methods of gang experts and what Hallsworth, Robert Garot (2010), John Hagedorn (1994), Johnathan Ilan (2013), and other researchers find to be the informal, fluid realities of gang life on the streets. It's a problem that originates in perception, in the flawed "conceptual lens by and through which we make sense of complex street worlds" (Hallsworth 2013, 111, 112, 124).

But which conceptual lens would better serve the study of street gangs and street life? Hallsworth recommends the sort of nomadic thinking developed by Deleuze and Guattari (1987), a loose conceptual frame better attuned to the unstable, precarious lives of many street denizens. He recommends "reading the street as a rhizome," understanding the street as an emergent process, where people and their identities come and go, where incidents bubble up one moment and dissipate the next, where boundaries are negotiated more than enforced, where seemingly stable phenomena like "gang membership" or "gang structure" are in reality always in the process of being accomplished (Garot 2010; Hagedorn 1994). He suggests that trying to get to the essence or the truth of street gangs, or any other informal social phenomenon, may be not only impossible but imprudent—that we might be better served by looking around and beyond that which we study than looking too directly at it. And he concludes with a recommendation that is surely anathema to any gang "'expert," to any social "scientist," or to anyone else unprepared to imagine the methods of drift. "Think fuzzy thoughts about fluid institutions that are only ever always interstitial," Hallsworth (2013, 124, 196) says, "and you are halfway there."

See what I mean about method? It's really not a matter of selecting the proper coding procedure, or seeing that the forms are filled out thoroughly, or abiding by one set of investigative rules or another. It's more important than that. Method shapes how we see the world around us, how we connect with it, what we make of it. The use of static, bureaucratic methods—the methods of stable arrangements, hierarchical organizations, and those settled souls who occupy them—make a world of drift into something it's not, spawning dangerous delusions of hobo mafias and tightly organized gangs. As before, this mismatch moves in the other direction as well; a new generation of writers, artists, and filmmakers cut loose from career certainty and social stability can hardly afford to bring along the heavy historical baggage of bad bureaucratic method as they move today between one situation and another. A century ago the "bindle stiff" had a similar problem. An iconic hobo character who carried his few possessions and maybe a bit of bedding in a bindle strapped to his back, or sometimes suspended from the end of a stick carried over his shoulder, his personal poverty and peripatetic existence precluded excess baggage. As a result, bindles weren't big— just a little collection of the few items that a life of hard traveling had taught the stiff were essential. Now, a century later, what methods might today's intellectual bindle stiffs find worth carrying along? Grant and Hallsworth would suggest a bit of uncertainty, a rhizomatic outlook, and some fuzzy thinking—and I'll add a few more to the bindle as we go along. But in any case, we do know what's not worth lugging with us: Big textbooks turgid with fixed methodological procedures. "Social science," and the accumulated weight of its staid, bureaucratic ethos. Static, singular notions of truth and essentialist knowledge. And concrete slabs—definitely no concrete slabs.

CONCRETE SLABS

According to conventional academic understandings, method is the foundation on which research is built, and against which the validity of research findings is measured. A competent researcher constructs this methodological foundation carefully, choosing method that is efficient in its production of data and legitimate in its standing before the wider academic community; deciding and developing a priori protocols for designing questions, collecting data, ensuring confidentiality, and coding findings; and submitting this elaborate methodological foundation for approval by university or governmental review committees. Once completed and approved, this methodological design becomes the sturdy, steady base on which the research rests; day after day, interview after interview, survey after survey, the preset methodological protocols guarantee research consistency and guard against unintended bias or intellectual tangent on the part of the researcher. When the research is subsequently published, method reappears as foundation, this time establishing the evaluative basis for the findings presented and arguments made in the article or book. In this sense, those trained in sociology, political science, criminology, governmental studies, and related fields generally see good method as a well-laid concrete slab—a level, reliable foundation for constructing research, a firm footing for investigating the social world.

In many of these fields, survey research and subsequent statistical analysis constitute the preferred foundation. Quick and quantifiable, with preset questions and preset answer options that structure in replication and reliability, surveys flood the social sciences with information on subjects ranging from sexual habits and housing preferences to voting tendencies and crime fears. Yet what surveys spew forth in quantity, they lack in quality. Shallow in its conceptualization, abstract in its approach to the lived social world, dehumanizingly reductionist in its statistical manipulations, this sort of survey research is questionable at best—the foundation for a sort of prefabricated intellectual housing thrown up with little craft or care. As a foundation for research on drift and drifters, survey research and statistical analysis are especially inappropriate;

by the necessities of their design and execution, they constitute a uniquely wrongheaded and heavy-handed slab of methodological misdirection. Survey research generally assumes a social world defined by static, discrete factuality—degree of fear, amount of sexual activity, number of housing units, overall student satisfaction with college—a factuality foreign to the fluid arrangements and emergent identities of those whose lives float on movement, uncertainty, and change. Based in models of statistical probability and sampling, surveys are almost never administered to the entire population under study; instead they are administered to a statistically representative sample of a set, knowable population. Of all ten thousand students enrolled at a university, a hundred might be surveyed; of a hundred thousand homeowners, perhaps three hundred. By definition, though, drifters offer no definable population, and thus no possibility of accurate sampling. The lives of homeless folks, FTRA adherents, episodic gang members, illicit migrants, and unknown others are defined by, if nothing else, a sort of sacred immeasurability. And even if survey researchers could know the precise population of homeless wanderers or international migrants—which they can't—how would they locate a sample in order to administer the survey? You can't read a survey to someone you can't find. You can't call someone without a phone or mail a survey to someone without an address. You can't elicit a response to an online survey from someone without a computer.

When researchers nonetheless attempt to lay down slabs of survey research amid situations shaped by emergence and ambiguity, the results are predictably disfiguring. Interested in an important contemporary issue of dislocation and movement—the extent to which direct or indirect crime victimization shapes "neighborhood change" and "helps prompt households to leave an area"—the authors of a 2008 study decided to utilize data from the US National Crime Survey (NCS). Its name notwithstanding, the survey was in actuality administered to only a sample of housing segments drawn from a sample of districts drawn from a sample of metropolitan or county "primary sampling units"—with this model utilized, the researchers note, in order to "minimize travel and other administrative costs." Moreover, given that new confidentiality protocols installed in 1985 limited the usefulness of NCS data from subsequent years, the researchers decided to utilize NCS data from 1980–85—data collected more than two decades before their research. The researchers' subsequent analysis of this stale data—remember, so as to examine issues of mobility and household dislocation—in turn excluded mobile homes, "living quarters hotels or motels occupied by transient guests," and "group quarters (such as dormitories or rooming houses) because too few observations are found to support separate analyses" (Xie and McDowall 2008, 809, 816–17). To analyze an emergent issue, then, the researchers used a sampled stack of decades-old data that was itself prejudiced toward a finding of stability. Not to be outdone, the National Gang Center uses US federal funding to conduct its annual National Youth Gang Survey. This survey avoids the rhizomatic complexities of gang life and identity by simply ignoring gang members altogether; the survey is sent only to law enforcement agencies or, more accurately, to a mixed sample of agencies. For years, the survey declined to provide a definition of "youth gang" on which respondents might base their answers, on the grounds that "little agreement has been reached on what constitutes a gang, gang member, or gang incident" (OJJDP 1999, 7); now the survey offers the oddly elastic nondefinition of "a group of youths or young adults in your jurisdiction that you or other responsible persons in your agency or community are willing to identify as a 'gang'" (www.nationalgangcenter.gov). Despite its inability to define a phenomenon that is itself inherently fluid and amorphous, the survey produces definitive categories and findings—the number of gangs, gang members, and gang homicides nationwide, for example—that offer the sort of illusional positivistic certainty that Hallsworth's antigang industry hustlers can appreciate and put to use. The conclusions that my colleagues and I reached regarding the National Youth Gang Survey characterize other survey slabs as well, and their inadequacy for the task at hand: "That which is not to be studied directly can nonetheless be surveyed definitively, based on the records, or perhaps the personal perceptions, of those whose job it is to eradicate that which they cannot define accurately" (Ferrell, Hayward, and Young 2015, 203).

This commitment to pre-established method as the stable foundation for social research, and the parallel determination to administer rigid methodological models to even the most emergent of people and situations, reveals some deeper predilections as well—predilections we might summarize as the "fetishism of methodology." In general terms, *fetishism* denotes particular relationships between meaning and the material world. One is the attribution of animating powers to an inanimate object, so that the object itself is seen to embody what otherwise might be understood as larger forces of human action or cultural practice. A second suggests a sort of unnatural preoccupation with some small dimension of a larger totality. For the anthropologist, then, fetishism can be investigated as a form of religious mysticism, whereby groups imbue fetish objects with spiritual powers. For the Marxist, the "fetishism of commodities" implies not so much mysticism as mystification—an essential capitalist conceit, according to which commodities are imagined to embody value in such a way that the creation of this value through human labor is forgotten. For the sexual fetishist, the toe, the earlobe, or the high-heeled shoe emerges as the object of affection, a focused substitute for broader currents of sexuality and allure.

Slabs of contemporary method often operate in just these ways. Researchers imagine that survey research and statistical analysis are somehow mystically imbued with the power of "objectivity," and that such methods embody the spirit of scientific inquiry, mathematical precision, and dispassionate analysis. They imagine that these methods somehow operate independently from the flux of human emotion and human action—that such methods can distil objective "data" from those who are their targets, can produce results that are valid and "replicable" no matter the changing circumstances, can expunge "error" and "subjectivity" from the research process. As Karl Marx said of commodity fetishists, "There is a definite social relation . . . that assumes, in their eyes, the fantastic form of a relation between things. . . . In that world the productions of the human brain appear as independent beings endowed with life, and entering into relation both with one another and the human race. . . . To them, their own social action takes the form of the action of objects, which rule the producers instead of being ruled by them" (Marx 1970, 52–53, 57). Like sexual fetishists, researchers in turn focus so tightly on the minutiae of their methodology, and on the social minutiae that their methods are designed to investigate, that they regularly, and inevitably, miss larger dynamics of movement and emergence. Like other fetishists, they obsess over their fetish objects—"a one-way ANOVA random effects model," "hierarchical linear modelling (HLM) software," and "estimated variance of the random intercept" in the study of victimization and household mobility (Xie and McDowall 2008, 820, 823, 824)—with a sort of unnatural intensity, turning them over in their minds and in their computers, and so forgetting the fluid world beyond answer sets and data sheets. This fetishizing of methodology—this preoccupation with methodological minutiae and the particles of "data" they produce—pervades contemporary social science, converting emergent issues and fluid populations into static data sets available for ceaseless statistical manipulation. And indeed all of this is mostly fetishistic, and mostly masturbatory as well—available for the self-contained pleasure of a small circle of journal editors, tenure committees, governmental operatives, and anticrime experts but mostly unintelligible to the larger social world.

In this way, contemporary slabs of methods sit heavier still. The solidity of the method stills the fluidity of the world it is allegedly designed to investigate; the foundation comes to matter more than the intellectual edifice that might be built upon it. How immeasurably mistaken is this fetishized methodology of measurement? How incalculably distant is it from the lived experiences of those on the move between locations, identities, and employment? Build thee more stately mansions, oh my soul (Holmes 1858)—build soaring survey constructions and palaces of estimated variance if you must. But understand that these methodological mansions and the slabs on which they sit offer no home for drifters, wanderers, and the displaced. On the contrary: they're engineered to exclude them.

HISTORICAL UNCERTAINTIES

In 1923, Nels Anderson published one of the classic works in sociological criminology: *The Hobo: The Sociology of the Homeless Man.* As earlier chapters have suggested, though, the research that Anderson undertook for the book was hardly the start of his hoboing history. Anderson's own father had immigrated to the United States from Sweden by way of Germany, and once in the United States had become "a real hobo worker," traveling between jobs as a farmhand, miner, and lumberjack (Anderson [1923] 1961, v, vii). Marriage did little to settle him down, at least initially. Anderson's parents wandered the West and Midwest, Nels and the other children in tow, moving ten times in the first sixteen years of their marriage. Anderson himself soon enough abandoned high school to work and wander, joining other hobo workers who made up a team of railroad mule skinners. After six months with the mule skinners, Anderson was on the road again, working other railroad jobs, finding work in lumber camps and metal mines, and learning to hop freight trains like his old man. He also ran out of money more than once and, as seen in chapter 5, learned how to survive by begging on the streets and at homes for food. Some years later, after getting through college, he hopped his final freight—to attend graduate school in sociology at the University of Chicago.

Once at the University of Chicago, Anderson began his focused research and writing on hobos—and yet even here, as Anderson recalls ([1923] 1961, xi–iii), "I found myself engaged in research without the preparation a researcher is supposed to have. I couldn't answer if asked about my 'methods.'" What methodological guidance Anderson did encounter was decidedly less than formal. "Of the guidance I received at the University of Chicago from Professors Robert E. Park and Ernest W. Burgess," Anderson remembers, "most was indirect. The only instruction I recall from Park was, 'Write down only what you see, hear, and know, like a newspaper reporter.'" Years later, a methodological textbook described Anderson as "an intimate participant observer" of hobo life—but as Anderson admits, he had never heard the term at the time, and anyway, he was mostly just trying to earn a living and get by in his graduate work.

Seventeen years later, Nels Anderson published another book, *Men on the Move,* this one focused on the spatial and occupational dislocation caused by technological change and the Great Depression. In the introduction to this second book, he thought back to *The Hobo,* now concluding that it might best be characterized as a piece of "journalistic sociology" (1940, 2). As Park's earlier advice to him suggests, this was an apt description; much of the early ethnographic work undertaken at the University of Chicago had been animated by a journalistic sensibility oriented toward person-to-person interviewing, deep investigation, and on-the-street observation. Frederic Thrasher's research for his 1927 book, *The Gang,* for example, spooled out over a seven-year period, and in this book he not only presented in fine detail his impressions of "the thrilling street life of the gang" but included his own in situ photos of gang rituals and juvenile gang life (1927, xiii, 79). But as for *The Hobo,* Anderson (1940, 2) now came to another conclusion as well: he was weary of the book, and the attention it had drawn, and was aware of how much he had omitted from it. In fact, he doubted that it held up in comparison to "better contributions of earlier date" like Alice Solenberger's *One Thousand Homeless Men* (1911) and Jack London's *The Road* (1907).

The definitive article in his original book's title notwithstanding, Anderson and his research in these ways embody a striking intellectual and methodological modesty. Rolling into the University of Chicago by freight train, carrying with him a family history of itinerant manual labor, Anderson knew more about migrants than he did about sociological method. Later on, taking the oral examination for his master's degree—*after* the completion and publication of *The Hobo,* by the way—Anderson still "was not able to answer most of the questions put to me," as one of his examining professors noted. "You know your sociology out there better than we do, but you don't know it in here," the professor said. "We have decided to take a chance and approve you for your Master's degree" (Anderson [1923] 1960, xii). This chancy situation was in part of the professors' own making; they themselves were apparently comfortable enough with a sociology mostly invented by a researcher "out there" in the streets. Yet for all that time in the streets, Anderson himself never found his own street research fully "convincing" (Anderson 1940, 1) and seemed increasingly aware of its omissions and limitations. Still beset seventeen years later by the sorts of "fuzzy thoughts" and uncertainties that Hallsworth endorses, Anderson doubted that his work even added much to the findings of earlier researchers. But what of that earlier research by Solenberger and London, and its methodological acumen in comparison to Anderson's?

An official with the Chicago Bureau of Charities, Alice Solenberger had in 1911 published the book *One Thousand Homeless Men*—or, more accurately, had the book published on her behalf, since she had passed away in December 1910, when the book was not quite complete. Because of this, her colleague Francis McLean wrote a foreword to the book that was meant to stand in for the preface and final chapter that Solenberger had planned but had not written. In it McLean (1911, xiii–ix) argued that Solenberger's method of engagement with the homeless men she studied—a method that was critical but also oriented toward compassionate verstehen—was essential to her findings. "Her very quests, the splendid spirit of her work—intelligent, not to be hoodwinked, but human, natural, and discerning—promoted a mutual understanding," he wrote, "failing which no one may hope to get very far with that most elusive and compulsive creature, the homeless man." McLean also noted that Solenberger took care to familiarize herself not only with homeless men, tramps, and runaways, and with their trajectories over a number of years, but with the cheap "lodging houses" and impoverished South Side neighborhoods through which they moved. And McLean emphasized the emergent nature of Solenberger's methods, arguing that this lack of formalization in fact allowed her to develop a deeper understanding of the men. "At the beginning of the work there was no long look ahead to its possible uses as a study and interpretation," McLean says. 'She had no thesis to prove; her discriminating analysis of facts reveals this again and again."

Jack London's research methods were looser and more emergent still—if they can be called research methods at all. In 1907, London published *The Road*, a collection of largely autobiographical accounts recalling his early years tramping and hoboing around America. Indeed, the book is a detailed compendium of hobo slang, train-hopping techniques, on the road arrests, begging episodes, and more than a few itinerant adventures. London is of course aware of the need to make all this into a series of engaging stories, and he's good at it—but he's also aware that he is undertaking a narrative sociology of hobos and other early American drifters (Lennon 2014). In this light, he includes in the book a self-effacing statement of purpose that in its own way also defines his method—or maybe stands the very idea of method on its head. He writes,

> Every once in a while, in newspapers, magazines, and biographical dictionaries, I run upon sketches of my life, wherein, delicately phrased, I learn that it was in order to study sociology that I became a tramp. This is very nice and thoughtful of the biographers, but it is inaccurate. I became a tramp—well, because of the life that was in me, of the wanderlust in my blood that would not let me rest. Sociology was merely incidental; it came afterward, in the same manner that a wet skin follows a ducking. I went on "The Road" because I couldn't keep away from it; because I hadn't the price of the railroad fare in my jeans; because I was so made that I couldn't work all my life on "one same shift"; because—well, just because it was easier to than not to. (London 1907, 85)

Like Nels Anderson, and his father before him, Jack London's "method" was mostly ungrounded—or if it was grounded in anything at all, it was more in a wanderlust for the road than an affinity for the formalities of research. And if, as Anderson modestly claimed in *Men on the Move*, Solenberger's and London's were "better contributions" to understanding drifters than his own, it was certainly not because their methods constituted better-built concrete slabs. It was because their methods remained sympathetic, emergent, and largely adrift from the formalities of method itself.

Whatever the relative merits of these various works, Anderson's *Men on the Move* did push beyond Solenberger, London, and others with one significant advance. Like Thrasher, Solenberger, and other early researchers, Anderson had included rudimentary photographs in his earlier book *The Hobo*—straightforward photographs of street scenes, hobo jungles, and mission sleeping quarters. But in *Men on the Move*, he incorporated a whole other order of photography: the photographs produced in the 1930s by the Farm Security Administration (FSA). Charged with addressing rural poverty and publicizing the need for rural rehabilitation as part of Franklin Roosevelt's New Deal, the FSA during the 1930s assembled a team of documentary photographers who eventually produced some hundreds of thousands of images. The FSA's photographic project was led by former economics professor Roy Stryker, who consulted with sociologist Robert Lynd to produce "shooting scripts" by which to orient FSA photographers to comparative social conditions. Visual sociologist Douglas Harper (2012, 31; see also Harper 1982) sees in these scripts the origins of "sociological photography"—though notably he adds that "it is not at all clear that [the photographers] paid a great deal of attention to the scripts" other than to introduce themselves to new cities or situations. On the FSA's roster were pioneering and now well-known photo-documentarians like Walker Evans, Gordon Parks, Russell Lee, and Arthur Rothstein, and indeed *Men on the Move* features numerous photographs with the credit lines "Farm Security Administration, by Lee" and "Farm Security Administration, by Rothstein." Even more numerous and prominent in *Men on the Move* are the photographs credited to "Farm Security Administration, by Lange." These are images that belong not just to the FSA but to the photographer Dorothea Lange, and to the methodology of collaborative drifting through which she produced them.[1]

THE PHOTO-DOCUMENTARY TRADITION:
WANDERING, WAITING, MISSING, CONNECTING

Abandoning a career as a successful San Francisco portrait photographer, Dorothea Lange decided in the 1930s to take her camera out into the tragedy created by the Great Depression's economic collapse. Around this time, she also married Paul Taylor, a professor of economics at the University of California, and the two of them set out to crisscross the country with those forced onto the road by economic and agricultural failure. This wandering research with migrants continued into the early 1940s, when Lange also photographed another sort of forced dislocation: the herding of Japanese Americans into West Coast internment camps. The power of these internment photos was such that the US Army had them impounded so as to remove them from public view (Gordon and Okihiro 2008). In 1939, though, she and Paul Taylor brought the first phase of their work to a close with the publication of the book *An American Exodus*. A landmark in the development of documentary inquiry, the book stood on what Lange and Taylor (1939, 15) called "a tripod of photographs, captions and text"—that is, it attempted an innovative integration of Lange's photographic images, Taylor's written analysis, and the words spoken by those photographed.[2] The book's subtitle—*A*

Flood refugee family near Memphis, Texas. (Photo by Dorothea Lange, 1937. Original caption.)

Record of Human Erosion in the Thirties—suggests a second innovation. Lange and Taylor undertook to situate the human tragedy of the Great Depression within its parallel ecological tragedy, to show both people and places that had been worn down and worn away from their roots. Indeed, the book documents countless degradations of land and people alike; time and again Lange's photographs show both human faces and abandoned farms creased by starkly weathered lines of erosion.[3]

Traveling through Dust Bowl desolation and on to California squatter camps, Lange and Taylor—a professionally trained photographer and a professor of economics—employed an approach that might strike some as neither professional nor professorial. As Robert Coles (1997, 113–14)

Family walking on highway, five children. Started from Idabel, Oklahoma. Bound for Krebs, Oklahoma. Pittsburg County, Oklahoma. In 1936 the father farmed on thirds and fourths at Eagleton, McCurtain County, Oklahoma. Was taken sick with pneumonia and lost farm. Unable to get work on Work Projects Administration and refused county relief in county of fifteen years residence because of temporary residence in another county after his illness. (Photo by Dorothea Lange, 1938. Original caption.)

argues, *An American Exodus* was prophetic in documenting the interplay of human and ecological destruction, but "also prophetic and important was the manner in which this project was done: informally, unpretentiously, inexpensively, with clear, lucid language and strong, direct, compelling photographs its instrument. For some of us . . . this particular piece of research stands out as a milestone: it offers us a guiding sense of what was (and presumably still is) possible—direct observation by people interested in learning firsthand from other people, without the mediation of statistics, theory, and endless elaborations of so-called methodology." Notably, this evaluation comes from Coles's 1997 book *Doing Documentary Work;* sixty years after Lange and Taylor, sixty years on in the development of documentary analysis, a leading documentarian like Coles still considers *An American Exodus* a documentary masterwork precisely because of its informality, humanity, and disinclination to reify

Family who traveled by freight train. Washington, Toppenish, Yakima Valley. Aug. (Photo by Dorothea Lange, 1939. Original caption.)

its own methodology. And lest this lack of pretention be seen as indicative of some sort of naïveté on the part of the book's authors, we can consider Paul Taylor's own ideas on the subject. In a section of the book subtitled "Nonstatistical Notes from the Field," he addresses his "statistician friends" in economics and other disciplines. They "demand numbers"— but instead he and Lange purposely "decided to place primary reliance on personal observation of people in the situation to be studied in the field close-up." His statistician friends "seem to love averages"—but Taylor prefers the empathetic to the arithmetic, and wonders, "If the average reveals, doesn't it by the same token conceal?" (Lange and Taylor 1939, 136).

Looking east down the railroad track, near Calipatria, California. Single men, itinerants with 'bindles' waiting for the freight. (Photo by Dorothea Lange, 1939. Original caption).

The trek of bums, tramps, single transients, and undesirable indigents out of Los Angeles County because of police activity. (Photo by Dorothea Lange, 1936. Original caption.)

This grounded methodological fluidity directly informed Lange's photographic work as well. As one 1930s critic put it, her photography was "motivated by no preconceived photographic aesthetic. Her attitude bears a significant analogy to the sensitized plate of the camera itself. For her, making a shot is an adventure that begins with no planned itinerary." Indeed, in describing the process by which she shot the photo "White Angel Bread Line" and other iconic Depression-era street images, Lange recalled, "I can only say I knew I was looking at something. You know there are moments such as these when time stands still and all you do is hold your breath and hope it will wait for you. And you just hope you will have enough time to get it organized in a fraction of a second on that tiny piece of sensitive film" (quoted in Coles 1997, 149, 153–54). Nor was this open, immediate methodology limited to

Lange's work. For Walker Evans, another FSA photographer whose images illuminate the classic Depression-era ethnography *Let Us Now Praise Famous Men* (Agee and Evans [1939] 2001), "The point was to dream, to wander from topic to topic, and then, finally, to find the specific time and place, so that the eyes were free to follow the reasons of heart and mind both" (Coles 1997, 127). In this context Susan Sontag (1977, 29) describes Evans as "the last great photographer to work seriously and assuredly in a mood deriving from [Walt] Whitman's euphoric humanism." Yet Evans (1989, 13) highlights the rigor that underwrote this humanism as well. "I stare and stare at people, shamelessly," he says. "Stare. It is the way to educate your eye, and more."

Dedicated to capturing the lives of those cut adrift and pushed to the margins, Dorothea Lange, Walker Evans, and other documentary photographers in these ways employed a photographic orientation that ran parallel to such lost lives. This approach mixed the open road of intellectual and physical wandering with those little moments that emerge, unplanned and otherwise unnoticed, along that road. For the photographer, the key was to remain open to such immediacies and to understand how to catch them as they came. Those familiar with the history of documentary photography will notice in this method of informed immediacy something else as well: Henri Cartier-Bresson's definitive notion of "the decisive moment." A street photographer par excellence, whose work in the 1930s shaped the emergence of modern photojournalism, Cartier-Bresson roamed Paris and the world beyond, his beloved Leica camera in hand, his eye ready for what might emerge. "I prowled the streets all day," he recalled, "feeling very strung up and ready to pounce, determined to 'trap' life—to preserve life in the act of living. Above all, I craved to seize the whole essence, in the confines of one single photograph, of some situation that was in the process of unrolling itself before my eyes" (quoted in Miller 1997, 23).[4] Yet capturing these *images à la sauvette* (images on the run), Cartier-Bresson understood, required more than a fast finger on the shutter button; it required a sense of the decisive moment. For Cartier-Bresson, the decisive moment incorporated "the simultaneous recognition, in a fraction of a second, of the significance of an event as well as the precise organization of forms which give that event its proper expression." In the flicker of this decisive instant, sociology and criminology intersect photography; employing a "developed instinct," the photographer is able to catch the social meaning of an event as well as its appropriate visual representation. Within the inherent and ongoing motion of the social world, the skilled photographer captures an instant of ephemeral equilibrium (Cartier-Bresson quoted in Miller 1997, 102; see Ferrell and Van de Voorde 2010).

Robert Doisneau, another pioneer of street photography, embraced the same sort of photographic flâneuring as did Evans, Cartier-Bresson, and others; as he said, he worked by "feeling his way . . . prompted by feelings of attraction and repulsion, tossed hither and thither by events, allowing intuition its head—even when it kicked over the traces" (quoted in Gautrand 2003, 7). Doisneau highlighted another aspect of his work as well: temporal inefficiency. "Paris is a theatre where you book your seat by wasting time," he said, "and I'm still waiting" (quoted in Gautrand 2003, 15; see Doisneau 2001). Decades later, other visual documentarians are still waiting, too. Gianfranco Rosi's documentary film on the ring road that surrounds Rome and the people along it won the top prize at the 2014 Venice Film Festival. Commenting on his making of the film over a two-year period, Rosi echoed Doisneau's dawdling methodology. "I hate filming," he said. "I don't go around with the camera filming everything. I like to miss things, constantly, missing missing missing missing and waiting for that moment that I know is going to be the right moment. Once I'm there and O.K., this is the right moment to take out the camera and film, I don't know what is going to happen. And that's the magical thing, the unexpected happens" (quoted in Hale 2014, C5). Again we see the understanding of the decisive moment and of the wandering and waiting necessary to discover it. And as opposed to social science methodologies that promise comprehensive substantive coverage and the efficient production of knowledge, we glimpse in the work of Doisneau and Rosi a methodology of omission and delay, and with it a necessary aesthetics of absence.

This photographic embracing of omission and absence—this orientation toward disorientation—is perhaps best seen in the work of "the world's pre-eminent living photographer" (Dawidoff 2015, 40), Robert Frank. In 1958 Frank, who had emigrated from Switzerland some years earlier, published the photographic book *The Americans*—a collection of eighty-three photographs drawn from the twenty-seven thousand that Frank had taken in his travels across the continent. Frank admired, and had worked as an assistant to, Walker Evans, and his work mirrored—but also pushed onward and outward—the fluid approach earlier developed by Evans, Cartier-Bresson, Lange, and others. An accomplished photographer from a young age—a restless and impetuous one as well—Frank immigrated to New York, then traveled to South and Central America, Spain, and France before returning to the United States. Once back, he undertook three car trips around and across America to shoot the photos for *The Americans,* circling the United States almost in its entirety during the third trip. Wandering from city to city, sliding in and out of situations, Frank created a "disturbed and mournful song-of-the-road portrait" of America, doing so in a way that caught something of Cartier-Bresson's decisive moment and *images à la sauvette,* with Frank's quick reflexes and "dancer's combination of precision and abandon" (Cotter 2009, C27, C30) deployed during instantaneous events.

Yet where Cartier-Bresson sought the equilibrium of the decisive moment, Frank embraced what might be called the undecisive moment. Like Doisneau and Rosi, Frank was waiting as he wandered—but he was "waiting for the moment of revealing disequilibrium, to catch reality off-guard, in what he calls the 'in-between moments'" (Sontag 1977, 121). As Frank said, he was in search of "some moment I couldn't explain"; and as for the photographs themselves, "I leave it up to you. They don't have an end or a beginning. They're a piece of the middle" (quoted in Dawidoff 2015, 42, 43). Holland Cotter (2009, C30) records something of this ambivalent interstitiality, and its lasting influence, in his description of the final photograph in *The Americans,* an image of Frank's wife and son huddled together in an automobile, the automobile itself only half captured by the photo: "Like many of Frank's pictures, it isn't about an event but about an uncertain moment between events, when emotional guards are down, and dark feelings can flow in. . . . The ostensibly throwaway style of this and other pictures [by Frank] had a huge influence, from the 1960s forward, on young artists who understood that traditional models of resolution and wholeness, in art as in life, are unstable, if not illusory." Considered "among the foremost art photographers of his time" (Fox 2013, B9), Saul Leiter was like Frank also an influential street photographer—and like Frank, a photographer of the in-between and the out-of-focus. Undertaking to capture something of New York City's everyday human rhythms, Leiter shot photos of shadows, marginal spaces, and ephemeral intersections of people and places. "Unplanned and unstaged, Mr. Leiter's photographs are slices fleetingly glimpsed by a walker in the city," says Margalit Fox (2013, B9). "People are often in soft focus, shown only in part or absent altogether, though their presence is keenly implied. Sensitive to the city's found geometry, he shot by design around the edges of things."

If dawdling, delay, and a distinct disinclination to reify method suggest something of the distance between the photo-documentary tradition and contemporary social scientific methodologies, the interstitial approaches of Frank and Leiter confirm it at the level of ontology. Positivist methods such as survey research assume an objectively knowable world made up of discrete factual components and therefore go about portraying this world through data sets, statistical summaries, and other accumulations of atomized information. Frank, Leiter, and other photo-documentarians see a world that is largely unknowable and ambivalent at best—an unfolding, uncertain process in which the action occurs not on the spot but in the spaces in between—and go about portraying it through images that are themselves partial and imperfect. In doing so, they replace the totalizing gaze of social science with something more akin to the fleeting glance or the furtive observation (in this sense, it is surely no accident that both Frank and Leiter were ambivalent about their own work and largely disinterested in career advancement). The difference between a statistical table and a Robert Frank photograph is there for all to see, in the contrast between number and image, between ordered data and visual design. But before that, beneath that, is a deeper difference: the underlying assumption as to the nature of the world that each attempts to apprehend.

The depth of this difference can be seen in a final dimension of the photo-documentary tradition. Dorothea Lange, Walker Evans, and many others focused their work on the downtrodden, with the intent of recording their plight and perhaps even granting them a modicum of dignity by way of attentive photography. Robert Frank (quoted in Dawidoff 2015, 40) is explicit about this. "I photographed people who were held back, who never could step over a certain line. . . . My sympathies were with people who struggled," he says. "There was also my mistrust to the people who made the rules." Indeed, Susan Sontag (1977, 55) argues that "photography has always been fascinated by social heights and lower depths"—and that "documentarists (as distinct from courtiers with cameras) prefer the latter." This "sustained look downward" (Sontag 1977, 57) has of course not been without its dangers, among them class voyeurism and easy romanticism. Yet at its best, the photo-documentary engagement with those on the margins has produced distinctly important photographs out of distinctly human relationships. Mary Ellen Mark, for example, drew on the work of Cartier-Bresson, Lange, and Franke to become "one of the premier documentary photographers of her generation" (Grimes 2015, A17), photographing homeless teenagers and families, autistic children, heroin addicts, and street prostitutes. Living for two months in the maximum security women's wing of a state mental hospital, her rapport with the inmates was such that it "translated into strikingly de-dramatized representations of humans in extreme circumstances" (Grimes 2015, A17)—into a hard-earned photographic reversal, that is, of what Tannenbaum (1938) famously called the "dramatization of evil."[5]

Significantly, Mark also maintained connections with many of those she photographed, allowing her to revisit them photographically, sometimes decades later. Similar intensities of rapport and long-term commitment animated the work of Milton Rogovin. A progressive, whose early career was destroyed by the 1950s McCarthy-era investigations, Rogovin spent half a century photographing the poor around the United States—"the rich ones have their own photographers," he said (quoted in Genocchio 2011, B14). Like Mark, he worked slowly to gain trust and establish relationships, to the point that he was able to produce, for example, a series of triptychs of impoverished families spanning some twenty years of their lives.[6] In the deeply committed work of Mark and Rogovin, then, we see again the issue of *verstehen* (Weber 1978; Ferrell 1997)—an empathic understanding of those under study, certainly, but more than that, an informed, fluid subjectivity in place of the distanced objectivity that characterizes positivistic social science methods. We can quite literally see this informed subjectivity as well in the photographs themselves. A photograph is after all neither an objective recording of an external reality nor a purely subjective construction of the photographer but instead a visual documentation of the relationship between photographer and those photographed (Ferrell and Van de Voorde 2010)—and the photographs of Mark, Rogovin, and other photo-documentarians are photographs *of* their unfolding, empathic relationships with those who are their focus. Without these relationships, the photographs would be impossible—impossible to take in the first place and impossible to produce in the form in which we see them. As is the case for ethnographers and other qualitative researchers, the verstehen achieved by documentary photographers is no simple nicety; it is a human relationship essential to their work and its emotional and visual accuracy.

TOWARD METHOD ADRIFT

The approaches developed throughout the photo-documentary tradition bring the dynamics of dislocation, immediacy, uncertainty, and engagement directly into the lens of the camera. Drifting with drifters, prowling Paris streets, wandering American highways, photographic flâneurs like Lange, Cartier-Bresson, and Frank didn't know what they were seeking, but they knew how to find it and how to recognize it when they did. Certainly photographic plans were formed and decisions made, but mostly in the moment of their execution; they remained emergent in extremis. As with great musicians, great dancers, and other skilled performers, the "developed instinct" to which Cartier-Bresson referred is not a technical straightjacket nor an end in itself but rather a careful preparation for letting go, a method by which method can be abandoned in the interest of situational immediacy and human engagement. Unlike the fetishized reifications that shape positivistic social science method (Ferrell 2009, 2014), this photo-documentary approach is supple, fluid, best perhaps when it disappears into instinct and intuition. "We never, never talked about photography," Cartier-Bresson recalls of his time spent working in Paris with Robert Capa, Chim, and other pioneers of documentary photography. "Never! It would have been monstrous, presumptuous" (quoted in Miller 1997, 24).

Then again, that Cartier-Bresson quote comes from around 1935, about the same time that Walker Evans was photographing Southern sharecroppers, that Dorothea Lange and Paul Taylor were wandering America with Dust Bowl refugees, and that Nels Anderson was including the photos of Lange and other FSA photographers in *Men on the Move*. Even the best-known work of later photo-documentarians like Robert Frank is itself now a half-century old. So, despite some recent renewed interest in documentary traditions (Stallabrass 2013), and some powerful, contemporary photo-documentary work (for example, Salgado 2000; Maimon and Grinbaum 2016), perhaps this fluid approach is now mostly outmoded, a relic of the naïveté inherent in the early days of sociological ethnography and documentary photography, an unsophisticated embarrassment that we've moved past as these fields and their methods have continued to develop. Or perhaps it's that these photographers are particularly inarticulate in giving voice to their methods, uncomfortable outside their own medium of visual expression; in any case, they are certainly more artists than scientists, and so perhaps they simply remain unconcerned with the formal rigor of scientific method.

Perhaps so—but there's an alternative historical interpretation to consider. Since those early days of sociological ethnography and documentary photography, more and more money has poured into sociology, criminology, criminal justice, and related disciplines—money earmarked for quantifiable social scientific research, for producing the sorts of methodological fetishism and numerical analysis most useful for the governmental agencies and foundations from which the money comes. Increasingly since those early days, social scientists interested in disciplinary legitimacy—and money—have learned to build their research on these positivist methodological foundations, to imitate what they imagine to be the methods of the natural sciences. Intent on defining their disciplines as legitimate social science, and on marking them off from other forms of human inquiry, they have made of method a slab-like foundation on which all disciplinary edifices must be built and evaluated (Ferrell 2009, 2014). At the same time universities themselves have increasingly succumbed to risk management and the rationalization of knowledge, and under these regimes they have found a growing intolerance for social research that they consider undisciplined, unorthodox, unscientific, or unquantifiable.

By this alternative historical interpretation, then, it's not that social researchers have moved beyond the work of Nels Anderson, Dorothea Lange, and Paul Taylor; it's that they've been induced to forget it, or made to dismiss it, in the name of progress toward disciplinary rigor and rationality. By this view, social scientists have now come to the point that they engage in precisely the sort of monstrous and presumptuous behavior that Cartier-Bresson disavowed: the fetishism and reification of method as something exterior to, even more important than, the fluid social worlds they seek to understand. Absent a critical, reflexive theory of these social worlds—relying all too readily on the sorts of ontological, epistemic, and political assumptions that documentary photographers regularly challenged—social scientific disciplines construct method as a self-important impediment to attentive human inquiry. If this is so, our task is not to forget this earlier work, nor to move beyond it, but to remember and reinvent it—to pry up the methodological slabs under which it has been buried and to rediscover the power and importance of spontaneity, incompletion, and engagement.

"Beneath the paving stones, the beach," the Situationists said, imagining the possibilities that lay lost under the weight of modernist administrative conformity. Beneath and before today's methodological slabs, the liquid lessons of the past—and with these lessons, intimations of what method might usefully become were it cast adrift.

8

Drift Method

To chase after drifters is to chase after ghosts. Undocumented immigrants, the homeless, freight-hopping gutter punks—in the practice of
their own lives and in the imagination of lawmakers, settled citizens, and
the media, folks like these exist less as persons than as apparitions. Their
presence is haphazard; between their own peripatetic movements and
the ongoing attempts to exclude them from public space and public life,
they float in and out of social experience more than they inhabit it. Constructed as threats to social order and public decency, they haunt the
lives of the more secure, moving through the margins to seek shelter or
beg for money, leaving vague reminders of their unauthorized presence
in alleyways, on walls, along migrant trails. Ghostly also is their habit of
standing in the shadows, moving through the night, spectral figures out
there somewhere beyond the surveillance screens and mood lighting of
late modern living.

For a quarter century I've been working those same shadows, attempting to understand various sorts of marginal people and practices. You
might even say that my research has accumulated over the years into a
sort of unintended handbook, titled something like *How to Get Near a
Ghost*, that exists only in my head. To avoid apprehension and prosecution, I found, underground radio operators broadcast at odd hours and
stay on the move, sometimes going live from the back of a bicycle; as
discussed in chapter 3, groups like Critical Mass, Reclaim the Streets,
and Food Not Bombs embrace dis-organized, decentralized strategies

that shape their practices along lines of mapless fluidity and flow (Ferrell 2001). Urban trash pickers haunt the city's alleys and burrow in its trash bins, taking care to maintain their invisibility so as to avoid detection, confrontation, or arrest; in becoming one myself, I realized how skilled I had become at hiding behind Dumpsters and down dark passageways (Ferrell 2006). Another time, wandering the back roads of the American West, documenting the roadside shrines that accumulate there, I found these shrines to be lovely, fragile memorials to those lost along the highway—with the shrines themselves getting lost, too, decaying over time into the welter of roadside waste (Ferrell 2003). When it all started, it wasn't my intention to study ghosts, nor was it my intention to write that handbook, even in my head—yet this lack of intentionality now seems all the more appropriate and revealing. Setting out to document certain sorts of subcultures and social movements, I discovered drift, and ended up lost amidst its ghosts.

Contemporary graffiti—a focus of my research on and off throughout that quarter century (Ferrell 1996, 1998, 2013, 2016, 2017; Ferrell and Weide 2010)—constitutes its own sort of ghost. It's mostly an urban ghost, a ghost in the machine of the late modern neoliberal city described in chapter 2, a spectral presence that has only grown as contemporary graffiti has mutated and spread worldwide (Bofkin 2014; A. Young 2016). Today graffiti both eludes surveillance and invites it, tangled up with and often indistinguishable from legal street art and graffiti-style corporate street advertising. It is there and not there, pervasively visible in one sense but also hidden beneath an accumulating urban palimpsest of spray paint, whitewash, and erasure. It comes and goes, surreptitiously painted by underground artists while the city sleeps, or made to unexpectedly disappear the next day amidst urban redevelopment or enforcement campaigns. It creates urban audiences that come and go as well. As I've written elsewhere,

> Graffiti writers and street artists have been writing and rewriting a secret history of the city for a long time now, even when they've been writing it in plain sight. Their role has remained consistently inconsistent, off and on the radar, legal and illegal, caught somewhere between notoriety and acclaim, between the act and the art, moving in and out of the street and the gallery. . . . You see street art and you don't; you figure it out and you never figure it out. It shakes your hand and picks your pocket and then pays you back—sometimes. The more you know about the streets, the community, the traditions, the beefs and the alliances, the more it reveals itself to you; the less you know, the less it has to offer. Because of this street art and graffiti hide in the light . . . they always know more than they say, always paint their own riddles. (Ferrell 2013)

Spectral in its appearance and disappearance, graffiti exists as a series of urban apparitions, its authors an army of nocturnal drifters, street merchants of illicit meaning.

When this graffiti is itself set in motion, the ghosts go with it. Increasingly, contemporary graffiti is painted not only in urban spaces but on the freight trains that travel from one urban rail yard to the next (Ferrell 1998; Weide 2016). Cut loose from spatial context, this freight train graffiti flows across the country, creating sliding juxtapositions of color and meaning as one painted freight car passes another, or as the open doors of one freight car frame, for a moment, the mural on the car passing behind it. Moving between cities, this graffiti also comes to rest in the next urban rail yard and then the next, with these rail yards now haunted by local graffiti writers and graffiti aficionados, who attend to them as vast open-air art galleries. In this way contemporary graffiti gets entangled with some other ghosts: with contemporary train hoppers like Zeke and Goddamn It Dale, themselves easing around the rail yards, catching rides on outbound freights and signing in their illicit identities on rail cars and urban walls. It also gets tangled up with some older ghosts: the long-standing ghosts of hobo graffiti—signatures, coded markings, and little drawings written on the sides of railcars by hobos and rail workers for a century and a half, and still written and rewritten today, disjointed memories of time and place left for the world to find (Daniel 2008; Ferrell 1998; Lennon 2016; Rogers 2016). Often the apparitions do indeed appear together; if you look closely enough at most any freight car, you're likely to see little hobo markings amidst the bigger and more colorful work of contemporary graffiti writers, one dislocated image dancing next to another.

For a century and a half, hobos have themselves been floating and fading, too, ghosts of the great American West and points beyond. "In the course of my tramping I encountered hundreds of hobos whom I hailed and who hailed me . . . and who passed and were seen never again," recalled Jack London (1907, 71) in 1907. "On the other hand, there were hobos who passed and repassed with amazing frequency, and others, still, who passed like ghosts, close at hand, unseen, and never seen." Two decades later the hobo and wandering thief Jack Black ([1926] 2000, 17) chronicled a similar life of illicit movement, invisibility, and absence:

> At thirty I was a respected member of the "yegg" brotherhood, a thief of which little is known. He is silent, secretive, warty; forever travelling, always a night "worker". He shuns the bright lights, seldom straying far from his

kind, never coming to the surface. Circulating through space with his always-ready automatic, the yegg rules the underworld of criminals. At forty I found myself a solitary, capable journeyman highwayman; an escaped convict, a fugitive, with a background of twenty-five years in the underworld.

Like trash pickers and graffiti writers, hobos have long learned to make themselves disappear; melting into the machinery of the train at the moment of catching out, camouflaging themselves inside dark clothes and railroad grime, traversing "the spaces where those of us in polite society fear to look or travel" (Cresswell 2011, 239), the hobo negotiates an ongoing absence, a life of being there and not there. By the mid-twentieth century, writers like Jack Kerouac had come to see such hobos as "ghosts, spiritual guides circulating around the country ready to lead those who can recognize them" (Lennon 2014, 158). But spiritual guides or not, the train ghosts continue to roll today. When I was hanging out and hopping freights with Zeke, he told me ghost stories about secretive groups like the Tramp Family Shadow People and reminded me of the old hobo creed: "you just want to be least visible as possible."[1]

Then again, sometimes you don't have much choice but to be least visible as possible. Cast out from one town and another, millions of vagabonds in the 1930s became what Tom Kromer (1933, 115) said of himself, as I noted in chapter 4, wandering lost and hungry through the economic ruins of the Great Depression: a "restless ghost." Today, as chapter 2 documented, consumerist urban economies and aggressive urban policing combine to enforce a similar invisibility on the homeless, herding them out of high-traffic areas, erasing them from public space, and sending them into perpetual motion, staggering zombie-like from place to place as they struggle to negotiate bulldozed encampments, banishment orders, and inhospitable park benches. As I pointed out in chapter 2, Kristina Gibson (2011, 3–4, 16) argues that when homeless street kids "are pushed out of public spaces around the city, their plight not only is worsened, it also is made invisible." Echoing Jack London's circulating world of hobos "unseen and never seen," she adds that, amidst enforcement campaigns against such kids in New York City, "workers report that while they are still finding large numbers of street kids, they are not able to find the same kids consistently." Likewise, when contemporary graffiti writers haunt the nighttime urban margins, hiding in alleys and abandoned buildings, they do so not only out of a sense of nocturnal adventure but because high-profile antigraffiti campaigns have left them little else; recalling one such campaign, graffiti writer Eye Six notes that he and other writers were "pushed into real obscure places where all we're basically doing is . . . puttin' up wallpaper for winos and bums" (quoted in Ferrell 1996, 104). Similarly, street gangs' fluid identities and rhizomatic dynamics reflect the organic realities of urban street life, but they also operate as adaptions to the aggressive criminalization of such gangs and imposed legal categorization of their members. And this is not to mention perhaps the most prominent contemporary example of imposed invisibility: the extralegal lives of migrants and immigrants who have been stashed away in isolated refugee camps, or who have managed to avoid such a fate only by keeping to back roads and hidden bivouacs, surreptitiously crisscrossing borders and serially moving away from and toward the wrong situation.

This dialectic between the enforced invisibility of drifters and their own strategies for maintaining such invisibility points to a larger issue: conceptualizing drifters as ghosts suggests some sort of ghostly post-death presence and so demands at least some inquiry into the nature of that death. Twenty-five years into chasing drifters and ghosts, I suggest that this death is distinctly social in nature—a *social death,* whose pervasiveness identifies it as endemic to the contemporary social order. A social system built around economic inequality and social exclusion (J. Young 1999) systematically withdraws from its marginalized members the lifeblood of citizenship. Just as inclusive social life is defined by acceptance, mutuality, and shared respect, so this social death results from the enforced failure of such mutuality. Those who are today socially murdered are defined as outside the realm of warranted acceptance, stigmatized for their supposed failings, aborted in their attempts to gain and maintain cultural dignity, and erased from the spaces of shared social life. As a result they live as social and cultural ghosts, dead to those who would condemn them, for others little more than specters sometimes glanced in a parking lot or beneath a freeway overpass, or in a headline. Even when they are made visible—as in the Australian and American phenomenon of police officers and citizens photographing the homeless without their permission, then posting the photos to Instagram with derisive comments—it is a visibility begot by the glare of public ridicule (*Daily Telegraph* 2015).

Decades ago, Harold Garfinkel (1956, 420) noted that there existed a certain type of demeaning social ritual that involved "communicative work"—a ritual aimed at lowering an individual's social status and communicating this lowered status to a particular audience. Garfinkel's focus was on the dynamics of small groups and everyday interactions, and so this notion of what he called "degradation ceremonies" has most often been applied to events like ritualized hazing in the military or among fraternity members. When executed on a larger scale, though, degradation ceremonies can be thought of as the ongoing mechanisms of social death; they can exist not just among small groups and within organizations but in the pronouncements of national politicians, in sequences of sensationalist newspaper headlines and articles, and in the broader flow of social interaction and cultural meaning. "These men do their life sentences on the installment plan because they have been discredited and stigmatized by other Americans," James Spradley said of skid row habitués a half century ago (1970, 17)—and, he might have added, discredited and stigmatized by serial arrests, by political accusations of laziness and moral turpitude, and by the practiced indifference of passersby. In the same way, when corporate, political, and media elites conspire to stage elaborate campaigns aimed at defining graffiti writers as somehow outside the boundaries of urban community—as in fact violent invaders of such community—they assassinate graffiti writers' social and cultural existence, redefining them in terms of animalistic inhumanity and aesthetic rape and leaving them to flee police and vigilantes alike (Ferrell 1996; Austin 2001). Globally, migrants and political refugees, who are imagined as the carriers of exotic disease, the thieves of honest labor and good jobs, even the Trojan horse of terroristic violence, are effectively made dead to those who have learned to fear them. As the 400 or 4000 blows accumulate (Truffaut 1959), the installment plan continues, demanding payment in the form of serial exclusion and social death.

This degradation and death spawn subsequent spirals of social and physical invisibility. To be homeless and publicly visible, for example, is to invite all manner of social and legal abuse and, all but certainly, to set in motion social reactions that will result in further harassment and stigmatization. As a result, homeless folks learn how to haunt and hide, how to slouch down back alleys and disappear into bombed out, postindustrial estates. Hanging out years ago with my old friend Harry Lyrico, generally homeless and a graffiti writer to boot, I witnessed this first hand. Socially dead, sans legal counsel or other self-protection, Harry had learned to undertake some uncanny magic—to spot a cop two blocks away and slip off before the cop's arrival, to make himself invisible in most any social situation, to remove himself from public recognition as needed (Ferrell 1996, 2001). After all, Harry taught me, you can survive after social death—as a ghost, that is—but only if you learn to enforce your own invisibility, only if you agree to cooperate in your own exclusion. When in such circumstances a local politician subsequently claims that we certainly don't seem to have a homelessness problem here, when an upstanding homeowner later remarks on how seldom she sees refugees living on the streets, well, that's part of social death as well. Perception intersects practice; all involved conspire in the construction of ghosts, in not seeing those who are not to be seen.

During the Argentinian "Dirty War" of the 1970s and 1980s, military and security forces worked with right-wing death squads to abduct, torture, and dispose of thousands of Argentinian citizens, who came to be known as "desaparecidos"—"the disappeared." Removed from everyday life, secreted away in clandestine torture centers, many of their bodies later disposed of at sea, they were not only tortured and murdered. They were made to disappear from the society itself, their captors' intention being to erase their social and political presence as well—to impose on them, that is, both physical death and social death. Sadly, our contemporary world retains its own torture chambers and death squads; yet in many cases it is a different set of mechanisms by which people are made to disappear. The desaparecidos of everyday life are produced more by the workings of immigration law and exclusion orders, by political pronouncements and economic inequality, by urban gentrification and anticrime campaigns. Disappeared from the shared spaces of social life, dismissed from membership in imagined forms of stable community, they are left to drift in and out of public perception; constructed as organized criminals and moral menaces by the media and by the law, they haunt the margins, circulating more as an imaginary presence than as an identifiable threat. Members of a ghost army adrift, they necessarily live as occasional apparitions among the living.[2]

Japan's "evaporated people" constitute another sort of desaparecidos—ghosts who don't make even occasional appearances among the living. Shamed by unemployment and debt, bankrupted by Japan's financial crisis or its reliance on "irregular" jobs, they forego suicide for social death. Leaving behind their family, friends, and identities, they disappear into a shadow world of unmapped slums dotted with tiny living quarters. Serviced by a shadow economy of illicit home movers and off-the-books employment, they become thoroughgoing social ghosts, invisible and untraceable. Estimates are that a hundred thousand Japanese evaporate in this way each year, but who would know? There's no national database on the missing, and, more importantly, discussing the phenomenon is itself taboo—so much so that families often don't report missing members. "Look at me. I look like nothing. I am nothing," says one man who evaporated after losing his job as an engineer. "If I die tomorrow, I don't want anyone to be able to recognize me." Another, bankrupted by the costs of parental care, understands himself to be among ghosts. "You see people on the street," he says, "but they have already ceased to exist" (quoted in Callahan 2016; see Mauger, Remael, and Phale 2016).

The ghostly consequences of systematic social death in turn operate in a larger contemporary context—one that further spawns the pervasive if apparitional presence of drifters and ghosts. After all, we live in a time after time—a time of ghosts, aftermaths, and absences. The ecological consequences of modernist state conflict and capitalist avarice have come due; mortgaged to the future for so long, we've likely exhausted our run. The death of the Fordist model and the economic carcass of neoliberalism leave us looking over our shoulders, wondering how it is that we imagined the American Dream into reality in the first place. Migrants, temporary workers, and the unemployed wander from one lost opportunity to the next, zombies crossing cities and continents and oceans in search of, well, something. Decades of mass incarceration have left millions of convicted felons to go about their lives "civilly dead" (K. Hernandez 2014, 418), disenfranchised and denied basic legal rights. Ghostly times indeed: dead careers, dying planet, the ship of the nation-state dead in the water—a social order that stumbles ahead, a specter of its former self. In such times there are drifters and ghosts aplenty, and so it seems imperative that we think about and theorize the nature of ghosts and drifters, consider the torn cultural and social tissue that connects and disconnects them, and face up to the fraudulence behind which they are hidden. Undertaking to understand ghosts and drifters—for that matter, undertaking to find them in the first place—will require new ways of seeing the world and new methods for engaging with it. It will require constructing narratives that come closer to ghost stories than to social scientific summaries.[3] As the previous chapter suggested, it will require some mix of reorientation and disorientation; we can't count what we can't catch, and we can't usefully categorize those who remain endlessly on the move between categories. Ghostly lives will require ghostly method.

"By 'modernity' I mean the ephemeral, the fugitive, the contingent," wrote Baudelaire ([1863] 1964, 13), famously, "the half of art whose other half is the eternal and the immutable." By ghostly, I mean the ephemeral, the fugitive, the contingent as well, the drifting half of the contemporary world, whose other half is the settled, the sedentary, and the sentries of social order.

GHOST METHOD

Parts of the book were scrawled on Bull Durham papers in box cars,
margins of religious tracts in a hundred missions, jails, one prison,
railroad sand-houses, flop-houses, and on a few memorable
occasions actually pecked out with my two index fingers on
an honest-to-God typewriter.

—Kromer, *Waiting for Nothing,* 1935

One way to think about ghosts and drifters is to think about absence. Putting aside for a moment supernatural considerations, we can understand ghosts as embodying, if nothing else, the presence of absence. A long-dead, one-time occupant, who to this day seems to haunt an old house and its new owners; a deceased father, who stays alive in the memories of a grieving daughter; a series of wartime horrors that still rattle decades later in a veteran's head—all suggest that the absent and the missing remain with us. Put another way, these and other shared cultural experiences suggest that absence constitutes a phenomenon in its own right, a void as sensually immediate and emotionally present as any matter that might fill it. For drifters this is the case as well; by the nature of their dislocated wanderings, they are less likely to be present in any one place than to be absent from it—less likely to be here, that is, than to have been here, to have just departed or disappeared altogether. The homeless shopping cart left up under a bridge, the bus on the way out of town, the faraway horn of a freight train and its transient human cargo—all denote the inevitability of the drifter's absence. "There is no there there," Gertrude Stein once said of Oakland, California. For drifters, it's not just Oakland; "there" is a fixedness seldom available. By turns enforced and embraced, this absence forms much of the drifter's lived experience; it shapes the experience of those who encounter drifters, and those who fear them, too. For them, drifters seem mostly to offer up their absence, pending or accomplished, and with it the sort of apparitional uncertainty that discomforts those who seek stable circumstances, clear vision, and firm understanding. Ghosts and drifters alike haunt the social worlds of these more sedentary citizens, present in their absence, visible in their invisibility.

As a researcher, my preferred method is ethnography—immersive, in-depth research with subjects of study—a method, I would argue, that is far more useful and humane than the abstracted, fetishized slab methods outlined in the previous chapter. Where slab methods are fixed before the research begins, ethnography tends to be supple and emergent, more an informed sensibility about what is being studied than a pre-established framework for inquiry; where slab methods are designed for statistical abstraction and intellectual generalization, ethnographic methods are meant for attentiveness and fidelity to the situation under study. Yet for all its strengths, ethnography harbors a problem. Ethnography has traditionally been attuned to the careful study of definable groups and settled subcultures, and to long-term research involvement with them and the settings they occupy. It has also been dedicated to precise documentation of the people, objects, and interactions that the ethnographer finds to be present in such settings; as with the instructions given to Nels Anderson ([1923] 1961) in the previous chapter: "Write down only what you see, hear, and know, like a newspaper reporter." For ethnography and ethnographers, then, the problem comes when the subjects of study are drifters and ghosts, coming and going haphazardly, moving through settings more than occupying them—a problem once again of how to get near a ghost, or to find one in the first place. The problem is redoubled when ethnographers, trained to record what is present, and on its own terms, are faced mostly with what is absent. Absence may be present, but knowing how to notice it, record it, and account for it is another matter.

A solution to this problem would retain the attentive sensibility of ethnography while reorienting it, or perhaps disorienting it, to the shape-shifting world of ghosts and drifters. Certainly a foundation for this solution appeared in the previous chapter with the work of documentary photographers like Dorothea Lange, Robert Frank, and Saul Leiter, their minds and their cameras aimed at human exodus and erosion, at gaps in time and interaction, and at the lost spaces of social life. Contemporary ethnographers have begun to consider such possibilities too. "The ethnographic project has changed because the world that ethnography confronts has changed," argues Norman Denzin (1997, xii). "Disjuncture and difference define this global, postmodern cultural economy we all live in. National boundaries and identities blur. Everyone is a tourist, an immigrant, a refugee, an exile, a guest worker, moving from one part of the world to another." I and others have begun to explore practices like "instant ethnography" and "liquid ethnography," with the goal of developing research approaches that can account for ephemeral moments, unstable social circumstances, and the sorts of ceaseless movement that Denzin describes (Ferrell, Hayward, and

Young 2015). Independent filmmaker Kelly Reichardt has likewise "made a career of silence and suggestion" while shooting a series of films about the lives of "lonesome, seminomadic searchers." She has done so by embracing the pain and hardship of such living, and by situating herself and her actors inside its sustained and often incommunicable discomfort. "Google is not research," she says. "Research is a lived thing" (quoted in Gregory 2016, 37–38). Following her lead and that of others, how might we live inside the thing that is drifters and ghosts, and their absence?

Excavating Absence

In an essay entitled "The Geography of Emptiness," Gary McDonogh (1993, 13) argues that "we must recognize and explore empty places as culturally created and socially meaningful zones rich in interest for our analysis of the city," since "such spaces do not define a vacuum, an absence of urbanness, so much as they mark zones of intense competition: the interstices of the city." McDonogh's notions of emptiness as constructed from cultural and competitive forces points to a critical analysis of absence—that is, an investigation of the social and cultural forces from which absence is built. By this logic absence is neither natural nor inevitable; it is a residue of particular social conflicts and social arrangements. When for example nineteenth-century European settlers declared the Australian outback to be terra nullius—"nobody's land"— it was not in fact because the land was absent inhabitants; it was because the settlers sought to eradicate the land's aboriginal population, to erase their history and culture, and to render the aborigine "socially invisible" (Morrison 2004, 75). Spaces of emptiness and absence are in this way often spaces of social death, sometimes the killing grounds on which citizenship and social visibility are exterminated, other times the spatial residues of such cultural violence. Emptiness is never fully emptied of its origins; absence is never absent the echoes of the forces that formed it. If we are to understand drifters and ghosts, our task is to find these origins, to listen to these echoes—to excavate absence for what remains present in it.[4]

As a starting point, absence can be excavated in search of those *not there*. This sort of excavation requires not only an ethnographic attentiveness to the particulars of absence but an application of the sociological imagination—an ability to look past the overwhelming immediacy of presence to see those not allowed to be present, a willingness to dig beneath the obvious and unearth the residues of embedded exclusion. In the sort of exclusive society already noted, and in the proliferating spaces in which such exclusion is enforced, far more people are denied access than are invited in. It's simple enough to notice those with invitations—but our job is to see those without access and to glimpse the way their ghosts haunt the privileged pleasures of inclusion. A fine restaurant in a fine neighborhood, and a fine evening for those dining there as well—but notice that the undocumented immigrants preparing the meal are kept invisible in the kitchen, that those without the money for such a meal are absent altogether, and that homeless folks and street populations are carefully policed away from such places, left to circulate unseen in the darker districts of the city. The first day of school, the bustle of students and teachers—but notice the refugees who aren't in attendance, lacking the official paperwork needed for registration, or excluded entirely by law, economy, or public condemnation from those in the settled neighborhood in which the school sits. Televised coverage of a street protest somewhere around the globe, and the reporter's comments on the "thousands of citizens in the street"—but notice the enforced gender segregation by which all the "citizens" in the streets are men. Such situations are defined by who is absent as much as by who is present; in all such cases, the presence of absence is the politics of absence as well.

This absence of those not there often echoes the absence of those *no longer there.* Excavating this second sort of absence requires not only a sociological imagination but a historical sensibility, a sensitivity to the politics of historical evolution and social change. If that fine restaurant sits in a recently gentrified neighborhood, as is increasingly likely, then its presence also hides the absence of the little shops and low-rent apartments that once defined the neighborhood, as well as the absence of the homeless folks once allowed to congregate there. The big box store out on the highway not only draws our attention but in doing so diverts our attention from the now-boarded-up shops a few miles away on the town square and from all the nearby farms lost to foreclosure (Tunnell 2011). Over time, as cities enforce banishment and exclusion orders, the daily removal of street populations from public space accumulates into a history of removal—a history that hides the earlier vitality of such space, leaving it not only empty but emptied (see McDonogh 1993). As the wars on drugs and gangs drag on, generations of young black men are pulled from their communities, the result being that these communities are increasingly haunted by those no longer present, shaped by those who are both in prison and out of the neighborhood;

over time, villages in Central America likewise empty out and confront a recalibration of their social lives as men and boys who were once there continue to migrate north in search of jobs that may be somewhere else. To be both not there and no longer there is to endure a double absence; it is to live as one of the desaparecidos, a ghost of circumstances changed and memory evacuated.

The absence of those not there and no longer there can coalesce into particular sorts of spaces as well. Justin Armstrong (2010, 244) describes these as "un-spaces"—"the abandoned and unseen locations that exist at the edges of everyday life and experience . . . the hollowed-out spaces that are left to their own devices . . . shadows of former places cast aside in the drifting of time"—spaces that he argues are amenable to a "spectral ethnography" attuned to the cultural resonances of past occupation. More generally, Michael Bell (1997, 813, 822; emphasis in original) argues that "ghosts—that is, *the sense of the presence of those who are not physically here*—are a ubiquitous aspect of the phenomenology of place" across a range of locations. For Armstrong the unspatial location is the North American High Plains, with their endless, empty roads and decaying, all-but-abandoned towns "haunted by their departed human agents," who once migrated there and have now moved on (244). For Bell, such locations include a generations-old family vacation area and a century-old faculty office, both still "filled with ghosts" of past experiences and departed colleagues. If for Armstrong and Bell such places resonate with a mix of warmth and chill, a mélange of fond memories and sorrowful loss, for criminologists like Travis Linnemann and Mark Hamm, there is often something more akin to cold sweat. Noting presidential assassination sites and Holocaust locations, exploring in particular the cultural residues of the *In Cold Blood* murders, Linnemann (2015, 517) has written of "the haunting power of human creation and indelibility of meaning—specters of remembrance that transmit and inherit across generations," adding that "to speak of ghosts then is to speak of the phenomenology of place—the lasting presence of those who are not physically there." Undertaking an "ethnography of terror," Hamm (1998, 115) tracked down the seedy Kingman, Arizona, motel room Timothy McVeigh had occupied a year earlier, as McVeigh had prepared to truck-bomb the Murrah Building in Oklahoma City. McVeigh was by this time long gone, but Hamm moved in for a couple of nights anyway—and found his own distinctly terrifying, ghostly mélange of black auras and night panic. Whatever their differences, though, all of these are places of absence and loss, places in which those once there are no longer, having drifted or been drawn away—and yet places where such absence remains palpably present.[5]

A final sort of absence requires anticipatory excavation. The economic and political trajectories outlined in the previous chapters strongly suggest that the contemporary world consists not only of those not there, and those no longer there, but those who will soon not be there—those scheduled to be put adrift and made absent. The next corporate or university reduction in full-time staff; the next war, and with it the next wave of forced refugees and bombed-out veterans; the next consumerist urban development plan—all will empty out social spaces, enforce absence, and cast lives adrift as surely as the ones before them. "Speculative emptiness," McDonogh (1993, 7) calls it—and excavating such speculative emptiness will mean decoding official pronouncements about economic progress and efficient growth, watching carefully for the early signs of absence and emptying out, and confronting the insidious mechanisms of power by which such targeted absence is engineered, enforced, and forgotten. When Eye Six and other Denver graffiti writers were pushed out of lower downtown and its rail yards, and into the "real obscure places" that Eye Six recalled earlier, the antigraffiti campaign that did the pushing was operating, we now know, as the forward edge of a long-term plan to cleanse the area of graffiti writers, runaway kids, and homeless folks, so it could be redeveloped for high-end consumption, housing, and entertainment. The plan was a success—and save for the arguments of a few critics like myself (Ferrell 1996, 2001), it was also a success in redefining these areas as having all along been an empty terra nullius, awaiting only developmental salvation. Likewise, when Zeke recounted (see chapter 5) being approached by a city cleanup crew near the rail yards, and getting the crew to wait while he and other train hoppers made breakfast, he wasn't just putting one over on the crew; he was seeing his own ultimate absence. I saw it too, hanging out with Zeke and other train hoppers around those yards: the amassed bulldozers, the surveyor's stakes, the arriving work crews, all portending—if you knew how to read them—the new toll road that would be built right over the to-be-razed hobo jungles that had dotted that area for decades. Soon enough, speculative emptiness begets the presence of absence and amnesia.[6]

Aftermath: Residues

In the aftermath of enforced absence, in the afterlife of social death, ghosts drift away to circulate along the shadow margins of social life.

For them, the aftermath is an ongoing echo of the calamity by which they were initially made absent, a lingering reverberation of the social forces that conspired to construct their exclusion. This aftermath is itself a cultural and temporal space shaped by absence and ambiguity, a borderland "space of nonexistence" that "excludes people, limits rights, restricts services, and erases personhood," as Susan Bibler Coutin (2003, 172) writes in describing the everyday lives of undocumented El Salvadoran immigrants in the United States. To live inside it is to move about in a suspended state, to hide out in the temporal ruins of enforced nonexistence. Itself a ghost of the immediate, the aftermath is also the place where the ghosts of immediate injustice gather and disperse.[7]

This aftermath is a residual phenomenon, powder burns after the explosion, lipstick traces on a cigarette (Marcus 1989)—and its residual dynamic doubles as ghosts and drifters move through it. Made to be always on the move, pushed out repeatedly by immigration policy or urban redevelopment plans, drifters have no choice but to leave behind residues of themselves. And so, just as they are more likely to be absent than present, they are more likely be visible in the vestiges that remain than in the person now departed. "A ramblin' man he has his troubles hangin' on to all that he owns," sang Jerry Jeff Walker (1972), lamenting a lost guitar—but a woman or man *made* to travel, forced to move on time and again, has a whole other order of troubles in hanging on to what little is owned. If we want to understand drifters—if we want to get near ghosts—we had best reorient ourselves to their residues and commit to developing a sociology of the residual.

Those who've tangled with ghosts can tell us something of residues, and of the ways they provide a lingering presence amidst human absence. Decades ago, James Agee trained his phenomenologist's eye on the modest possessions of the farm family he studied—and amidst this modesty he found the sacred remembrances of the family's past—fancy baby dresses and old talcum powder boxes, traces of family life tucked away in a drawer that he came to understand as their private tabernacle (Agee and Evans [1939] 2001, 145–49). More recently, exploring the possibilities of spectral ethnography, Armstrong (2010, 244, 247) has argued for "a subtle rethinking of ethnographic space—that fluid and transient expanse in which cultural analysis takes place—as a possible location for the study of the accumulation of cultural time . . . and space in the wake of human occupation. In this form of ethnographic inquiry, the traces, artifacts, and other resonances that people leave behind act as the focal point of an investigation of spectral ethnographic space."

For Armstrong, this "archeology of hauntedness" has meant documenting disused sidewalks, boarded-up storefronts, and abandoned farm
machinery to create a parallel "archeology of the abandoned present."
Exploring the "ghosts of place," Bell (1997, 816) has likewise investigated the ways in which we mix "souls with things" and "souls with
spaces," thereby imbuing long-held objects and well-worn environments with the residual ghosts of past relationships and experiences (see
Stallybrass 1993; Linnemann 2015). In sorting through the cultural
detritus of Timothy McVeigh's violent paranoia, Hamm (1998, 122)
discovered a distinctively disturbing ghost. Immersed in the music,
books, and movies that McVeigh had consumed just before the Oklahoma City bombing, noticing the cigarette-burned carpet and snot-
smeared walls of his motel room, Hamm found that he had summoned
"the ghost of Earl Turner," the truck-bombing protagonist of *The
Turner Diaries*, the book that had been McVeigh's inspirational blue-
print for the attack.

   As seen in the previous chapter, Dorothea Lange and Paul Taylor
([1939] 1969) pioneered their own sociology of the residual, and a visual sociology at that, during the Dust Bowl and the Great Depression.
Weathered, eroded, worn down—for Lange and Taylor, these were
descriptions of the land and the people alike. Through Lange's photographs and Taylor's writings, they showed what was left of a farmer
and a farm in the aftermath of ecological tragedy: Emptied-out houses,
domestic dilapidations of the sort that Armstrong would document decades later and a thousand miles north. Barbwire twisted and splayed
along a lost fence line in a way that no working farmer would counte-
nance. And once that former farmer and his family, desperate to escape,
gathered what little they had and took to the road: broken truck parts,
abandoned alongside the highway; tin cans tossed away from improvised campsites; and, in one of Lange's photos, captioned "squatter
camp on outskirts of Holtville," a foreground piled with discarded
buckets, bottomless cans, and meat tins. "A record of human erosion in
the thirties," they subtitled *An American Exodus*, the book in which
this all appeared, and as they well understood, that erosion inevitably
left behind the worn-down vestiges of human misery. For those forced
into hard traveling (Guthrie 1943), the privilege of spatial stability and
careful conservation of possessions is left behind. Drift soon enough
devolves into discards.

   Perhaps the magnitude of a tragedy and the amount of suffering it
imposes cannot later be measured by its residues—but the ghosts of

Dust storm. It was conditions of this sort which forced many farmers to abandon the area. Spring. New Mexico. (Photo by Dorothea Lange, 1935. Original caption.)

tragedy and the sensuality of suffering can certainly be glimpsed in their traces. This remained true six decades after Lange and Taylor, by the way. Living along Route 66 in the 1990s, hiking stretches of it now abandoned to later road realignment, I continued even then to find mangled 1930s and 1940s hubcaps, early model car jacks, and decades-old tin cans rusted paper thin, all preserved by the hot, dry desert environment though which western migrants had suffered. This remains true today as well. Over the past few decades, countless undocumented migrants have undertaken the dangerous crossing of the Sonoran Desert of Arizona in an attempt to enter the United States. Hiking ahead at night, sleeping in hidden campsites, ducking the border patrol, they have remained not only undocumented but often unnoticeable. Yet along the journey they discard what they can no longer afford to carry, so over time gullies near campsites fill with worn clothing and empty water bottles—to the point that "hundreds of thousands (if not millions) of water bottles, backpacks, shoes and other items have been left in the deserts of Arizona since the 1990s" (De Leon 2013, 327; 2015). More than this, these discards document a sensuality that otherwise remains itself undocumented: the profound suffering that accompanies those of little means as they illicitly cross a vast desert. As De Leon (2013, 321, 333) has shown, for example, their discarded shoes display holes worn through their soles, desperate on-the-fly repairs, menstrual pads inserted to cushion blistered feet, and cactus spines pushed through their sides. The vast, accumulated residues of generations of undocumented migrants suggest at least something of their sheer numbers; they also record what De Leon calls "the materiality of habitual suffering."

For anthropologists like De Leon (2013, 330), the "use-wear patterns" of a migrant's discards can be read in much the same way that archaeologists read use-wear patterns in the material artifacts left by ancient societies. An exhibition based on De Leon's work, "State of Exception/Estado de Excepción," accumulates and displays these patterns, presenting for example hundreds of discarded, dirt-encrusted backpacks (Cotter 2017). For artist and activist Ai Weiwei, the dirtiness of migrants discarded clothes can likewise be read as a record of their vulnerable instability. With contemporary European refugees kept haphazardly on the move, Ai says, "There is no time to wash. They have to throw away dirty stuff." And in this way "the migrants are there but they're not there" (quoted in Pogrebin 2016, C18). But where De Leon, and Lange and Taylor before him, documented this displacement of possessions, Ai has staged an artistic intervention. Collecting the soiled clothes and blankets that migrants were forced to abandon as they were hustled from the Idomeni refugee camp along the Greek-Macedonian border, Ai has cleaned and washed them, paired them with a documentary on Idomeni and photos of the other refugee camps he has visited, and presented these as part of his "Laundromat" exhibition—all as a component of his broader focus on "uprootedness and displacement" (Pogrebin 2016, C18). For artists, anthropologists, and others attentive to drifters and their lives, drifters' residues are indeed a text written by and about them, a trail of notes left behind—but appropriately enough, a ghost text compiled in fragments, an unsteady and unfinished trail, a moving absence, whose lost passages are sometimes inscribed in invisible ink. Human erosion and material erosion, a discarding of personhood and possessions—each is a residue of the other. "A poetics of suggestion and conjecture recovers stories that might not allow themselves otherwise to appear through more direct methods," Caitlin DeSilvey (2007, 420–21) says. "By allowing the equivocation and discontinuity sedimented in these material residues to remain present in the re-telling, I foreclose the possibility of a tidy ending. . . . Incoherence, in this sense, does not have to signal incomprehension, but may instead open a working space which respects the complexity of the historical subject we study."[8]

Aftermath: Ruins

Ruins are their own sort of residues. A beat-down abandoned building stands—and eventually falls—as the material aftermath of an economic and social moment now passed, a ghostly residue of long-ago commercial plans and structural accomplishments. Its emptiness is not only physical; inside its decaying walls is an absence of what once was, save perhaps for residual reminders encoded in faded wall advertisements or broken equipment. Because of this, temporal ruins and physical ruins demand once again an excavation of absence, and a critical inquiry into what is no longer there. The ruins of little stores and small businesses that dot Appalachia are, as Ken Tunnell (2011) has documented, also the ghosts of obliterated local economies; the regionally made merchandise that once filled their now deteriorating shelves is today globally manufactured and piled inside a nearby WalMart, at half the price and twice the social cost. The shells of shuttered mid-America factories harbor the ghosts of Fordist jobs now lost to globalization, with those who once held those jobs now out of work or drifting around the part-time service economy. Awaiting the bulldozer, boarded up public housing in its emptiness anticipates the consumer-driven urban development that will replace it. So pervasive are such ruins amidst the predations of globalized late capitalism that the notion of "ruin porn" has now emerged—the aesthetic appropriation of burned-out factory buildings and decaying shopping malls by photographers, urban explorers, and global tourists. Now I'll admit, there can be something seductively pleasing in stylish photographs of such ruins, especially photographs of the big ruins—a visual confirmation that the past hubris of urban developers and corporate planners has now been humbled. Still, this isn't the real ruin porn; the real pornography of ruins lies in the obscenities of exploitation that they both hide and reveal, and in the absences that they hold.

For drifters and ghosts, there is also a sad sort of circularity. Cast out from the local factory by the logic of neoliberalism, cut off from job or career, the unemployed drifter now returns to the factory's ruins in search of scrap metal or social invisibility; lacking the funds to purchase what the shopping mall sells, banished from the thriving commercial district lest its upscale patrons be offended, the urban ghost later finds in the now-boarded-up mall or the dying commercial district a bit of temporary shelter; priced out of an old housing block now converted to condominiums, the homeless wanderer squats for a night or two in a nearby block of flats, themselves awaiting demolition. Consigned to the social margins, made to conspire in their own invisibility, ghosts tend to gather in those spaces and structures that have themselves been rendered marginal; ruined social reputations tend to play out in ruined spaces. To put it in Lange and Taylor's terms, human erosion often accumulates, at least for a while, amidst physical erosion. "The thousand-and-one hiding holes of industrial night," to which Jack Kerouac ([1960] 1970, 172) referred, and in which ghosts and drifters secret themselves away, have more times than not been carved out by long-flowing currents of economic erosion and spatial decay.

Little wonder, then, that a drifting, alienated war veteran like Timothy McVeigh would wash up in that dilapidated Kingman motel—the sort of low-end, rent-by-the-week place that offers cheap, temporary sanctuary to truckers, road hustlers, fugitives, runaways, and refugees (Grant 2003). And little wonder, as Christopher Dum's (2016, xiii) ethnographic case study has documented, that those who suffer particularly thoroughgoing social death—ex-convicts, registered sex offenders, the mentally ill, families on welfare—would find themselves housed in a single dilapidated motel, "hidden from the public eye, in squalid conditions that many of us would consider unfit for habitation." The old motel that Dum studied was indeed squalid and ruined, its residents confronting sewage leaks, mold and bug infestations, and piles of debris. But it constituted ruins in a broader sense as well. Built in 1960, the motel sat on the town's Main Street—the old highway through town, a once-prosperous strip that by the mid-1990s had declined to the point of being nicknamed "desolation row." Now the motel survived amidst other rent-by-the-week motels (some in even worse shape), a trailer park, a church food pantry, and various small restaurants and businesses. It constituted a residential ruin full of ghosts and, more broadly, one of the many little lost islands in the archipelago of flop motels to which the ghosts of social death are consigned. For registered sex offenders, of course, this consignment is legally enforced; local residency restriction ordinances often leave them with nowhere to reside but in such motels or, lacking those, in the shadows beneath bridges and viaducts.[9]

Amidst such ruined circumstances, we can find yet another echo of Lange and Taylor, and their twined notions of human and physical erosion. Those made socially dead are often consigned to places of ecological death as well, to areas ruined not only by social and economic decay but by overcrowding, chemical contamination, or consumer waste. The nature of environmental racism and environmental classism is such that those groups discarded from social life are regularly left to survive in ruined ecological zones that have themselves been discarded from con-temporary economic arrangements—and in both cases the hope, among the better classes of people, is that the problem can be kept out of sight and at a distance. So, drifters and dead-end nomads camp amidst the abandoned recreational properties that border the dead waters of the Salton Sea. And globally, one underclass after another lives on and from the towering landfills that grow outside major cities (Walker, Harley, and Jardim 2010). In rusted-out places like Camden, New Jersey—one-time industrial powerhouse, now one of the poorest cities in the United States and home to sewage plants and trash-burning facilities—"those discarded as human refuse are dumped, along with the physical refuse of postindustrial America" (Hedges 2010, 15). On the outskirts of Rome, migrants from Africa and elsewhere have for years now squatted a large, abandoned tower block. Some of the hundreds ensconced inside the building at any one time use it as a way station en route to northern Europe, and some make it their permanent home; of late it has become so crowded that new arrivals, many of them suffering from scabies and other afflictions, sleep on dirty mattresses on the floor of its underground parking garage. So well known is the place among African migrants that it has acquired an ironic nickname: Salaam Palace (Povoledo 2014). But if this place is a palace, it's a distinctly brokedown palace (Garcia and Hunter 1970)—and like other places frequented by ghosts and drifters, one ruined by abandonment, contagion, and overcrowding.

Earlier it was suggested that reading the residues of drifters and ghosts requires an openness to shards of discontinuity and incomple-tion. Ruins require a similar style of engagement. Piles of lost possibil-ity, ruins preserve something of their own history while hiding that his-tory amidst the absence and loss that animate their present form; ruins, as Tim Edensor (2008, 123, 129) says, are "often replete with obscure signs of the past," often places where "counter-aesthetics and alterna-tive memories might emerge." In reading ruins and trying to understand their occupants, then, a linear narrative is less likely than a series of evocative insights and incomplete accounts. The materiality of ruins is such that these instabilities of meaning are replicated in instabilities of structure—in sagging walls, broken tiles, jumbles of disjointed furni-ture, missing floorboards, and fixtures. Navigating such ruined spaces as visitor or temporary occupant demands a certain forfeiting of inten-tionality, a willingness to embrace the clumsy, staggering pace that ruins require of those traversing them. Reporting on the experience of walking through ruins, Edensor (2008, 127) notes the "lack of any evident sequence in a path to nowhere" and realizes that it is "often impossible to progress in an uninterrupted, purposive fashion toward a predetermined destination." My quarter century of chasing ghosts and shadows has led me into many such ruins—and I now realize this has been precisely my experience as well. Stumbling across scrabbled metal and piles of discarded ties in dark rail yards, dodging deep holes in an abandoned flour mill frequented by Denver's down-and-out, picking my way through demolished buildings as an urban scrounger, a slow pace and uncertain progress have defined my experience. No wonder drifters find comfort in ruins; the ruins themselves embody drift and offer those who can embrace it a spatial epistemology of uncertainty and delay.[10]

As regards drifters, ghosts, and others on the margins, though, there's another way to think about ruins. If one kind of absence is the absence of those no longer there, then the structures that replace those marginal populations no longer there—the high-end condominiums covering what was once a working-class neighborhood, the factory farm super-imposed over what were once many little family operations—constitute the ruins of these populations and their lives. The shiny efficiency of such places hides the emptied-out spaces on which they have been built and the cultural destruction on which they are predicated—but they are ruins nonetheless. That abandoned Denver flour mill, once the domain of graffiti writers, hobos, and runaways, is now the exclusive Flour Mill Lofts; cleansed of its graffiti and its past, it sits like a sarcophagus atop decades of now-dead subcultural history (Ferrell 2001). The new Fort Worth toll road that Zeke and I saw coming now runs right over the top of the old rail-yard hobo jungles, entombing them beneath acres of concrete and erasing their memory from the city's spatial structure. And in yet another twist, a "tramp stockade" that the city of Los Angeles built in 1908 still stands, just north of downtown. Constructed back then as part of the city's "war on tramps," the stockade was designed to hold two hundred of the "vicious, filthy brutes," as the local newspaper called them, so that they could profitably be put to work on city chain gangs or on the adjoining rock pile (Hernandez 2014, 433, 443–46; Municipal League of Los Angeles 1908). Today the building remains but with the ghosts of all those imprisoned drifters hidden away behind its current consumerist functions: home to a boxing gym and a theater troupe.

Always, a double question haunts the world of ghosts and drifters: What was ruined, and what remains?

Spaces In-Between

This world of drifters, and within it the ghosts of social death, requires that we notice absence as much as presence, and that we explore ruins and residues rather than the obvious and the overbuilt. It also requires new ways of looking and seeing. Instead of looking head-on at the thing itself, this world invites us to look sideways, glancingly, at the spaces in-between one thing and another—and to think about the ways in which these spaces in-between constitute, like absence, phenomena in their own right. Of late, there have been important attempts by Keith Hayward (2012a, 13; 2012b) and others to theorize place and space in the dynamics of transgression and control. But as Hayward himself recognizes with his notion of "parafunctional spaces"—"the abandoned, anonymous, and seemingly meaningless spaces within our midst"— there is more to space and place than material location. To understand the social lives of ghosts and drifters, we must also theorize "no place"— that is, those situations that have no place in the political economy of consumerist development, no place in the legal grid of the city, no place on conventional maps of meaning. Like the drifters and ghosts that traverse them, such situations exist in-between places; they are neither here nor there.

This interstitiality has long animated the lives of drifters. Traveling from work site to work site, riding the rails from state to state, hobos lived much of their lives between jobs and on the move between the places where such jobs sometimes existed. "The true hobo was the in-between worker, willing to go anywhere to take a job and equally willing to move on later," Nels Anderson ([1923] 1961, xviii) concluded a century ago. John Lennon (2014, 8) adds more broadly that, "with one foot in the environments where they labored and the other in the machines that brought them to these jobs, they were precariously positioned along the fault-lines of the new realities of post-Civil War America." The jungles in which hobos camped and IWW organizers worked were themselves in-between spaces, self-organized by hobos, wedged into derelict areas near railroad tracks or switching yards, hidden by brush and trees, generally not in the city itself but near enough to it, and so not rural either. Don Mitchell (2013, 69) argues that it was in part this interstitial status that made the jungle seem so dangerous to local authorities. "Its hiddenness together with the seeming impenetrability of its mores—its very status as an interstice—together with the obvious fact that it was a space of radical organizing, added to its threatening power." The sedentary and the settled could hold a steady job, reside in one place, perhaps even celebrate their stability; hobos by necessity moved between jobs, continually leaving one and anticipating the next, along the way camping in places that were officially no place at all.

Ruins constitute such in-between places as well. They occupy, often tenuously, the space spanning a structure's original construction and its ultimate destruction; in this they hover somewhere between past and future, between the assemblage of intentions through which the building initially came to exist and future, perhaps as-yet-unimagined possibilities for its location. Ruins are "terrain vague" and "interstitial spaces," Edensor (2008, 126) concludes—and so are many of the absences that permeate contemporary social life. The "un-spaces" of absence that Armstrong (2010, 244) earlier described—"the abandoned and unseen locations that exist at the edges of everyday life and experience"—catch something of the hobo jungle, the shuttered factory, and the flop motel as well. All exist in the darkness at the edge of town, in the cracks that open when cities and economies collapse. Decorated by graffiti that itself floats like an urban specter somewhere between visibility and invisibility, occupied by a shifting cast of drifters and ghosts, such spaces hang in the air, ready always to evaporate into something else.

"Spectral housing," Arjun Appadurai (2000, 635–37) calls such living arrangements in Bombay, India—and with these arrangements the "experience of shortage, speculation, crowding, and public improvisation . . . the absent, the ghostly, the speculative, the fantastic." For some in Bombay, Appadurai notes, "homes" of a sort are available in the form of outlying shantytown shacks, "unstable products—a bricolage of shoddy materials, insecure social relations, poor sanitation, and near-total lack of privacy." For occupants of these homes, the long train ride to work in central Bombay offers a sort of interstitial transformation, an opportunity to morph into the proper clerks and secretaries that they will be for the duration of the workday. For others, "home" is less even than this, a no place that is interstitial in its entirety. As Appadurai reports, a large segment of Bombay's citizens

> lives on pavements—or, more exactly, on particular spots, stretches, and areas that are neither building nor street. These pavement dwellers are often able to keep their personal belongings with others in shops or kiosks or even inside buildings (for some sort of price, of course). Some actually live on pavements, and others sleep in the gray spaces between buildings and streets. Yet others live on roofs and on parapets, above garages, and in a variety of interstitial spaces that are not fully controlled by either landlords or the

state. . . . Almost every one of these kinds of housing for the poor, including roofs, parapets, compound walls, and overhangs, is subject to socially nego-tiated arrangements.

This is indeed life lived in the spaces in-between—and of course such living is hardly confined to Bombay. A fiery tragedy recently exposed the extent of similar "negotiated arrangements" in the Bay Area of Califor-nia and elsewhere in the United States. When an inferno engulfed an old Oakland warehouse known as the Ghost Ship, some three dozen people were killed—not warehouse workers but instead a mix of partygoers and residents, who had illegally colonized the warehouse as an alterna-tive living and gathering space. The Ghost Ship, it turns out, was one of countless such illegal, patched-together living spaces in the city—so many that firefighters, police officers, and building inspectors found themselves overwhelmed in their attempts to regulate them. Such spaces have proliferated as part of a "vast gray economy of live/work spaces" in Oakland, San Francisco, New York, Seattle, and other cities, owing to increased economic inequality and with it soaring rents that effectively price young, part-time workers and working-class families out of the legal housing market (Dougherty and Turkewitz 2016, A16; see Turke-witz, Fuller, Perez-Pena, and Dougherty 2016). As a result, an army of artists and low-wage workers floats between one Ghost Ship and another, negotiating arrangements with building owners, dodging eviction and hiding mattresses when the inspectors come, and caught in an ongoing netherworld between legality and illegality—since illegal housing, if legalized, quickly becomes unaffordable. As one ex-resident of such warehouses said, recalling the precarity movement seen in chapter 3, "The fire in Oakland was not an unlikely accident, but rather an inevita-bility given the dangerous precarity of the spaces in which underground D.I.Y. culture exists nationally" (quoted in Dougherty 2016, A23).

Those with even fewer resources suffer their own sort of interstitiality. Mitchell (2013, 67) argues that it is not only the old North American hobo jungles that were interstitial. Equally so are today's version of those jungles: the self-organized tent cities that the homeless construct "under bridges, in abandoned lots still waiting development, on the grounds of old factories, in the scrub and silt of the rivers that run through town." Certainly these tent cities exist in the city's in-between spaces. A recent report noted that one San Francisco tent city, with some 350 residents, had formed "between a food truck court . . . and a vegetarian grocery co-op that sells tofu in bulk," and that a nearby shantytown had taken shape "along a narrow strip of concrete between a street that clogs with rush-hour traffic and a railway that roars with commuter trains in the shadow of a sprawling new biotech center" (Duane 2016, 6). These encampments exist in-between time as well. Like other ruins, the disused lot awaiting development and the old factory scheduled for removal offer tenuous sorts of temporary space in which to form a community, an indeterminate interregnum between one regime of urban development and the next. And for the residents of contemporary tent cities, the next legal and economic regime will be enforced soon enough. As Mitchell shows, and as chapter 2 documented, the prevalence of consumerist development schemes and "place-based" policing strategies means that tent city residents will be regularly rousted and tent cities repeatedly razed. In the case of San Francisco, spatial interstitiality was itself impermanent; new construction projects had forced the homeless from the vacant lots in which they once slept and into the new in-between spaces they now occupied. Even if residents intend a degree of permanence, life in a tent city remains unsettled, suspended as it is between the fragility of present circumstances and the inevitability of outside interruption.

A homeless tent city under one bridge, exiled sex offenders living under the next, the many gutter punks with whom I've shared a beer or some summer shade under another, not to mention musical invocations of under-the-bridge drug use (Flea, Frusciante, Kiedis, and Smith 1992)—all of these grant a distinct materiality to the usual sense of a marginalized "subculture," and along the way highlight a further sort of space in-between. For ghosts and drifters, under is often the scene of the action—as much so for the homeless folks who camp beneath Las Vegas in its storm drains or live in a New York City train tunnel as for those hunkering down below the bridge (Toth 1995; Snyder 2009; see Ballard 1973). Across the bridge roll cars and buses, their occupants on the way to work or home; under the bridge gather the jobless and the homeless, at least for a while. The bridge is an obvious urban artifact; the space beneath it is uncertain, shadowy, and interstitial, a forgotten residue of construction plans and abutment specifications. Others of these little *lost ecologies* are scattered around city and country as well—triangles of land isolated between freeway ramps, streams channeled through concrete corridors, slivers of disused land overgrown between buildings, grassy strips along roadways—and these too are the in-between terrain of those adrift. For the more privileged, they are little more than the collateral damage of development; for drifters, they are islands of invisibility and survival. Over my years chasing ghosts, I've seen it time and again, stumbling upon a hidden homeless encampment burrowed into an embankment between a freeway interchange, finding other camps in flood plains or along railroad tracks. Oh, and under the bridge downtown—as seen in Alison Murray's documentary *Train on the Brain*, that's where the police beat some train-hopper kids until they drew some blood.

The lives of past hobos and present Ghost Ship residents remind us that the spatiality of interstitial survival—in a hobo jungle or a tent city, on the pavement or in an old warehouse—is in turn often intertwined with what might be called occupational interstitiality. Hobos camped in jungles because they remained on the move between jobs; Ghost Ship residents resorted to one illegal warehouse or another because low-wage and part-time work left them unable to afford legal housing. In the con-temporary part-time service economy described in chapter 2, millions of others likewise live occupationally in-between. For many in an older generation, being temporarily "between jobs" may have been little more than an interlude, a brief journey from one stable situation to the next. Today, being between jobs—piecing together part-time work, moving always from one gig to another—constitutes its own liminal reality; it is life lived inside the interlude. To negotiate this sort of life is to traverse gaps in space *and* time, to remain in motion between memory and antic-ipation. The precarity of today's contingent arrangements doubles down—and so if we hope to find those trapped in these arrangements, we'd best look for them not on the job but between jobs, not at their nonexistent home but on the move from one temporary living space to the next. In such a world, unemployment often means an indeterminate space between a job lost and the next one sought, and with it couch surf-ing or tent city survival. But even for those with jobs, there's the travel between them, the train car or automobile as rolling office, the hours lost waiting between split shifts, the netherworld of being always "on call," the daily trips between day care, work, and housing.

For millions of prisoners and ex-prisoners, the contemporary mania for mass incarceration adds still other layers of interstitiality; they traverse and occupy the various spaces between prison and community. After all, the pipeline that connects marginalized communities to impris-onment runs in both directions, with the flow of people both in and out of prison shaping their individual and collective experiences. Edward Green (2016) has found that prisoners often occupy extended states of liminality, caught as they are between their preprison identities, their emerging circumstances in prison, and the anticipation of life postprison. Jamie Fader (2013) spent three years with young black men confined to reform school—young men who, once released, attempted to transition back into their old urban neighborhoods. She found that such young men must negotiate a double transition, between reform school and the community and between adolescence and young adulthood. Now free from confinement, they must nonetheless conform to the demands of probation officers and reintegration workers, all while attempting to restore relationships with their families and friends. Determined to avoid the sort of trouble that would send them back to confinement, they must also finesse the dangers of old haunts and old friends. Fader (2013, 219–20) summarizes the in-between lives of these young men: "They appeared to move back and forth between employment and unemployment, offending and conforming on an almost day-to-day basis. . . . Employment, fatherhood, romantic relationships, and housing were all characterized by intermittency and precariousness for the majority of these young men. Offending followed the same intermittent patterns as youth moved back and forth across the relatively fluid boundary between the legal and underground economies." Family and friends of those still imprisoned find a similar string of interstitial experiences emerging. As its title suggests, Brett Story's (2016) poignant film *The Prison in Twelve Landscapes* documents these experiences, as the fortressed solidity of the prison leaks out into the everyday spaces of prisoners' families. Waiting for the next visitation day, enduring the long bus rides to and from the prison once the day arrives, carefully putting together a prison-approved care package, planning for a prisoner's eventual release and return home, the families endlessly navigate the lonesome distance between their lives and the lives of those imprisoned.

Of course it's not only prisoners who wait for their release, or their families who wait to visit them while they are still imprisoned; waiting pervades the lives of drifters and ghosts. From old Jimmie Rodgers (1928) hobo songs to the contemporary gutter punks seen in earlier chapters, train hoppers wait for trains more than they ride them. Trash pickers learn to wait, too—to wait for an event to end or for objects to be discarded (Ferrell 2006, 186–92). Refugees wait interminably in isolated camps, wait to cross borders, wait to claim legal status. For drifters and others, waiting calibrates the degree to which those made to wait lack power and control; waiting also constructs a kind of absence, a suspension of action, a time out of time not unlike that found amidst an aftermath. In this way waiting is the time in-between, an experience of temporal interstitiality, an elongated moment that leaves its occupants suspended between what was and what may yet be. No wonder that waiting wears out its welcome—that those made to wait often find themselves afflicted with boredom (Ferrell 2004; Bengtsson 2012; Steinmetz, Schaefer, and Green 2016); waiting carves out an absence of meaning and action, a lacuna between the last purposeful moment and the next. Interwoven with other forms of interstitiality—train hoppers waiting in the brush beside the track, trash pickers waiting not in the street but in the alley, contingent workers waiting out split shifts, migrants waiting in social and geographic borderlands—waiting grinds open one final gap, one further experience of absence, for those left with little but to live in-between the spaces of social life.

Given this, it seems to me that learning to look in-between may be the most useful aspect of ghost method—for all sorts of people, the key to seeing, understanding, and engaging with a world of ghosts and drifters. For architects and urbanists, this interstitial reorientation might mean rethinking architecture in terms of illicit mobility (Cairns 2004) and "exploring cities through their gaps" (Levesque 2013, 21). As David Burney notes, "In the past 10 to 12 years there has been a paradigm shift in thinking about planning and urbanism, from a primary focus on buildings to a focus on the spaces between buildings—public space" (quoted in Pogrebin 2015, C3.) For contemporary activists, this might mean imagining the ways in which an interstice, as Andrea Mubi Brighenti (2013, xviii) argues, "is not simply a physical space, but very much a phenomenon 'on the ground,' a 'happening,' a 'combination' or an 'encounter.'" As seen in chapter 3, the Situationist *dérive* is a style of drifting, experiential politics designed to liberate participants from the spatial constraints of everyday life; in light of Brighenti's insight, it can also be understood as an interstitial experience, a "happening" that lures participants into the unmapped spaces that hide between the structures of daily life (see Rubin 2012). A politics beyond the experiential also become imaginable in these spaces. Having reviewed the essential interstitiality of hobo jungles and tent cities, Mitchell (2013, 82; emphasis in original) suggests something of their contemporary potential: "If the bourgeoisie *still* has no solution to the housing problem, then we need to find a *non*-bourgeoisie solution. And here, ironically, tent cities, though they must be eliminated if a just city is to arise, provide the model: as a taking of land, as a non-commodified and cooperative form of property and social relations, as (potentially) an organization space, tent cities, and their progenitors like the hobo jungle, have much to teach us." For drifters and ghosts, the action is often on the fly, behind or beneath the social order—and as they squat the cracks in that order, perhaps widening them along the way, the action also emerges in-between.

"Improvement makes straight roads," William Blake wrote in 1790, "but the crooked roads without improvement are the roads to Genius." Today, as ghosts and drifters wander those crooked roads, they remind of us something else: genius—or at least some understanding of the contemporary world—can also be found alongside those roads, beneath their bridges and viaducts, behind their barricades, hidden in the lost ecologies that encircle them. Drifters and other denizens of social death remain on the move, perpetually absent and invisible, navigating the temporal and spatial residues of social life. To find them, to understand them, we will have to make their movements and their methods our own. Deleuze and Guattari (1987, 380) once proposed that "the life of the nomad is in the intermezzo"—that the nomad's knowledge of the world remains uncontained and comparative as it forms between and beyond particular places. For more and more people today, the intermezzo constitutes the main performance. What kind of music emerges from this world of intermezzos, and how might we learn to listen to it?

In this context other questions arise, too, a couple of which I'll consider in the following, final chapter. How might we think about images of ghosts and drifters, and with them images of interstitiality and absence? And just how far might this world of drifters and ghosts take us—or how far might we take it—in exploring its disorientations?

9

Ghost Images and
Gorgeous Mistakes

This last chapter offers neither summary nor conclusion. That sort of straight-line finality would undermine the shifting dynamics of drift that have, I hope, been revealed throughout the book. But as I hope the book has also shown, drift is not simply a synonym for random variation, either; it's more a matter of calibration and recalibration, of courses tentatively set and soon enough changed. So I'll not just wander off, either; instead I'll suggest a few further possibilities among the many that drift presents. And I'll try my best to avoid the mistake of employing a grammatical conceit that, I'll admit, does appeal as a way of closing a book on drift: the ending of the last line of the last chapter with ellipses, to indicate incompletion and ambiguity.

GHOST IMAGES

The previous chapter proposed that drift often intertwines with departure and social death, and because of this drift can be understood in terms of ghosts, aftermaths, absence, and interstitiality. There I also suggested that the traditional hallmarks of good research—paying attention to what is present, recording what one sees and hears—must be reconsidered if we are to engage with this absent, apparitional world. Issues of the image follow. Seeing and photographing what is present are difficult enough—when, as photographers and photographic theorists have long known, present circumstances inevitably include the contingencies of relationships, decisions, and mechanical capabilities (Sontag 1977). All the more challenging is the process of seeing and photographing what is not present—still a matter of manifold contingencies but now one dimension removed. Sometimes this challenge can be met by aiming the camera in-between or beyond; sometimes by watching as images themselves drift and float; and sometimes by producing portraits of ghosts themselves.

Photographing Drifters and Ghosts

In the mid-1950s, the great documentary photographer W. Eugene Smith shot some seventeen thousand photographs in and around the city of Pittsburgh, Pennsylvania. Intending to produce a sweeping photographic chronicle of the city, Smith shot flaming furnaces and factory smokestacks, bridges and rail yards, and with them images of industrial laborers and industrial production, hard-won leisure, social class, and urban identity. An "attempt at photographic penetration deriving from study and awareness and participation," Smith's project was to document a living people and a living city, though true to Smith's critical vision, one replete with inequality, contradiction, and unintended consequence (Smith, quoted in Lybarger 2015; see Trachtenberg, Stephenson, and Smith 2003). More broadly, Smith's work produced images of a particular time in American history—a moment of relative Fordist stability characterized in Pittsburgh, at least, by cacophonous steel and aluminum mills, the Pittsburgh Screw and Bolt Factory, and rows of soaring skyscrapers and solid housing.[1]

Certainly some ghosts haunted Smith's Pittsburgh—including more than one factory worker visually lost to flame, smoke, and steel—but today those ghosts have become legion and are more likely to haunt a shuttered factory than a working one. To capture the present moment, then, the camera must now aim less at skyscrapers and humming factories and more at ruins and residues—at the ghosts of that earlier time that Smith documented. Ken Tunnell's (2011) Kentucky photographs accomplish this; in showing shuttered stores, faded advertisements, and abandoned trailers, his photographs create their own negatives, catching shadows of what was and what is now lost. The previous chapter recounted Justin Armstrong's (2010) ethnographic writings on the "un-places" of the contemporary North American High Plains, their rusting machinery, empty roads, and abandoned towns testament to lost agricultural prosperity. Armstrong has produced his writing's visual doppelgänger as well: a short documentary, *Everywhere Is Nowhere*. A lonesome journey through these same lost spaces, the film has the feel of

Springsteen's album *Nebraska* (1982), dark and windy in its despair and narrated by a ghost—a former local resident who overlays the film's images with her recollections. And speaking of Springsteen's *Nebraska,* Nancy Warner and David Stark's (2014) book *This Place, These People* collects the photographs that Warner shot in the Great Plains of Nebraska around the same time, pairing them with the recorded memories of local people in the manner of Lange and Taylor's ([1939] 1969) *An American Exodus.* The visual ghosts here are especially poetic: old drapes entangled in broken windows, doors latticed with crackled paint, rainwater stains abstracted onto exposed wallpaper. The more recent spatial and architectural ghosts of Los Angeles's outward expansion are likewise the subject of *Discarded* (2016), Anthony Hernandez's exhibition of large-format color photographs. Having previously photographed hidden homeless encampments and other marginal urban spaces, Hernandez in *Discarded* documents the bankrupt housing developments and abandoned street grids that are the underside of endless urban sprawl (see Lubow 2016). In these discards the developer's failure, and the developer's absence, remain palpably present; a distinctly shoddy sort of late-modern ruins, they seem unlikely to outlast those of Greece and Rome.

This spectral dialectic of absence and presence, visibility and invisibility, also plays out in the interstitial spaces that drifters and ghosts inhabit. Images of such spaces require a camera pointed not at the solid phenomena we assume to make up daily life but at the unnoticed spaces that flicker between these phenomena. Here the photo-documentary tradition discussed in chapter 7 provides an invaluable foundation. In that chapter, this tradition was offered as a methodological and ontological counterpoint to the rigid abstraction of social science methodology; here it can be reconsidered for its wide-ranging orientation to the in-between. Recall for example that the street photographer Saul Leiter shot photographs in which there was no singular subject, only social edges and fleeting interactions. "Where other New York photographers of the period were apt to document the city's elements discretely—streets, people, buildings," says Margalit Fox (2013, B9), "Mr. Leiter captured the almost indefinable spaces where all three intersect." Recall that Robert Frank not only drifted around the globe, and back and forth across the United States in photographing *The Americans,* but did so with an eye for social disequilibrium and "in-between moments" (Sontag 1977, 121). As for the resultant photographs, "I leave it up to you," Frank said. "They don't have an end or a beginning. They're a piece of the middle" (quoted in Dawidoff 2015, 43). Recall also that Robert Doisneau drifted through social situations in search of images while embracing the waiting that accompanied such unplanned excursions, and that the documentary filmmaker Gianfranco Rosi today employs a similar strategy of "missing and waiting" on the way to that "magical thing," the moment when "the unexpected happens" (quoted in Hale 2014, C5). If we're looking for ghosts, the photo-documentary tradition has much to teach us; its practitioners have been well attuned to the presence and potential of absence, to the ways in which social life plays out in spatial and temporal gaps, and to the power of interstitial image-making.

For photographers like Lange, Frank, and Doisneau, this orientation toward ruin and erosion, and toward the interstitial dimensions of time and space, was interwoven with a willingness to wander and drift in search of—or, more accurately, in accord with—these phenomena. For them, the best way to find the spaces that ghosts frequented was not to look for them but to give oneself up to the rhythms that might take you to them. The visually seductive films of Agnes Varda embody something of this, too; her "fiction films, documentaries and first-person film essays share a fascination with the fleeting and the serendipitous" (Hoberman 2015, AR13). So does the work of the photographer Alex Webb. Known for his images of fraught borderlands and tense political interruptions, he is a photographic flâneur, a modern-day Doisneau. "I wander and I walk and one thing leads to something else," he says. "In a car-oriented culture like ours a lot of times you can't just walk, you've got to drive. But I try to keep the experience of wandering basically the same" (quoted in *New York Times* 2012a, AR22). The photographer Lise Sarfati describes her photographic practice in terms of a particular form of drift, and one that has recurred throughout this book: the Situationist *dérive*. For one project she "drifted through Hollywood, staying several months," and producing images of women who frequent "street corners, sidewalk strips, recesses" (Sarfati 2012, SR8).[2] Though less visually sophisticated, the countless amateur images that urban explorers and "place hackers" today produce of abandoned buildings and industrial ruins share this same dynamic: the interstitial image as a residue of the dislocated process that made it possible.

Absence expands outward, though, and it seems to me that the potential for photographing the absent and the spectral can likewise develop beyond ruins, residues, and in-between spaces. The previous chapter proposed various forms of absence—that which is not there, that which is no longer there, that which will soon not be there—and this fluid plurality of absences points toward some of these possibilities. More than once in the previous chapters, for example, I've mentioned the old hobo jungle that ran along the Fort Worth rail yards and recounted the story of how Zeke and his friends, camped out in that jungle, encountered the work crew that was a portent of the new toll road that would soon enough replace it. Indeed, the jungle is now dead and gone, obliterated, bulldozed, and paved over by the tollway, over-run each day by automotive traffic. But we can still catch sight of its ghost, and photograph its absence. The presence of this tollway is, quite literally, the absence of the jungle, and with it the hidden history of a thousand hobos. From the view of city authorities, of course, the jungle never existed in the first place, never produced markings on a city map or revenue for city tax rolls, never supported a legitimate population—and now that which officially never was is no more, entombed under tons of concrete. None of this prevents our photographing its ghost.

Now imagine a photographic project on the order of Smith's seventeen thousand Pittsburgh photographs—only this time seventeen thousand photographs of urban ghosts. Smith had been sent to Pittsburgh on assign-ment to shoot photographs for a book celebrating Pittsburgh's bicenten-nial, in conjunction with the Allegheny Conference on Community Devel-opment, a local booster organization. As was his style, though, Smith rebelled—against the editorial constraints and deadline demands of pro-fessional photography and against the scripted promotional photographs he was meant to shoot. So he overstayed his assignment by months and years, endlessly wandering Pittsburgh's neighborhoods and undertaking to produce a critical visual encyclopedia of the city. "Each time I pressed the shutter release, it was a shouted condemnation hurled with the hope that the pictures might survive through the years," Smith wrote of his photography more generally, "with the hope that they might echo through the minds of men [sic] in the future, causing them caution and remem-brance and realisation" (quoted in Miller 1997, 140). Today, seventeen thousand captioned photos of urban ghosts like the hobo jungle ghost image above might echo in the same way. Imagine: not a photo captioned "Exclusive Spicewood Condominiums" but one captioned "Ghost of Flop Hotel," not "First National Bank Tower" but "Ghosts of Seven Workers Killed during Construction," not "Washington Avenue, Rush Hour" but "Ghost of Bike Lane Never Built, not "Christ Chapel Bible Church Expan-sion" but "Ghost of a Hundred Razed Working-Class Homes"—this last an actual megachurch and an actual ghost that today haunt my decimated neighborhood near the Fort Worth rail yards. Such a project would craft a visual encyclopedia of absence and dislocated drift, of land appropria-tion and consumerist development. It would call to life a ghost town while writing a ghost atlas of urban space. Like Smith's work, it would constitute a subversive exercise in realization and remembrance.[3]

If in photographing ghosts absence can expand outward to become an encyclopedia of urban displacement, it can also seep into the interiors of photography itself. Put differently, a photographer can wander the streets, attuned to the resonances of absence and disorientation—but a photographer can also introduce absence and disorientation into the photographic process, in such a way that ghosts come to appear there as well. Photographer Larry Sultan, for example, "always thought of a great photograph as if some creature walked into my room; it's like, how did you get here? . . . The more you try to control the world, the less magic you get" (quoted in Dyer 2016, 14). For Sultan, the photographer's technical mastery and practiced vision, yes, but within these a forfeiting of intentionality. This is indeed a kind of ghostly magic, an absent space in which apparitions can appear, and the very sort of in-the-moment magic pioneered by earlier photo-documentarians. In this context, the writer and photographer Teju Cole (2016a, 18–19) contrasts formally surrealist photography with photography that emerges as surreal. Certainly surrealist writers and photographers have long sought to escape conscious intent in the interest of producing alternative visions of the world. But to the extent that surrealist photographers *intend* to accomplish this escape, and employ techniques to do so, they undermine the indeterminacy of their own projects; a surrealist photo is seldom surreal, Cole argues, precisely because it intends to be. Instead, Cole suggests that photographs that are "productively accidental, enchantingly dreamlike and charged with a palpable but irretrievable meaning" may come closer to the surreal. Echoing Sultan, he argues for images that embody "inadvertency and the element of surprise—the sense that the power of the image is independent of the photographer's plans." Cole concludes in a ghostly register. "Surrealism of this kind often relies for its effect on humanity on the absence of actual humans," he says. "Rather, it arrives like a metaphysical gift, showing up when it is least expected to conquer logic and haunt the imagination" (see Cole 2015).

In this light, Cole argues that attentive photo-documentarians like Walker Evans, Helen Levitt, and Henri Cartier-Bresson have generated many a surreal image. I agree, and in fact I would argue that Cartier-Bresson's definitive photographic concept—"the decisive moment"— itself harbors a surreal interplay of presence and absence. Recall from chapter 7 that Cartier-Bresson defined the decisive moment as "the simultaneous recognition, in a fraction of a second, of the significance of an event as well as the precise organization of forms which give that event its proper expression" (quoted in Miller 1997, 102). This is the street photographer's consummate, synthetic skill: to perceive an event's social significance and, in that instant, to organize that event visually within the lens of the camera. After years of training, that is, the photographer learns to see what others don't see and can't see—to see what is not visibly, recognizably present for others—and to visualize it in a way that only the photographer can. The resulting image is a precise visual document of what was in actuality present in the moment—but it's also a ghost, an image of what was just as surely absent, *not perceptibly there,* for anyone else. If we accept the most basic of sociological tenets—that everyday reality is socially constructed, built from shared interactions and perceptions—then the photographer is introducing *unreality* into this everyday world, loosing a visual apparition among the innocent. To master the decisive moment is to catch sight of ghosts that otherwise float unseen, to catch them with the camera as well and to deploy them among the population. The brilliance of Cartier-Bresson's concept lies not only in its invocation of instantaneous perception and visual organization but in its uncanny interplay of presence and absence.[4]

Images Adrift

We live in a world saturated with circulating images. The images that pervade cell phone and computer screens, televisions and digital billboards appear and disappear, coming and going with the flick of a key or at the whim of some unseen algorithmic calculation. This empire of images in turn loops and spirals back on itself; images from one media source soon enough show up in a thousand others, later to be circulated digitally among friends or recycled into documentary films or website compilations. Like train hoppers, temp workers, and refugees, images today may settle for a while in one location or another—but they are mostly on the move, continually transferred or discarded or repositioned, in many ways defined by their ongoing migration. Endlessly adrift in time and space, images offer a series of flickering moments; the image we saw yesterday on a news channel we glimpse today on a subway passenger's phone, or forget as the next visual wave arrives. Each iteration of image becomes the ghost of a former incarnation.

Beneath this digital swirl of drifting images are other sorts of dislocated images, ghostly in their own right—perhaps more so. These are the millions of prints produced by decades of predigital camera and film.

Wedding photos taped into commemorative albums, "snapshots" accumulated in cardboard shoe boxes, "home movie" film reels stored in old trunks—all find themselves stashed away in abandoned basements and musty attics, arrayed in flea market stalls, left to molder in trash heaps or landfills. Apparitional images from an earlier time, a ghost army of grandmothers and half-remembered holidays, they take on additional dimensions of dislocation as marriages fail, families dissolve, or houses change hands. Left behind or unceremoniously discarded, these images now drift farther from the contexts of their production, so that by the time they are rediscovered by a building's new owner or purchased from a flea market stall, the women and men they picture have been recast as ghostly, nameless figures. The haphazard hurry of late modern life may be mirrored in the flurry of its digital images—but it is reflected in the ghostly, free-floating afterlife of earlier analog images, too.

In the physicality of such photographic prints reside other ghostly residues. Fundamentally, the photographic prints themselves are physical residues of a particular, historically situated image-making process, one that involved the exposure of film, the decisions made in the dark room, and the specific technologies of developing and printing images— all lingering still in the color, shape, and paper of each photo. Beyond this, each photo hints at its individual physical history, with the presence or absence of stains and tears telling uncertain stories about care, neglect, and context. These are ghost stories indeed—narratives that the contemporary viewer of the photo is left to construct from shadow,

stain, and photographic scar tissue. When in addition such a photo features handmade markings, made directly on the print, the mystery deepens. Now the residues of someone's postphotographic intentionality seem to remain but in a way that is largely indecipherable and unknowable. An obscure design tattooed on a hobo's hand, a refugee's

counterfeit passport, an ink mark on an old photo—all are apparitions, hiding what they reveal.

As the decades of digital image production accumulate, the residual nature of these earlier analog photo prints only increases—as does the likelihood that those portrayed in them are now deceased. The ghost army grows; each year that an old print survives, its subjects are less

likely to. The same is true of the photographers, of course, who haunt the photos as surely as do their subjects. Each photo embodies what was for the photographer a decisive moment –not in the sense of Cartier-Bresson's practiced artistry, of course, but decisive nonetheless. In pressing the shutter button, a proud parent or a bemused traveling companion decided in each case that *this* was indeed a moment worth capturing and then, with more or less forethought, set up the photo and posed its subject. As a result, the photographs recall what mattered in the lives of those now gone and suggest something of the cultural contexts in which such moments were made to matter. As John Prine (1971) put it, "Photographs show the laughs recorded in between the bad times." Beyond this, amateur photographers often physically appear in their own photographs, through their shadows. Following the rudimentary photographic rule of putting the sun behind your camera and in the face of your subjects, these photographers unintentionally allow the sun to put them in the picture, too. The shadowy specter of the photographer haunts what was meant to be an image of others, imprinting the photo with suggestions as to the photographer's clothing, stance, and gender—even hints as to the particular photographic technology in use at the time, which might, for example, require looking down into a waist-high camera's viewfinder.[5]

The haunting power of these dislocated analog images circulates beyond the old attics and flea markets in which they are found. A few years back, a box of unidentified photo negatives, repossessed from an unpaid storage locker, was put up for auction in Chicago. John Maloof bought the box at that auction, and in it he found the work of Vivian Maier—a previously unknown street photographer now destined, in light of Maloof's chance discovery, "to take her place as one of the preeminent street photographers of the twentieth century" (J. Scott 2012, 27; see Maloof and Siskel 2013). During her lifetime, Maier had apparently been largely uninterested in printing or exhibiting the more than one hundred thousand photographs she shot—or perhaps she had been financially unable, as a woman working as a nanny and later living on her Social Security payments. Similarly, over the past few years the photographer Zun Lee (2016) has gathered old Polaroid prints from garage sales, flea markets, and eBay, most of which feature African Americans at home or at gatherings. For Lee the prints document a long and mostly ignored history of African American self-representation and, in so doing, provide a positive visual counterpoint to racialized stereotypes that circulate through popular culture. The ready availability of such prints through commercial channels, though, carries with it a sadness as well. "Why had so many families lost their things to secondhand dealers and estate sales?" asks Teju Cole (2016b, 29). "Behind these photos . . . lay the invisible stories of evictions, dispossessions or separation. The Polaroids were evidence of joy, but the fate of the photos themselves was unhappy." Historians know that individual status and social power

privilege the careful preservation of some histories over others; the narratives of a stable, wealthy family are more likely to survive the ages than those of a poor wanderer. So it is with ghost images. From Maier's negatives to Lee's Polaroids, photographs cut adrift from their original owners often carry with them larger ghosts of poverty, gender inequality, and ethnic discrimination.[6]

The drifting analog images reproduced in this section don't come from an auction house or a flea market, though, but from the trash—specifically, from the trash bins and Dumpsters of Fort Worth, Texas. I've been a trash picker—a "Dumpster diver," in common American parlance—all my adult life. Some years ago, in fact, I spent most of a year surviving as a full-time trash picker, later recounting my adventures in *Empire of Scrounge* (Ferrell 2006); since that time I've continued to trash pick on a daily basis, for reasons of ecological intervention, charitable donation, and existential independence. In exploring the residues of lives lost to the trash bins, I included a few of my trash-picked photos in *Empire of Scrounge*—but since then the old photos have continued to accumulate, hundreds and thousands of them, a dozen found one day amidst the detritus of a remodeled house, twenty found another day stuffed in a folder inside a plastic trash bag. Dumpster diving is all about digging up ghosts; an outgrown shirt, an old wrench, a box of tax returns, a garbage bag filled with toys or party favors are all residues of lives lived, decisions made, circumstances changed, opportunities taken

or lost. But the photos—as already argued, they are ghosts of another order. Freeze-frames from the lives of people I can't know, images of human apparition, they haunt the spaces of urban life and urban waste, and they haunt me, too. So I rescue them, resurrect them (these verbs revealing something of my near-religious devotion to trash picking), occasionally exhibit them (Ferrell, Morrison, and Stables 2016), and mostly wonder what to do with all the ghosts.

Of one thing I'm sure: the sort of inadvertent surrealism advocated by Cole adheres to many of those lost photos. Certain of them have the ghostly, absent aura that Cole described—an aura all the more surreal for its assumed unintentionality on the part of the photographer. But beyond this is the surreality of their circumstances. Dislocated from their origins, the photos achieve the oddest of temporary juxtapositions—and because of this induce in me moments of genuine disorientation and surprise. Digging through a Dumpster layered with yard waste, lumber, old shingles, and . . . wait, what's this atop that last board, an old sepia-toned photograph of an infant? Tearing open a big trash bag, spilling out old clothes, last year's calendar, shopping receipts, and . . . there, in between the pages of that paperback novel, a set of graduation photos.

But of course, as with Cole, this accidental surrealism can't be engineered; ghosts can't be made to go where we want. So I'll leave it to you. What ghosts do you find in these trash-picked images?

GORGEOUS MISTAKES

Interwoven with ghost images and their occurrence is a hint of something else, something larger perhaps. The practices of the photographers and filmmakers just considered, and the language through which they describe these practices, suggest this larger dynamic. Filmmaker Gianfranco Rosi waits and waits, missing shot after shot, until the "magical" and "unexpected" occurs; photographer Larry Sultan finds himself surprised by his own photos, and argues that less control over the photographic process likewise yields greater "magic." Filmmaker Agnes Varda is inspired by the ephemeral, and the "serendipitous"; photographer Teju Cole advocates for a visual surrealism that substitutes accident, inadvertency, and surprise for the photographer's own intentionality. For these and other visual artists, the path to the ghostly, the absent, and the surreal is itself paved by a particular sort of absence—the absence of the artist's intentionality and control—and illuminated by the glow of surprise and serendipity. Even the more general process by which critical insight is attained and creativity produced appears to operate beyond rationality, as well as individual responsibility, instead emerging in some other, "magical" realm.

Actually, though, I would argue that the magic of the accidental and the unexpected has been here all along, interleaved throughout the pages of this book, inherent in the dynamics of drift. As seen from the start, drift can be a dangerous and disorienting process—certainly this is so for millions across the globe today—but by way of this same dangerous disorientation, through the very mistakes and missteps that drift guarantees, it can also make magic. Early sociologists saw this—saw that the dislocation and cultural marginality of drift could engender in the drifter an unexpectedly cosmopolitan, comparative sensibility. Political activists and cultural theorists found this among flâneurs and those engaged in the *dérive*—found that abandoning spatial certainty and embracing accidental encounters could create ways of knowing the world. Today, Critical Mass and Food Not Bombs activists birth alternative forms of community by "dis-organizing" drifting events—by making room for mistakes and surprises within collective endeavors—and Precarity activists embrace ambiguity and the startling commonalities that can emerge amidst uncertain conditions. Long before, of course, North American hobos had already come to understand the potent politics that could be crafted from uncertainty on the move—and today, their train-hopping progeny embrace their own form of what they call "the drift," with its abandonment of control over time and space, and the liberating existential unpredictability that results. Even academic sociologists and anthropologists these days urge us to "think fuzzy thoughts," as Simon Hallsworth said back in chapter 7—to make peace with uncertainty and ambiguity if we are to understand gangs, jobs, gender, urban spaces, and maybe contemporary social life itself.

For some, mistakes even constitute a kind of methodology. Ethnographer Stephanie Kane (1998, 142–43) argues that chaotic "moments of extreme or unusual conditions" offer a researcher invaluable perspectives on social situations. She adds that mistakes and misdirections in research, moments of stumbling serendipity, are, therefore, to be valued—maybe even sought—for the otherwise unimaginable insights they offer. Just such a mistake—a moment of "brutal serendipity"—allowed criminologist Carl Root to transform an episode of egregious police violence into an otherwise unattainable, first-person analysis of state crime, silence, and victimization (Root, Ferrell, and Palacios 2013). No less a social scientist (and sociologist of science) than Robert K. Merton likewise acknowledged, late in his career, the "differences between the finished versions of scientific works as they appear in print and the actual course of inquiry. . . . Typically, the scientific paper or monograph presents an immaculate appearance which reproduces little or nothing of the intuitive leaps, false starts, mistakes, loose ends, and happy accidents that actually cluttered up the inquiry" (quoted in Cullen and Messner 2007, 6; see Livio 2013). Historian and philosopher of science Paul Feyerabend (1975) would agree with Merton and add that those who fetishize and enforce rigidities of "method" as a safeguard against error and subjectivity may mostly be ignoring insight and inhibiting creativity. Methodological mistakes, it turns out, may often be the best method.

As before, the photo-documentarians are worth recalling as well. Walker Evans was a precise and disciplined documentary photographer, but, as noted in chapter 7, he was also a photographer for whom "the point was to dream, to wander from topic to topic"; Dorothea Lange of course wandered as well, and coming upon a scene that would become one of her best-known photographs, admitted, "I can only say I knew I was looking at something. You know there are moments such as these when time stands still and all you do is hold your breath and hope it will wait for you" (quoted in Coles 1997, 127, 149). Similarly, we now know that Kandinsky, Man Ray, Duchamp, Rauschenberg, Pollock, and de Kooning were all artists whose breakthrough works emerged out of mistakes and misperceptions, out of cracked printing presses and broken picture tubes—though as art critic Carter Ratcliff says, recalling Merton, "it wasn't part of the way they presented themselves to acknowledge this" (quoted in Lovelace 1996, 119). We also now know that iconic posters, album covers, and films from the 1960s emerged in part from a mix of forgetfulness, miscommunication, and—wait for it—drug-induced error (*New York Times* 2012b). More recently, digital filmmakers have begun creating filmic collages from "the unexpected glories of decaying film stock," and visual artists have exhibited works damaged by Hurricane Sandy, presenting them as "things made more interesting by entropy, chance and life" (Kehr 2012, AR10; Kennedy 2013, C25). Chronicling the "lovely accidents, purely serendipitous" that have shaped his writing, the writer Mark Helprin (2012, D1, D8) has argued that "accident is as much a part of fiction as anything else." Timothy Egan (2014, A19) agrees that, for creativity, "you need messiness and magic, serendipity and insanity," and he quotes Oscar Wilde: "A writer is someone who has taught his mind to misbehave." The Brazilian writer Clarice Lispector would agree, too. "I have an affectionate fondness for the unfinished, the poorly made, whatever awkwardly attempts a little flight and falls clumsily to the ground," she once wrote (quoted in Rafferty 2015, 19). Musician and engineer Daniel Wilson (2012, 35) has started exploring "miraculous agitations"—that is, "chaotic non-linear and emergent behaviour in acoustic vibrating physical systems." And John Maloof and those Vivian Maier negatives he bought at auction? That was all a mistake, too. Maloof, a realtor, bought them hoping they might yield useful illustrations for a book—which they didn't—but he was so inspired by Maier's images that he took a course in photography, built a darkroom in his attic, and turned his life toward professional photography and filmmaking.

Mistakes and more mistakes—"gorgeous mistakes," as Sinead O'Connor once sang (O'Connor and Pirroni 1990). The kind of mistakes that move you past the limits of your own intellect and imagination, taking you to places that intentionality can't map. Mistakes made into the magic of improvisation; mistakes that flower into beauty and surprise. And more than this: mistakes that situate us, humbly, amidst all that we don't know, reminding us of what might be possible out beyond our present perspective. In the rail yards I've more than once seen two freight trains on parallel tracks perform a slow-motion pas de deux, one pulling ahead and then the other, glimpses of the farther train appearing and disappearing between the gaps of the nearer. To stand and watch this is to see a series of gorgeous mistakes—to witness fleeting moments of light and shadow, ephemeral juxtapositions unbound by intentionality—and to consider how many other such moments emerge each day, seen or unseen, in a thousand other rail yards and a thousand other unknown places. To make mistakes, to embrace accidents and moments of serendipitous magic, is to be reminded of a world swirling around and beyond us, unknowable, uncertain, and endlessly emergent. In this world insights come and go, windows into alternative understandings open and close—and so our task is less to seek these insights than to be ready for them when they appear, less to master these unfolding moments than to imagine what gorgeous happenstance they may hold. Ordering such accidental assemblages along the lines of set taxonomies and settled understandings, imposing on them the arrogance of our own presumed intentionality—well, that would be a serious misrepresentation of their magic.

This, it seems to me, is the gift that drift grants us: a different sense of the world and our place in it, a sort of existential recalibration by which our own intentionality and importance are balanced against the liberations of accident and uncertainty. But in granting this gift and the creative freedom that accompanies it, of course, drift offers another sort of consequence, too: the pain of the many mistakes that are inevitably anything but gorgeous. Serendipity's dark side harbors all those accidents that accelerate not into happy coincidence but into tragedy, and drift's serial vulnerability guarantees their occurrence: the missed train out of trouble, the bus broken down between jobs, the wrong boat boarded to cross the Mediterranean, the camera or clothes or children lost along the way. This book's first chapter outlined four dialectics of drift, and this I would argue is its fifth—the dynamic by which drift's gorgeous mistakes are inseparably interwoven with its dangerous, disorienting vulnerability. As with Cole and his notion of the unintentionally surreal, seeking drift's liberating lessons while seeking to avoid its serial pains is to undermine drift itself; drift's gorgeous mistakes are only available to those willing to wander its tragedies as well. Missteps and mistakes inevitably emerge from drift's uncertain circumstances, and with them equal uncertainty as to their eventual meaning and consequence.

Pulsing with the magic of surprise, the anarchic energy of uncertainty, and the critical cosmopolitanism of ongoing comparison, drift can usefully be turned back against those forces that engender it—consumer-driven urbanism, ecological crisis, global inequality and injustice—and can help us imagine and enact progressive alternatives to them. By these same characteristics, drift can undermine contemporary regimes of risk management, big data prediction, and spatial surveillance—regimes that not only violate human freedom and autonomy but by design close off the free-flowing humanity of the accidental and the improbable. But employing drift in this way won't be easy. We'll need to learn the hard lessons of hobos and refugees, to embrace both the freedom and the hurt that come with serial dislocation. We'll need communities that float, cultures that flourish and flow in the margins, and a defiant sense that nowhere is home. And we'll need all the gorgeous mistakes we can get, even if . . .

Notes

CHAPTER TWO. DRIFT CONTEXTS

1. When, in the midst of a later, city-declared "homeless emergency," the Los Angeles mayor announced that, "this city has pushed the problem from neighborhood to neighborhood for too long," his comments could best be described as a form of confessional irony (quoted in Medina 2015, A1). In this context Kawash notes that the homeless remain on the move not "because they are going somewhere, but because they have nowhere to go" (quoted in Edensor 2008, 124). See likewise Charles Dickens's ([1852–53] 1997) *Bleak House*, with its characterization of a homeless boy repeatedly told to "move on."

2. Ward (2000, 49–57) similarly notes the contradiction by which English "travelers" are instructed to settle in one place and then denied the right to do so. In Rome, the city's decision to bulldoze the long-standing Ponte Mammolo migrant encampment was described by one observer as "paradoxical because so many ended up on the streets" (quoted in Povoledo 2015, A6). See also Pickering, Bosworth, and Franko (2018).

CHAPTER THREE. DRIFT POLITICS

1. Mixing commodification and commemoration, the Parisian-design house Hermes designated flânerie its "inspiration theme" for the year 2015 and created a pop-up museum in Paris to house the experiences of the flâneur (Sciolino 2015, ST14); see Elkin's (2016) critique of Hermes's undertaking and its gender politics. See also Atkinson (2017) on the contemporary "rise of the sad flâneur."

2. Critical Mass' direct, collective liberation of urban space from automotive traffic and traffic law has led to countless encounters with city officials and police, innumerable arrests, and a number of violent incidents with motorists,

including a Brazilian case in which an angry driver accelerated into a Critical Mass ride, injuring some thirty riders (Domit and Goodman 2011, A5).

3. In this, "precarity" recalls the ambiguity of "postmodernism." In referencing a world beyond truth and certainty, postmodernism raised the question of whether postmodernism constituted a historical period, an epistemic orientation, or an ethical prescription. This question in turn raises another: What kind of modernist question is that?

4. Thus we have Hannah Hoch, working amidst the everyday detritus of the magazine trade many decades before and photomontaging from it a subversive cultural vision (see Lavin 1993).

5. Naegler (2016) also finds that post-Occupy activists are engaged in creating shared social spaces on the model of European autonomous social centers.

6. A few years later in New York City, it did seem they were going to arrest everybody. After numerous arrests of Critical Mass riders during the Republican National Convention, the New York City police department demanded (unsuccessfully) that Critical Mass obtain a permit for its rides, posting fliers claiming that it was "dangerous and illegal to ride a bicycle in a procession" without a permit (quoted in Shepard and Smithsimon 2011, 174). Indeed—especially a dis-organized procession toward nowhere.

CHAPTER FOUR. HOBO HISTORY

1. For a different take on vagrancy law's historical emergence, see Adler (1989).

2. This "seemingly aimless motion," it should be emphasized, mostly seems that way to the law and to legal authorities. The dialectic between aimless motion and motion aimed at some anticipated destination in drifters' lives is in fact far more complex. Harper (1982, 98) says of the men with whom he hopped trains that his "understanding of the life included an appreciation, first, for the purposefulness rather than the aimlessness that lay at the basis of the movement, the work, even the drinking. These men were not 'drifters.'" See also Hernandez (2014, 444) on the criminalization of tramps and hobos in Los Angeles, 1880–1910, and on the key role that this criminalization played in the expansion of incarceration and convict labor in Los Angeles and the American West; by 1908, Los Angeles had even completed a special "tramp stockade" to house incarcerated hobos. See Bright (1995) for a Canadian case study.

3. See also Garon and Tomko (2006). And thus the opening line of Woody Guthrie's (1943, 19) autobiography, *Bound For Glory:* "I could see men of all colors bouncing along in the boxcar."

4. In light of the 1972 US Supreme Court case *Papachristou v. City of Jacksonville,* which ruled a vague vagrancy law unconstitutional, many traditional vagrancy laws have now been replaced with a welter of laws more specifically targeting the homeless and the transient. Citing Walt Whitman, Vachel Lindsay, and Henry David Thoreau, this ruling also suggested that vagrancy laws were in a sense anti-American to the degree that they impinged on American values of independence, nonconformity, and creativity (see Creswell 2011).

5. An interesting parallel can be seen between hoboing American Civil War veterans and the returning World War II soldiers who coalesced into the road-riding Hell's Angels. On images of the railroads' western expansion see Shawn Smith (2013, 99–127).

6. Harper (1982, 148) likewise notes that, "although the definitions vary, there was a popular notion that the hobo was a migratory worker and the tramp a migratory non-worker, and that the bum did not work or travel." Despite the relative consistency of these distinctions among itinerant groups and scholars, in everyday and folkloric linguistic usage the terms *hobo*, *bum*, and *tramp* have often intermingled, as is seen throughout this chapter.

7. Lennon (2014, 17–18) refers to the hobo as the "floating proletariat" and quotes Michael Davis's notion of the "nomad proletariat." See also DePastino (2003), Higbie (2003), and Ashleigh (1914). See Wyman (2010) on ethnicity and hoboing.

8. In 2015 the *New York Times* (Kurutz 2015, ST12) profiled the Bindle Brothers, a company that alleges to sell "locally-grown, naturally-fallen, artisanal bindle bags" as a critical commentary on artisanal culture and the appropriation of the past.

9. Likewise, Harper (1982, 147–48) notes,

> The tramp expected to set the pace of his work and to remain largely unsupervised, and the bosses knew that their control over the worker as a person was limited and temporary. A way of life—a culture—grew up in these circumstances. The character of the work, the need for migration, the extreme independence born out of necessity and sometimes a carefully cultivated ability to live without plans or possessions, an outlawry and the roguishness of the hustler, sprees of drinking in areas called skid roads . . . all came to be known as the way of the hobo, the way of the tramp.

10. This statement and its phrasing echo in Paul Kantner's (1969) Jefferson Airplane song "We Can Be Together": "We are all outlaws in the eyes of America. . . . We are forces of chaos and anarchy. Everything they say we are, we are. And we are very proud of ourselves." For updated research on Frank Little and his murder, see Carroll (2016).

11. As published in Industrial Workers of the World (1973, 9). "Hallelujah on the Bum" / "Hallelujah I'm a Bum" includes countless other verses, many of which have themselves continued to evolve over time. One that I have heard sung more than once over the years pertains especially to the vagrant hobo's status with the law: "If you can't find a job, and you're hungry for bread, find a good-hearted cop, and he'll beat in your head."

12. As published in Industrial Workers of the World (1973, 30).

13. In this sense the *Little Red Songbook* might be thought of as an early example of "social media." Essential to organizing a dispersed, drifting population of hobos, the songbooks in their prevalence constituted a form of mass-distributed, mobile media; beyond this, the collective singing of the songs contained therein created a radicalized social setting and an ongoing collective experience of resistance.

14. As published in Industrial Workers of the World (1973, 36–37).

15. At the 1908 IWW convention, a delegate responded to accusations of "anarchy" within the IWW: "Where can there be 'anarchy' when we advocate and stand for organization? Is organization anarchy?" (quoted in Foner 1965, 111). The hobo delegates at the same convention opposed reducing union dues, wondering "how an organization could exist without adequate funds" (Dubofsky 1969, 140–41).

16. Employment sharks and employers also colluded to hire and fire workers quickly and repeatedly, thereby collecting more employment fees—and thereby exacerbating the drifting circumstances of the itinerant worker.

17. See Woody Guthrie's song "Vigilante Man" and Steinbeck's (1936) account of vigilantes in his book *In Dubious Battle*.

18. Other hobo organizations of the time included the International Brotherhood Welfare Association (founded 1905), the Itinerant Workers' Union/Hoboe's Union of America (founded 1914), and the Agricultural Workers' Organization/Agricultural Workers' Industrial Union (founded 1915 within the IWW); see DePastino (2003) and Higbie (2003). It is also worth noting that, while the western IWW embraced both individual and organizational liquidity, it did at times attempt to limit individual movement as well, as with its "thousand mile picket line" designed to control worker movement.

CHAPTER FIVE. CATCHING OUT

1. In the 1930s film *Wild Boys of the Road* (Wellman 1933), a brakeman who sexually assaults a young hobo girl is in turn attacked by her male hoboing companions and thrown off the train to his death; on this, see Lennon (2014, 145–55).

2. As an old hobo, West Coast Blackie, is telling his story to Bill Daniel (2008, 97), a train horn blows in the distance. "I hear ya calling me baby," says Blackie, interrupting his story, "but you ain't getting me, not today anyhow."

3. In the context of ongoing hobo history, DePastino (2003, 265) refers to this phenomenon as the "hobo punk movement."

4. "So why am I living in self-imposed exile?," asks one of the young women in the chronicle *Off the Map* (CrimethInc. 2003, 107). "Because you get what you pay for. Pay a lot and you get an expensive life. Take what's free, and you get freedom." She continues, "But off the map and beyond the borders of fear, there are other formulas. Abandoned house – permission = free shelter and adventure. Rain + covered doorways = gratitude. Soon it's obvious that what you thought was flat actually has an underside, an edge, a core."

5. "The Bowery is the haven for hobos who came to the big city to make the big time by getting pushcarts and collecting cardboard," wrote Kerouac ([1960] 1970, 177, 180) sixty years ago. And when he interviews a Bowery bum, the following exchange occurs: "And I always carry this book with me—*The Rules of St. Benedict*. A dreary book. . . ." "Why do you read it then?" "'Because I found it—I found it in Bristol last year."

6. "Hobo punks hop trains, squat abandoned buildings, collect welfare, and Dumpster food," says Ferguson (1994, 70). "Anything, in short, to exploit and condemn the consumer culture they so despise."

7. Truman Capote (1966, 35), *In Cold Blood:* "'Anybody wearing the fraternity pin,' he added, and touched a blue dot tattooed under his left eye—an insigne, a visible password, by which certain former prison inmates could identify him." See likewise Genet (1964).

8. As Richard Grant observes while traveling with train hoppers in *American Nomads* (2003, 267), "The tramps pulled out their marker pens and signed in on the wall of the boxcar."

9. Hitchhiking is often disavowed by gutter punks and hobos as a form of begging or dependency as compared to the autonomy of train hopping; in Zeke's case, it was necessitated by the lack of trains between Pecos and his hometown. Harper (1982, 154) notes of the hobos and tramps with whom he train hopped, "The only other possibility of moving from one place to another, hitchhiking, is avoided and looked down upon because it makes the tramp a beggar." Ferguson (1994, 92) likewise notes that her train-hopping companion Dumpster "said there was no way he would hitch. He had principles."

10. Zeke tells me that another favorite catch-out spot for train hoppers is down by a nearby Jack in the Box. In an earlier book that I wrote about Dumpster diving (Ferrell 2006, 39–40), I recorded a 2002 encounter with a hobo near this Jack in the Box. Now, a long time later, I understand why he was there.

11. Sarah Ferguson's (1994, 69) train-hopping friend Dumpster ends up at a Rainbow Family gathering as well. See also Alice Stein's more recent documentary on "dirty kids" and Rainbow Gatherings, https://vimeo.com/135483549.

12. The video *Train Hopping—Michigan to Baltimore,* originally posted on Punk Nomad TV, includes a lengthy scene of kids waiting under a railroad bridge and the caption, "this is 90 per cent of trainhopping," www.youtube .com/watch?v=Jwn7zgZoIOc.

13. Lou Reed, "I'm Waiting for the Man," *The Velvet Underground and Nico* (1967).

14. While riding a freight train, Aaron Dactyl (2012, 52) noted, "The train must've had some priority because, after clearing Salem, it passed an Amtrak sided for us."

15. A few months later, on a beer run to the QuickWay in my old truck, I happened upon two train hoppers, who asked me how to catch out westbound. When we got confused over street names and directions, we agreed I'd just take them there, so off we went to this same spot. As usual, subcultural knowledge and community flourished even in the briefest of episodes.

CHAPTER SIX. FREEDOM IN THE FORM OF A BOXCAR

1. In *Railroad Semantics #1*, Aaron Dactyl (2012, 30) notes that, while being forced to ride a suicide porch, "for the most part I remained seated, but occasionally I couldn't help crossing porches side to side to capture a better picture." The cover of *Railroad Semantics* #2 (2012) shows a train hopper riding suicide.

2. Included in Industrial Workers of the World (1973, 31); see also Chaplin (1948). "It's just as close to, like, complete freedom as I've ever had," says a train hopper named Dumpster. "It's just a total adrenalin rush . . . there's just, like, the total rhythm of the train, too. Because it's all steady, it's like a steady

banging, and it sounds almost like a metal jam" (quoted in Ferguson 1994, 69–70).

3. Riding through southern Idaho, Aaron Dactyl (2012, 9) noted that "every now and then I spot a cattle carcass strewn alongside the tracks in a different stage of decomposition."

4. Hopping his first train, Ted Conover (1984, 4) immediately noticed that "my sleeves . . . had become stained with dirt and rust." Among certain sociologists and criminologists, an unpublished 1920's quotation from Robert Park—one of Nels Anderson's mentors at the University of Chicago—has become something of a sacred chant. In it, Park urges researches to engage in firsthand research, and he concludes, "In short . . . go get the seat of your pant dirty in real research." Riding the rails, I achieved Park's recommended degree of dirt—and it wasn't just the seat of my pants.

5. A quarter century ago, Ferguson (1994, 72) reported that "now more and more young women are seeking freedom on the rails," and I would estimate that a third to a half of the gutter punks and train hoppers I've met have been women. See also DePastino (2003, 85–91) on "hobosexuality" among earlier train hoppers; Nels Anderson ([1923] 1961, 144) concluded that "all studies indicate that homosexual practices among homeless men are widespread."

6. "Spotting tramps is an acquired skill," says Ted Conover (1981, 138). "Their dirty clothes are a natural camouflage in both industrial and wooded landscapes, and it's to their advantage to keep a low profile."

7. Zeke tells me that he is also a member of the Blue Rag Mafia crew, of which his other crew, Slow Drunk Krew, is a more elite subunit.

8. Douglas Harper (1982, 10) likewise records an old tramp's warnings about Yuma and the bull there; see also Conover (1981, 274).

9. A YouTube video for this song features remixed scenes from Bill Daniel's *Who Is Bozo Texino?* (www.youtube.com/watch?v=IqTPGzBpVCw). Over the past decade or so, a number of bomb scares have resulted from bicycles sporting stickers with the band's name.

10. Harper (1982, 19) recounts a similar moment of uncertainty regarding whether to stay on a train or get off with a companion's gear.

11. Thus graffiti writer Eye Six: "I was reading *Dharma Bums* by Jack Kerouac and it's amazing to me that thirty years ago they could see plain as day that the American culture was turning into something where there were rows of houses and in each house there was someone watching the t.v., seeing what people wanted them to see. . . . People just sit on their asses" (quoted in Ferrell 1996, 42).

12. Waters among train hoppers is (or was) a somewhat controversial figure, who apparently maintained a double life as a successful businessman and a well-known train hopper.

13. Sometime later, First would tell me that she was shaking and that her heart was racing the first time she boarded a unit, in an attempt to catch out from Fort Worth—and that Goddamn It Dale told her to calm down.

14. Railroad Workers United, http://railroadworkersunited.org; see also Industrial Workers of the World, http://iww.org. In 1913 the Western Federation of Miners led a copper miners' strike in Michigan's Upper Peninsula, in

part over attempts to introduce one-man drilling machines, thus eliminating half the mining jobs and increasing the danger for a single man who, once injured, would have no help.

15. Almost a century ago Jack Black ([1926] 2000, 144) described the technique of "springing" into a closed boxcar by using an iron bar to pop the boxcar door off its hasps or track. Douglas Harper (1982, 5) notes he used discarded rail-brake lines and linings to peg open a boxcar door.

CHAPTER SEVEN. BENEATH THE SLAB

1. As with the following decade's formation of the Magnum photographic collective (Miller 1997), the FSA's assembled roster of photographers was a historical moment that both crystalized and advanced the practice of documentary photography.

2. In a similar vein, see James Agee on the relative importance of his text and Walker Evans's photographs in their 1939 book *Let Us Now Praise Famous Men:* "The photographs are not illustrative. They, and the text, are co-equal, mutually independent, and fully collaborative" (Agee and Evans 2001, xi). Agreeing to provide the photographs for a book being written by Carleton Beals (1933), Evans likewise "imposed conditions for his participation: complete freedom to choose the photographs for publication, to establish the sequence, and to collect them at the end of the book so that they appear as an independent entity and not as an illustration of the text" (Mora 1989, 9).

3. In this sense *An American Exodus* might be thought of as a precursor to green cultural criminology (Brisman and South 2014).

4. As Susan Sontag (1977, 55) says, the photographer is in this sense a flâneur, "an armed version of the solitary walker reconnoitering, stalking, cruising the urban inferno, the voyeuristic stroller who discovers the city as a landscape of voluptuous extremes."

5. See Frederick Wiseman's (1967) related masterpiece of cinema vérité, *Titicut Follies.*

6. Vergara's (1995) longitudinal photography of changing urban spaces accomplishes something similar.

CHAPTER EIGHT. DRIFT METHOD

1. Kerouac (1958, 7), *The Dharma Bums:*

"When I told him I was planning to hop the Zipper first class freight train the next night he said, 'Ah you mean the Midnight Ghost.'"
"Is that what you call the Zipper?"
"You musta been a railroad man on that railroad."
"I was, I was a brakeman on the S.P."
"Well, we bums call it the Midnight Ghost cause you get on it at L.A. and nobody sees you till you get to San Francisco in the morning the thing flies so fast."

2. My thanks to Willem de Haan for this notion of today's ghosts and drifters as contemporary manifestations of "the disappeared." Well beyond the

Argentinian case, of course, is the widespread historical and contemporary global occurrence of what international human rights law labels "forced or enforced disappearance."

3. Relatedly, Linnemann (2015) characterizes true crime reporting as a form of ghost story; see also Gordon (1997), Dickey (2016), and Braudy (2016).

4. Similarly, Simon Hallsworth and Tara Young (2008, 131–32) argue, in regard to crime and silence, for "considering silence as the absent presence of crime," and for "a methodological approach for excavating silence," so as to understand the role of this "negative space" in constituting crime and crime control. See also Kunstler (1993) for a different take on the creation of spatial nowheres and cultural emptiness.

5. Emily Anthes quotes William deBuys regarding attempts to save the saola, a species of wild ox never seen in the wild by a Westerner, and a creature whose numbers are unknown—if any numbers of it now remain at all—in its habitat on the Laos/Vietnam border: "The challenges of saola conservation verge on epistemology: How do you save a ghost when you are not sure it exists? . . . Put a saola, even a saola you cannot see, in a forest, and the forest, as though it held a unicorn, acquires an energy that cannot be described. It becomes numinous; it gains the pull of gravity, the weight of water, the float of a feather" (Anthes 2015, D5).

6. Carl Sandburg (1970, 136) wrote of World War I battlefields:

Two years, ten years, and passengers ask the conductor:
What place is this?
Where are we now?

See Rappert (2010) for a different sense of the presence and potential of absence.

7. In another sense, gutter punks and other trash pickers occupy the aftermath of consumerism, living off its discards and material consequences (Ferrell 2006)

8. See similarly Ai Weiwei's film *Human Flow* (2017), the artist Maria Thereza Alves's "Seeds of Change" migratory project (Kennedy 2016, C2), and Katherine Biber's (2013) analysis of criminal evidence and its cultural afterlife. Operation Identification, based in Texas State University's Forensic Anthropology Center, utilizes deceased immigrants' residues and remains in an effort to identify them and thereby "give them their name back" (Fernandez 2017, A1). In another sort of deathly echo, many of the hundreds of dolls that mourners brought to the swampy site where young Caylee Anthony's body was discovered in 2008 remained there, mired in the muck, years later.

9. For a number of years, local sex offender residency restrictions in Miami, Florida, forced a colony of sex offenders to live under a causeway that spanned Biscayne Bay (DeGregory 2009). See also Brett Story's film *The Prison in Twelve Landscapes* (2016). "This drifting, at times dreamy documentary follows the tentacles of the confinement industry to stories that hide in plain sight," says the *New York Times* (Catsoulis 2016, C9), "like the small playground in Los Angeles constructed purely to prevent paroled sex offenders from moving into a nearby halfway house."

10. J.G. Ballard, *Concrete Island* (1973, 40–41): "He reached a low wall, and climbed a flight of steps that lifted into the air from the remains of a garden path. These ruins were all that remained of a stucco Victorian house pulled down years earlier. The surface of the island was markedly uneven. . . . A pile of worn headstones lay to one side."

CHAPTER NINE. GHOST IMAGES AND GORGEOUS MISTAKES

All photographs in this chapter were found/scrounged by the author.

1. In a similar vein, see Margaret Bourke-White's less insightful but visually dramatic images of industrial structure and production (Phillips 2003).

2. See also Rubin (2012) on the *dérive* as a form of urban pedagogy and image production. Salgado's (2000) remarkable work on migrants and migrations is also notable here.

3. Camilo José Vergara's (1995) encyclopedic visual survey of urban structural change works in a similar way. The artist JR has also reproduced old Ellis Island immigration photographs and restaged them at the island (see Ryzik 2014). See also Brown (2014) and Schept (2014) on the changing landscapes of imprisonment and the contested visuality that accompanies them.

4. "Watch the passing figures and await the moment in which everything is in balance," said Alfred Stieglitz (quoted in J. Scott 2012, 32). But who other than the photographer is watching and waiting in this way? On the seen and unseen in photography, see also Shawn Smith (2013), who draws on Benjamin's notion of the "optical unconscious."

5. "Photographs capture more than their intended subjects," says Shawn Smith (2013, 21). "Unwanted or unnoticed things sneak into the frame. People and animals walk in front of the lens. Discarded objects litter yards. . . . I am drawn to the people, objects, and shadows that populate the edges of family photographs, the details that were overlooked by photographers, the unintended subjects of snapshots. Such unanticipated details offer an unusual record of everyday life in family snapshots."

6. The same can be said of crime scene photographs and mugshots once they become disconnected from their original legal case and remade as art or entertainment (see Biber 2013). Similarly, the novelist Alexander McCall Smith (2016; see Light 2016) has written a series of fictional stories based on a small collection of old, unattributed photographs, and the writer Alexander Masters (2016), "ardent celebrant of the hidden and the rejected" (J. Parker 2016, 23), has written a book based on 148 anonymous diaries that a friend reclaimed from a trash bin. See also Thomas Sauvin's massive photographic salvage project Beijing Silvermine, http://www.beijingsilvermine.com/.

References

BOOKS, ARTICLES, AND BOOK CHAPTERS

Adler, Jeffrey. 1989. "A Historical Analysis of the Law of Vagrancy." *Criminology* 27 (2): 209–29.

Agee, James, and Walker Evans. (1939) 2001. *Let Us Now Praise Famous Men.* Boston: Houghton Mifflin.

Agier, Michel. 2002. "Between War and City: Towards an Urban Anthropology of Refugee Camps." *Ethnography* 3 (3): 317–41.

Algren, Nelson. (1935) 1966. "Somebody in Boots." In *The American Writer and the Great Depression,* edited by Harvey Swados, 319–48. New York: Bobbs-Merrill.

Allsop, Kenneth. 1967. *Hard Travellin': The Hobo and His History.* New York: New American Library.

Amin, Ash. 2008. "Collective Culture and Urban Public Space." *City* 12 (1): 5–24.

Amster, Randall. 2008. *Lost in Space.* New York: LFB.

Anderson, Nels. (1923) 1961. *The Hobo: The Sociology of the Homeless Man.* Chicago: University of Chicago Press.

———. 1940. *Men on the Move.* Chicago: University of Chicago Press.

Andreou, Alex. 2015. "Anti-homeless Spikes: 'Sleeping Rough Opened My Eyes to the City's Barbed Cruelty.'" *Guardian,* 18 February 2015. www.theguardian.com.

Anonymous. 2003. *Evasion.* Atlanta: CrimethInc.

Anthes, Emily. 2015. "Magical Beast in a Faraway Land." *New York Times,* 24 March 2015, D5.

Apel, Dora. 2015. "The Ruins of Capitalism." *Jacobin.* www.jacobinmag.com.

Appadurai, Arjun. 2000. "Spectral Housing and Urban Cleansing: Notes on Millennial Mumbai." *Public Culture* 12 (3): 627–51.

Armstrong, Justin. 2010. "On the Possibility of Spectral Ethnography." *Cultural Studies: Critical Methodologies* 10 (3): 243–50.

Arnold, Dennis, and Joseph Bongiovi. 2013. "Precarious, Informalizing, and Flexible Work: Transforming Concepts and Understandings." *American Behavioral Scientist* 57 (3): 289–308.

Ashleigh, Charles. 1914. "The Floater." *International Socialist Review* 15:34–38.

Aspden, Kester. 2008. *The Hounding of David Oluwale*. London: Vintage.

Atkinson, Sophie. 2017. "The Rise of the Sad Flâneur." *Millions*. www.themillions.com/2017/04/rise-sad-flaneur.html.

Aubenas, Florence. 2011. *The Night Cleaner*. Oxford: Polity.

Austin, Joe. 2001. *Taking the Train*. New York: Columbia University Press.

Ballard, J.G. 1973. *Concrete Island*. New York: Picador.

Barnard, Anne. 2014. "3 Years of Strife and Cruelty Put Syria in Free Fall." *New York Times*, 18 March 2014, A1, A5.

Baudelaire, Charles. (1863) 1964. "The Painter of Modern Life." In *The Painter of Modern Life and Other Essays*, edited and translated by Jonathan Mayne, 1–40. London: Phaidon.

Bauman, Zygmunt. 2002. "In the Lowly Nowherevilles of Liquid Modernity." *Ethnography* 3 (3): 343–49.

———. 2000. *Liquid Modernity*. Cambridge: Polity.

Beals, Carleton. 1933. *The Crime of Cuba*. Philadelphia: Lippincott.

Becker, Howard S. 1963. *Outsiders*. New York: Free Press.

Beckett, Katherine, and Steve Herbert. 2009. *Banished: The New Social Control in Urban America*. New York: Oxford University Press.

Bellafante, Ginia. 2015. "Giuliani and the Inconvenient Truth of New York City Homelessness." *New York Times*, 30 August 2015, 24.

Bell, Michael. 1997. "The Ghosts of Place." *Theory and Society* 26:813–36.

Bengtsson, Tea Torbenfeldt. 2012. "Boredom and Action—Experiences from Youth Confinement." *Journal of Contemporary Ethnography* 41 (5): 526–53.

Benjamin, Walter. 2002. *The Arcades Project*. Cambridge, MA: Belknap Press of Harvard University Press.

Berk, Richard, and John McDonald. 2010. "Policing the Homeless." *Criminology and Public Policy* 9 (4): 813–40.

Bey, Hakim. 1991. *T.A.Z.* New York: Autonomedia.

Biber, Katherine. 2013. "In Crime's Archive: The Cultural Afterlife of Criminal Evidence." *British Journal of Criminology* 53:1033–49.

Black, Jack. (1926) 2000. *You Can't Win*. San Francisco: Nabat/AK Press.

Blake, William. 1790. *The Marriage of Heaven and Hell*. London: William Blake.

Blumer, Herbert. 1956. "Sociological Analysis and the 'Variable.'" *American Sociological Review* 21 (6): 683–90.

Bofkin, Lee. 2014. *Concrete Canvas*. London: Cassell.

Bradatan, Costica. 2014. "The Wisdom of the Exile." *New York Times*, 17 August 2014, SR12.

Bradshaw, Kate. 2017. "In Tampa, Food Not Bombs Activists Arrested for Feeding the Homeless—Again." *Creative Loafing Tampa Bay*, 7 January 2017. www.cltampa.com/news-views/local-news/article/20848403/tampa-activists-arrested-for-feeding-the-homeless.

Braudy, Leo. 2016. *Haunted*. New Haven, CT: Yale University Press.

Braverman, Harry. 1974. *Labor and Monopoly Capital*. New York: Monthly Review Press.

Brighenti, Andrea Mubi. 2013a. Introduction to *Urban Interstices*, edited by Andrea Mubi Brighenti, xv–xxiii. Surrey, UK: Ashgate.

———, ed. 2013b. *Urban Interstices*. Surrey, UK: Ashgate.

Bright, David. 1995. "Loafers Are Not Going to Subsist upon Public Credulence: Vagrancy and the Law in Calgary, 1900–1914." *Labour/Le Travail* 36:37–58.

Brisman, Avi, and Nigel South. 2013. *Green Cultural Criminology*. London: Routledge.

Brown, Michelle. 2014. "Visual Criminology and Carceral Studies." *Theoretical Criminology* 18 (2): 176–97.

Buckley, Chris, and Austin Ramzy. 2015. "Thousands Wait in Southeast Asia, Lost in Time." *New York Times*, 26 May 2015, A1, A6.

Butler, C. T., and Keith McHenry. 2000. *Food Not Bombs*. Tucson: See Sharp Press.

Cairns, Stephen, ed. 2004. *Drifting: Architecture and Migrancy*. London: Routledge.

Calikoglu, Levent. 2012. "Half a Century of Urban Culture: The Recording of History and the Anatomy of Walls." In *Burhan Dogancay: Fifty Years of Urban Walls*, 14–16. Munich: Prestel Verlag. Exhibition catalog.

Callahan, Maureen. 2016. "The Chilling Stories behind Japan's 'Evaporating People.'" *New York Post*, 10 December 2016. http://nypost.com/2016/12/10.

Capote, Truman. 1966. *In Cold Blood*. New York: Random House.

Carlsson, Chris. 2002. "Cycling under the Radar—Assertive Desertion." In *Critical Mass*, edited by Chris Carlsson, 75–82. Oakland: AK Press.

Carroll, Rory. 2016. "The Mysterious Lynching of Frank Little." *Guardian*, 21 September 2016.

Catsoulis, Jeannette. 2016. "The Prison in Twelve Landscapes." *New York Times*, 4 November 2016, C9.

Caws, Mary Ann. 1989. *The Art of Interference*. Princeton, NJ: Princeton University Press.

Chambliss, William. 1964. "A Sociological Analysis of the Law of Vagrancy." *Social Problems* 12 (1): 67–77.

Chan, Sewell. 2015. "Global Warming's Role in Mass Migration Is Addressed." *New York Times*, 13 December 2015, 18.

Chaplin, Ralph. 1948. *Wobbly: The Rough-and-Tumble Story of an American Radical*. Chicago: University of Chicago Press.

Chronopoulos, Themis. 2011. *Spatial Regulation in New York City*. New York: Routledge.

Clark, Dylan. 2004. "The Raw and the Rotten: Punk Cuisine." *Ethnology* 43 (1): 19–31.

Clyde, E. M. (1911) 1988. "The March on Fresno." In *Rebel Voices*, edited by Joyce Kornbluh, 100–102. Chicago: Charles H. Kerr.

Cochrane, Joe. 2015. "Migrants Rescued from Sea Face Uncertain Future in Indonesian Camps." *New York Times*, 28 May 2015, A12.

Cohen, Albert. 1955. *Delinquent Boys.* New York: Free Press.

Coles, Robert. 1997. *Doing Documentary Work.* New York: Oxford.

Cole, Teju. 2015. "On Photography." *New York Times Magazine,* 22 February 2015, 62–70.

———. 2016a. "On Photography." *New York Times Magazine,* 1 May 2016, 26–29.

———. 2016b. "On Photography." *New York Times Magazine,* 23 October 2016, 16–19.

Colleoni, Elanor, Stefania Marino, and Manuela Galetto. 2014. "Radical Unionism in Italy—Back to the Future: Fiom and Chainworkers." In *Radical Unions in Europe and the Future of Collective Interest Representation,* edited by Heather Connolly, Lefteris Kretsos, and Craig Phelan, 137–56. London: Peter Lang.

Commando, Holden Caulfield. 2003. "How Much Can You Get Away With?" In *Evasion,* by Anonymous, n.p. Atlanta: CrimethInc.

Conover, Ted. 1984. *Rolling Nowhere.* New York: Viking.

Cooper, Marianne. 2014. *Cut Adrift.* Berkeley: University of California Press.

Cotter, Holland. 2009. "America, Captured in a Flash." *New York Times,* 25 September 2009, C27, C30.

———. 2015. "Allan deSouza: Notes from Afar." *New York Times,* 1 May 2015, C20.

———. 2017. "Things They Carried to the End." *New York Times,* 4 March 2017, C1, C2.

Coutin, Susan Bibler. 2003. "Illegality, Borderlands, and the Space of Nonexistence." In *Globalization under Construction,* edited by Richard Perry and Bill Maurer, 171–202. Minneapolis: University of Minnesota Press.

Cresswell, Tim. 2011. "The Vagrant/Vagabond: The Curious Career of a Mobile Subject." In *Geographies of Mobilities,* edited by Tim Creswell and Peter Merriman, 239–53. Farnham, UK: Ashgate.

CrimethInc. 2003. *Off the Map.* Salem, OR: CrimethInc.

Culhane, Dennis. 2010. "Tackling Homelessness in Los Angeles' Skid Row." *Criminology and Public Policy* 9 (4): 851–57.

Cullen, Frank, and Steven Messner. 2007. "The Making of Criminology Revisited." *Theoretical Criminology* 11 (1): 5–37.

Dactyl, Aaron. 2012. *Railroad Semantics #1.* Portland, OR: Microcosm.

Daily Telegraph. 2015. "Instagram Trend That Takes Photos of Homeless People and Posts Them Online for Cheap Laughs." *Daily Telegraph* (Sydney, Australia), 4 March 2015. www.dailytelegraph.com.au/news/nsw/instagram-trend-that-takes-photos-of-homeless-people-and-posts-them-online-for-cheap-laughs/story-fniocx12-1227247875002.

Daley, Suzanne. 2012a. "Spain Recoils as Its Hungry Forage Trash Bins for a Next Meal." *New York Times,* 25 September 2012, A1, A6.

———. 2012b. "Wave of Evictions Leads to Homeless Crisis in Spain." *New York Times,* 12 November 2012, A4.

Daniel, Bill. 2008. *Mostly True.* Bloomington, IN: Microcosm.

Dawidoff, N. 2015. "Hidden America." *New York Times Magazine,* 5 July 2015, 38–48, 51.

De Angelis, Massimo, and David Harvie. 2009. "'Cognitive Capitalism' and the Rat Race." *Historical Materialism* 17 (3): 3–30.

Debord, Guy. 1958. "Theory of the Derive." www.bopsecrets.org.

De Certeau, Michel. 1984. *The Practice of Everyday Life*. Berkeley: University of California Press.

———. 2008. "Walking in the City." In *The Cultural Studies Reader*, edited by S. During, 156–63. Abingdon, UK: Routledge.

DeGregory, Lane. 2009. "Miami Sex Offenders Limited to Life under a Bridge." *Tampa Bay Times*, 14 August 2009. www.tampabay.com/features/human interest/miami-sex-offenders-limited-to-life-under-a-bridge/1027668.

De Leon, Jason. 2013. "Undocumented Migration, Use Wear, and the Materiality of Habitual Suffering in Sonoran Desert." *Journal of Material Culture* 18 (4): 321–45.

———. 2015. *The Land of Open Graves: Living and Dying on the Migrant Trail*. Berkeley: University of California Press.

Deleuze, Gilles, and Felix Guattari. 1987. *A Thousand Plateaus: Capitalism and Schizophrenia*. Minneapolis: University of Minnesota Press.

Denzin, Norman. 1997. *Interpretive Ethnography: Ethnographic Practices for the 21st Century*. Thousand Oaks, CA: Sage.

DeParcq, William, and Charles Alan Wright. 1956. "Damages under the Federal Employers' Liability Act." *Ohio State Law Journal* 17:430–83.

DePastino, Todd. 2003. *Citizen Hobo*. Chicago: University of Chicago Press.

DeSilvey, Caitlin. 2007. "Salvage Memory: Constellating Material Histories on a Hardscrabble Homestead." *Cultural Geographies* 14 (3): 401–24.

Dickens, Charles. (1852–53) 1997. *Bleak House*. Hertfordshire, UK: Wordsworth.

Dickey, Colin. 2016. *Ghostland*. New York: Penguin.

Doisneau, Robert. 2001. *Mes Parisiens*. Paris: Nathan.

Domit, Myrna, and David Goodman. 2011. "Driver Accused of Injuring Brazil Cyclists." *New York Times*, 3 March 2011, A5.

Donohoe, Kevin. "Food Not Bombs Members Arrested for Feeding the Hungry." *Nation*, 27 June 2011. www.thenation.com/article/food-not-bombs-members-arrested-feeding-hungry/.

Dougherty, Conor. 2016. "Oakland Fire Leads Cities to Scrutinize Artists' Spaces." *New York Times*, 9 December 2016, A14, A23.

Dougherty, Conor, and Julie Turkewitz. 2016. "Pursuing Dreams in Illegal (and Risky) Warehouses." *New York Times*, 7 December 2016, A14, A16.

Duane, Daniel. 2016. "The Tent Cities of San Francisco." *New York Times*, 18 December 2016, 1, 6, 7.

Dubofsky, Melvin. 1969. *We Shall Be All*. New York: Quadrangle.

Dum, Christopher. 2016. *Exiled in America: Life on the Margins in a Residential Motel*. New York: Columbia University Press.

Durkheim, Emile. (1893) 1984. *The Division of Labour in Society*. Basingstoke, UK: Macmillan.

Dyer, Geoff. 2016. "On Photography." *New York Times Magazine*, 4 September 2016, 14–17.

Eck, John, and Emily Eck. 2012. "Crime Place and Pollution." *Criminology and Public Policy* 11 (2): 281–316.

Edensor, Tim. 2008. "Walking through Ruins." In *Ways of Walking: Ethnography and Practice on Foot*, edited by Tim Ingold and Jo Lee Vergunst, 123–41. Aldershot, UK: Ashgate.

Egan, Timothy. 2014. "Creativity vs. Quants." *New York Times*, 22 March 2014, A19.

Eichinger, Bernd. n.d. "Interview with Bernd Eichinger." www.baadermeinhofmovie.com/castcrew/eichenger_interview.html.

Elkin, Lauren. 2016. "Radical Flâneuserie." *Paris Review*, 25 August 2016. www.theparisreview.org/blog/2016/08/25/radical-flaneuserie/.

———. 2017. *Flâneuse*. New York: Farrar, Straus and Giroux.

Erlanger, Steven. 2012. "Young, Educated and Jobless in France." *New York Times*, 3 December 2012, A6, A11.

Evans, Walker. 1989. *Walker Evans: Havana 1933*. Paris: Contrejour.

Fader, Jamie. 2013. *Falling Back: Incarceration and Transitions to Adulthood among Urban Youth*. New Brunswick, NJ: Rutgers University Press.

Faleiro, Sonia. 2012. "Invisible Economy." *New York Times Book Review*, 25 November 2012, 22.

Fantone, Laura. 2007. "Precarious Changes: Gender and Generational Politics in Contemporary Italy." *Feminist Review* 87:5–20.

Farrell, Christopher. 2016. "Very Mobile Work Force, Never Far From Home." *New York Times*, 22 October 2016, B1, B4.

Ferguson, Sarah. 1994. "Meet the Crusties." *Esquire*, January, 69–75.

Fernandez, Manny. 2017. "A Northbound Path, Marked by More and More Bodies." *New York Times*, 5 May 2017, A1, A22–23.

Ferrell, Jeff. 1996. *Crimes of Style: Urban Graffiti and the Politics of Criminality*. Boston: Northeastern University Press.

———. 1997. "Criminological Verstehen: Inside the Immediacy of Crime." *Justice Quarterly* 14 (1): 3–23.

———. 1998. "Freight Train Graffiti." *Justice Quarterly* 15 (4): 587–608.

———. 2001. *Tearing down the Streets*. New York: Palgrave/Macmillan.

———. 2003. "Speed Kills." *Critical Criminology* 11:185–98.

———. 2006. *Empire of Scrounge*. New York: New York University Press.

———. 2009. "Kill Method: A Provocation." *Journal of Theoretical and Philosophical Criminology* 1 (1): 1–22.

———. 2011a. "Corking as Community Policing." *Contemporary Justice Review* 14 (1): 95–98.

———. 2011b. "Disciplinarity and Drift." In *What Is Criminology?*, edited by Mary Bosworth and Carolyn Hoyle, 62–75. Oxford: Oxford University Press.

———. 2011c. "Rondzwerven, Stedelijke Ruimte en Transgressie (Drift, Space, and Transgression)." *Tijdschrift over Cultuur en Criminaliteit (Journal on Culture and Crime*, the Netherlands) 1 (1): 34–50.

———. 2012a. "Anarchy, Geography, and Drift." *Antipode* 44 (5): 1687–1704.

———. 2012b. "Outline of a Criminology of Drift." In *New Directions in Criminological Theory*, edited by Steve Hall and Simon Winlow, 241–56. London: Routledge/Wilan.

————. 2013. "The Underbelly Project: Hiding in the Light, Painting in the Dark." *Rhizomes* 25. /www.rhizomes.net/issue25/ferrell/.

————. 2014. "Manifesto for a Criminology beyond Method." In *The Poetics of Crime*, edited by Michael Jacobsen, 285–302. London: Ashgate.

————. 2016. "Foreword: Graffiti, Street Art and the Politics of Complexity." In *Routledge Handbook of Graffiti and Street Art*, edited by Jeffrey Ian Ross, xxx–xxxviii. London: Routledge.

————. 2017. "Graffiti, Street Art and the Dialectics of the City." In *Graffiti and Street Art: Reading, Writing and Representing the City*, edited by Konstantinos Avramidis and Myrto Tsilimpounidi, 27–38. London: Routledge.

Ferrell, Jeff, Keith Hayward, and Jock Young. 2015. *Cultural Criminology: An Invitation*. 2nd ed. London: Sage.

Ferrell, Jeff, and Cecile Van de Voorde. 2010. "The Decisive Moment: Documentary Photography and Cultural Criminology." In *Framing Crime: Cultural Criminology and the Image*, edited by Keith Hayward and Mike Presdee, 36–52. Abingdon, UK: Routledge.

Ferrell, Jeff, and Robert Weide. 2010. "Spot Theory." *City* 14 (1–2): 48–62.

Feyerabend, Paul. 1975. *Against Method*. London: Verso.

Foner, Philip. 1965. *The Industrial Workers of the World, 1905–1917*. New York: International.

Fox, Margalit. 2013. "Saul Leiter, Photographer with a Palette for New York, Dies at 89." *New York Times*, 28 November 2013, B9.

Frank, Robert. 1959. *The Americans*. New York: Delpire.

Friedman, Thomas. 2013. "Egypt's Perilous Drift." *New York Times*, 16 June 2013, SR1, 7.

Galetto, Manuela, Chiara Lasala, Sveva Magaraggia, Chiara Martucci, Elisabetta Onori, and Francesca Pozzi. 2007. "A Snapshot of Precariousness." *Feminist Review* 87:104–12.

Garfinkel, Harold. 1956. "Conditions of Successful Degradation Ceremonies." *American Journal of Sociology* 61:420–24.

————. 1967. *Studies in Ethnomethodology*. Englewood Cliffs, NJ: Prentice-Hall.

Garon, Paul, and Gene Tomko. 2006. *What's the Use of Walking If There's a Freight Train Going Your Way? Black Hoboes and Their Songs*. Chicago: Kerr.

Garot, Robert. 2010. *Who You Claim: Performing Gang Identity in School and on the Streets*. New York: New York University Press.

Garrett, Bradley. 2013. *Explore Everything*. London: Verso.

————. 2015. "PSPOs: The New Control Orders Threatening Our Public Spaces." *Guardian*, 8 September 2015. www.theguardian.com/cities/2015/sep/08/pspos-new-control-orders-public-spaces-asbos-freedoms.

Gautrand, Jean-Claude. 2003. *Robert Doisneau*. Cologne, Germany: Taschen.

Genet, Jean. 1964. *The Thief's Journal*. New York: Grove Press.

Genocchio, Benjamin. 2011. "Milton Rogovin, Photographer, Dies at 101." *New York Times*, 18 January 2011. www.nytimes.com/2011/01/19/arts/design/19rogovin.html

Gibson, Kristina. 2011. *Street Kids*. New York: New York University Press.

Gillet, Kit. 2011. "Fast-Growing Mongolian Shantytown Holds Quarter of National Population." *Guardian Weekly*, 20 May 2011, 9.

Gill, Rosalind, and Andy Pratt. 2008. "In the Social Factory? Immaterial Labour, Precariousness, and Cultural Work." *Theory, Culture and Society* 25 (7–8): 1–30.

Ginsberg, Allen. 1956. *Howl and Other Poems*. San Francisco: City Lights.

Glick, Leonard. 2005. *Criminology*. Boston: Pearson.

Goffard, Christopher. 2009. "On the Run from Everything but Each Other." *Los Angeles Times*, 13 May 13 2009. www.northbankfred.com/run.html.

Goldsmith, Andrew, and Russell Brewer. 2015. "Digital Drift and the Criminal Interaction Order." *Theoretical Criminology* 19 (1): 112–30.

Gordon, Avery. 1997. *Ghostly Matters: Haunting and the Sociological Imagination*. Minneapolis: University of Minnesota Press.

Gordon, Linda, and Gary Okihiro, eds. 2008. *Impounded: Dorothea Lange and the Censored Images of Japanese-American Internment*. New York: W. W. Norton.

Gowan, Teresa. 2009. "New Hobos or Neo-romantic Fantasy?" *Qualitative Sociology* 32 (3): 231–57.

———. 2010. *Hobos, Hustlers and Backsliders*. Minneapolis: University of Minnesota Press.

Grady, Barbara. 2014. "Few Options for Homeless as San Jose Clears Camp." *New York Times*, 5 December 2014, A13–14.

Graeber, David. 2007. *Possibilities*. Oakland, CA: AK Press.

———. 2009. *Direct Action: An Ethnography*. Oakland, CA: AK Press.

Grant, Richard. 2003. *American Nomads*. New York: Grove.

Green, Edward L. W. 2016. "Weight of the Gavel: Prison as a Rite of Passage." PhD diss., Kansas State University. ProQuest (10127395).

Gregory, Alice. 2016. "The Precisionist." *New York Times Magazine*, 16 October 2016, 36–39.

Grimes, William. 2015. "Mary Ellen Mark, Who Photographed Street Life with Empathy, Dies at 75." *New York Times*, 27 May 2015, A17.

Guthrie, Woody. 1943. *Bound for Glory*. New York: Dutton.

Hagedorn, John. 1994. "Homeboys, Dope Fiends, Legits, and New Jacks." *Criminology* 32 (2): 197–219.

Hale, Mike. 2014. "Encircling Rome, On and Off the Road." *New York Times*, 5 June 2014, C1, C5.

Hallsworth, Simon. 2013. *The Gang and Beyond*. Houndsmills, UK: Palgrave MacMillan.

Hallsworth, Simon, and Tara Young. 2008. "Crime and Silence." *Theoretical Criminology* 12 (2): 131–52.

Hamm, Mark. 1998. "The Ethnography of Terror: Timothy McVeigh and the Blue Centerlight of Evil." In *Ethnography at the Edge*, edited by Jeff Ferrell and Mark Hamm, 111–30. Boston: Northeastern University Press.

Harper, Douglas. 1982. *Good Company*. Chicago: University of Chicago Press.

———. 2012. *Visual Sociology*. London: Routledge.

Harvey, David. 2008. "The Right to the City." *New Left Review* 53:23–40.

Hayward, Keith. 2012a. "Five Spaces of Cultural Criminology." *British Journal of Criminology* 52 (3): 441–62.

———. 2012b. "Using Cultural Geography to Think Differently about Space and Crime." In *New Directions in Criminological Theory*, edited by Steve Hall and Simon Winlow, 123–44. London: Routledge.

Hayward, Keith, and Mike Presdee, eds. 2010. *Framing Crime: Cultural Criminology and the Image*. London: Routledge.

Hazan, Haim, and Esther Hertzog, eds. 2012. *Serendipity in Anthropological Research*. Surrey, UK: Ashgate.

Healy, Jack. 2016. "Tensions Soar as Drifters Call National Parks Home." *New York Times*, 22 August 2016, A9, A12.

———. 2017. "Where Homelessness Can Be a Crime." *New York Times*, 10 January 2017, A8, A16.

Hebdige, Dick. 1979. *Subculture: The Meaning of Style*. London: Metheun.

Hedges, Chris. 2010. "City of Ruins." *Nation*, 22 November 2010, 15–20.

Helprin, Mark. 2012. "Bumping into the Characters." *New York Times*, 4 October, 2012, D1, D8.

Hernandez, Kelly. 2014. "Hobos in Heaven: Race, Incarceration, and the Rise of Los Angeles, 1880–1910." *Pacific Historical Review* 83 (3): 410–47.

Higbie, Frank Tobias. 2003. *Indispensable Outcasts: Hobo Workers and Community in the American Midwest, 1880–1930*. Urbana: University of Illinois Press.

Hirst, Caty. 2015. "Crime Rate Drops by 31% in City's Homeless District." *Fort Worth Star-Telegram Express*, 18 March 2015, 1AA–2AA.

Hoberman, J. 2015. "California, through a French Lens." *New York Times*, 9 August 2015, AR13, 16.

Holmes, Oliver Wendell. 1858. "The Chambered Nautilus." Poetry Foundation. www.poetryfoundation.org/poems/44379/the-chambered-nautilus.

Holmes, Seth. 2013. *Fresh Fruit, Broken Bodies*. Berkeley: University of California Press.

Hylton, Wil. 2015. "American Nightmare." *New York Times Magazine*, 8 February 2015, 24–29, 44–49.

Ilan, Jonathan. 2013. "Street Social Capital in the Liquid City." *Ethnography* 14 (1): 3–24.

Ince, Anthony. 2012. "In the Shell of the Old: Anarchist Geographies of Territorialisation." *Antipode* 44 (5): 1645–66.

Industrial Workers of the World. *Industrial Worker*. 1909–Present. Spokane, WA: Industrial Workers of the World.

———. 1973. *Songs of the Workers (The Little Red Songbook)*. 34th ed. Chicago: Industrial Workers of the World.

Irwin, Dave. 1998. "Train Gang." *Tucson Weekly*, 5–11 February 1998. www.tucsonweekly.com/tw/02-05-98/curr1.htm.

Jackson, Daniel. 2004. "Young Hobos Look to Rails for Adventure, Escape." *Rocky Mountain News*, 24 April 2004, 36A.

Johnson, Ian. 2013. "China Embarking On Vast Program of Urbanization." *New York Times*, 16 June 2013, 1, 10–11

———. 2014. "China Releases Plan to Incorporate Farmers into Cities." *New York Times*, 18 March 2014, A9.

Jordan, John. 1998. "The Art of Necessity." In *DiY Culture*, edited by George McKay, 129–51. London: Verso.

Kalleberg, Arne. 2009. "Precarious Work, Insecure Workers." *American Sociological Review* 74 (1): 1–22.

Kane, Stephanie. 1998. "Reversing the Ethnographic Gaze." In *Ethnography at the Edge*, edited by Jeff Ferrell and Mark Hamm, 132–45. Boston: Northeastern University Press.

Kawash, Samira. 1998. "The Homeless Body." *Public Culture* 10 (2): 319–39.

Kehr, David. 2012. "Symphony of Compositions from Decomposition." *New York Times*, 23 December 2012, AR10, 17.

Keith, Michael. 1997. "Street Sensibility? Negotiating the Political by Articulating the Spatial." In *The Urbanization of Injustice*, edited by Andy Merrifield and Erik Swyngedouw, 137–60. New York: New York University Press.

Kennedy, Randy. 2013. "The Poetry in the Ruins of New York." *New York Times*, 22 February 2013, C19, C25.

———. 2016. "Prize for Project on Human Migration." *New York Times*, 25 November 2016, C2.

Kerouac, Jack. 1955. *On The Road*. New York: Viking.

———. 1958. *The Dharma Bums*. New York: Signet.

———. (1960) 1970. *Lonesome Traveler*. New York: Grove.

Kindynis, Theo, and Bradley Garrett. 2015. "Entering the Maze: Space, Time and Exclusion in an Abandoned Northern Ireland Prison." *Crime, Media, Culture* 11 (1): 5–20.

Kornbluh, Joyce, ed. 1998. *Rebel Voices: An IWW Anthology*. Chicago: Charles Kerr.

Kromer, Tom. 1935. *Waiting for Nothing*. New York: Knopf.

Kropotkin, Peter. 1902. *Mutual Aid*. London: Heinemann.

———. 1975. *The Essential Kropotkin*. New York: Liveright.

Kruglanski, Aviv. 2005. "Precarity Explained for Kids (a Medley)." *Journal of Aesthetics and Protest* 4. www.journalofaestheticsandprotest.org.

Kunstler, James Howard. 1993. *The Geography of Nowhere*. New York: Simon and Schuster.

Kurutz, Steven. 2015. "Hobo Chic from the Bindle Bros. of Brooklyn." *New York Times*, 13 September 2015, ST12.

Lange, Dorothea, and Paul Taylor. (1939) 1969. *An American Exodus*. New Haven, CT: Yale University Press.

Langegger, Sig, and Stephen Koester. 2016. "Dwelling without a Home: Denver's Splintered Public Spaces." In *Order and Conflict in Public Space*, edited by Mattias De Backer et al., 140–59. London: Routledge.

———. 2017. "Moving On, Finding Shelter: The Spatiotemporal Camp." *International Sociology* 32 (4): 454–73.

Lavin, Maud. 1993. *Cut with the Kitchen Knife: The Weimar Photomontages of Hannah Hoch*. New Haven, CT: Yale University Press.

Lee, Elizabeth, and Geraldine Pratt. 2011. "Migrant Worker: Migrant Stories." In *Geographies of Mobilities*, edited by Tim Creswell and Peter Merriman, 225–37. London: Ashgate.

Lennon, John. 2007. "Too Dirty to Be a Hobo?" In *Youth Subcultures: Exploring Underground America*, edited by Arielle Greenberg, 212–23. New York: Pearson/Longman.

———. 2014. *Boxcar Politics: The Hobo in U.S. Culture and Literature, 1869–1956*. Amherst: University of Massachusetts Press.

———. 2016. "Trains, Railroad Workers and Illegal Rides: The Subcultural World of Hobo Graffiti." In *Routledge Handbook of Graffiti and Street Art*, edited by Jeffrey Ian Ross, 27–35. Abingdon, UK: Routledge.

Levesque, Luc. 2013. "Trajectories of Interstitial Landscapeness." In *Urban Interstices*, edited by Andrea Mubi Brighenti, 21–63. Surrey, UK: Ashgate.

Light, Alison. 2016. "Photos Finished." *New York Times*, 14 August 2016, 20.

Linnemann, Travis. 2015. "Capote's Ghosts: Violence, Media and the Spectre of Suspicion." *British Journal of Criminology* 55 (3): 514–33.

Liptak, Adam. 2014. "Begging Law Tests Ruling on Buffer Zones." *New York Times*, 9 December 2014, A20.

Livio, Mario. 2013. *Brilliant Blunders: From Darwin to Einstein*. New York: Simon and Schuster.

London, Jack. 1907. *The Road*. New York: MacMillan/Aegypan Press.

Lovelace, C. 1996. "Oh No! Mistakes into Masterpieces." *ARTnews* 95 (1): 118–21.

Lubow, Arthur. 2016. "Desperate Shadows Cast by California Sun." *New York Times*, 16 October 2016, AR20.

Lybarger, Jeremy. 2015. "Doomed to Pittsburgh: W. Eugene Smith in the City of Steel." *Belt Magazine*, 2 March 2015. http://beltmag.com/doomed-to-pittsburgh-w-eugene-smith-in-the-city-of-steel/.

MacLeod, Gordon. 2002. "From Urban Entrepreneurialism to a 'Revanchist City'?" *Antipode* 34 (3): 602–24.

Maimon, Vered, and Shiraz Grinbaum, eds. 2016. *Activestills: Photography as Protest in Palestine/Israel*. London: Pluto.

Maitra, Rob. 2007. "The Homeless Community of the Piers." In *Youth Subcultures: Exploring Underground America*, edited by Arielle Greenberg, 64–72. New York: Pearson.

Makeworlds. 2003. "Precarias: First Stutterings of Precarias a la Deriva." www.makeworlds.org/node/61.

Malik, Shiv. 2012. "Lost Generation Costing Europe 153bn a Year, Research Finds." *Guardian Weekly*, 26 October 2012, 3.

Mannheim, Karl. 1936. *Ideology and Utopia*. London: Routledge.

Marcus, Greil. 1988. "Myth and Misquotation." *Threepenny Review* (Fall): 3–4.

———. 1989. *Lipstick Traces: A Secret History of the Twentieth Century*. Cambridge, MA: Harvard University Press.

Markusen, Ann, and Greg Schrock. 2009. "Consumption-Driven Urban Development." *Urban Geography* 30 (4): 344–67.

Marston, Sallie A., John Paul Jones III, and Keith Woodward. 2005. "Human Geography without Scale." *Transactions of the Institute of British Geographers* 30 (4): 416–32.

Marx, Gary. 1981. "Ironies of Social Control." *Social Problems* 28 (3): 221–46.

Marx, Karl. 1935. *The Eighteenth Brumaire of Louis Bonaparte*. New York: International.

———. 1970. *Das Kapital*. Chicago: Gateway.

Massey, Doreen. 2006. "Landscape as a Provocation." *Journal of Material Culture* 11 (1/2): 33–48.

Masters, Alexander. 2016. *A Life Discarded*. New York: Farrar, Straus and Giroux.

Matza, David. 1964. *Delinquency and Drift*. New York: John Wiley and Sons.

———. 1969. *Becoming Deviant*. Englewood Cliffs, NJ: Prentice-Hall.

Matza, David, and Gresham Sykes. 1961. "Juvenile Delinquency and Subterranean Values." *American Sociological Review* 26:712–19.

Mauger, Lena, Stephane Remael, and Brian Phalen. 2016. *The Vanished: The "Evaporated People" of Japan in Stories and Photographs*. New York: Skyhorse.

McDonogh, Gary. 1993. "The Geography of Emptiness." In *The Cultural Meaning of Urban Space*, edited by Robert Rotenberg and Gary McDonogh, 3–15. Westport, CT: Bergin and Garvey.

McGreal, Chris. 2009. "Road of Battered Dreams." *Guardian Weekly*, 11 September 2009, 25–27.

McLean, Athena, and Annette Leibing, eds. 2007. *The Shadow Side of Fieldwork*. Oxford: Blackwell.

McLean, Francis. 1911. Foreword to *One Thousand Homeless Men*, by Alice Solenberger, vii–xv. New York: Charities Publication Committee/Russell Sage Foundation.

Medina, Jennifer. 2015. "Los Angeles Declares a Homeless Emergency." *New York Times*, 23 September 2015, A1, A20.

Merton, Robert K. 1938. "Social Structure and Anomie." *American Sociological Review* 3:672–82.

Miller, Russell. 1997. *Magnum: Fifty Years at the Front Line of History*. New York: Grove.

Mills, C. Wright. 1940. "Situated Actions and Vocabularies of Motive." *American Sociological Review* 5 (6): 904–13.

———. 1951. *White Collar*. New York: Oxford University Press.

———. 1959. *The Sociological Imagination*. London: Oxford University Press.

Milton, John. 1655. "When I Consider How My Light Is Spent." (sonnet 19). Poetry Foundation. www.poetryfoundation.org/poems/44750/sonnet-19-when-i-consider-how-my-light-is-spent.

Minder, Raphael. 2012. "Crowding and Austerity Strain Portugal's Prisons." *New York Times*, 27 November 2012, A12.

Minton, Anna. 2012. "An Undemocratic Model of Land Ownership Looms Large." *Guardian Weekly*, 22 June 2012, 17.

Mitchell, Don. 2003. *The Right to the City*. New York: Guilford.

———. 2013. "Tent Cities: Interstitial Spaces of Survival." In *Urban Interstices*, edited by Andrea Mubi Brighenti, 65–85. Surrey, UK: Ashgate.

Mora, Gilles. 1989. "Havana, 1933: A Seminal Work." *Walker Evans: Havana 1933*, by Walker Evans, 8–23. Paris: Contrejour.

Morrison, Wayne. 2004. "Lombroso and the Birth of Criminological Positivism." In *Cultural Criminology Unleashed*, edited by Jeff Ferrell et al., 67–80. London: Routledge.

Mudu, Pierpaolo, and Sutapa Chattopadhyay, eds. 2016. *Migration, Squatting and Radical Autonomy*. London: Routledge.

Municipal League of Los Angeles. 1908. "The Stockade." *Municipal Affairs* 3 (8): 2.

Naegler, Laura. 2016. "Resistance Post-Occupy. A Cultural Criminological Analysis of Resistance, Knowledge Production and Imagination in the Radical Movement in New York City." PhD diss., Universität Hamburg and University of Kent.

Nagourney, Adam. 2011. "For Honolulu's Homeless, an Eviction Notice." *New York Times*, 15 March 2011, A21, A24.

———. 2014. "Honolulu Shores Up Tourism with Crackdown on Homeless." *New York Times*, 23 June 2014, A1, A13.

———. 2016. "Aloha, and Welcome, Unless You're Homeless." *New York Times*, 4 June 2016, A1, A10.

Nazario, Sonia. 2006. *Enrique's Journey*. New York: Random House.

Neilson, Brett, and Ned Rossiter. 2008. "Precarity as a Political Concept, or, Fordism as Exception." *Theory, Culture and Society* 25 (7–8): 51–72.

New York Times. 2011. "California: Homeless Campers Evicted." 30 December 2011, A16.

———. 2012a. "Alex Webb." 24 June 2012, AR22.

———. 2012b. "Posters That Rocked." 15 June 2012, C25.

———. 2015. "Homeless Are Removed from Camp in Hawaii." 11 October 2015, A25.

Nolan, Ed. 1913a. "From Frisco to Denver." *Industrial Worker*, April 17, 1, 4.

———. 1913b. "From Frisco to Denver." *Industrial Worker*, April 24, 1, 4.

Nyong'o, Tavia. 2013. "Situating Precarity between the Body and the Commons." *Women and Performance: A Journal of Feminist Theory* 23:2. www.womenandperformance.org/ampersand-articles/introduction_to_precarious_situations.html.

O'Connell, Pamela Licalzi. 1998. "A Different Breed of Freight-Hoppers." *New York Times*, 20 August 1998. www.nytimes.com/1998/08/20/technology/a-different-breed-of-freight-hoppers.html.

OJJDP (Office of Juvenile Justice and Delinquency Prevention). 1999. *1996 National Youth Gang Survey*. Washington, DC: US Department of Justice.

O'Malley, Pat. 2010. *Crime and Risk*. London: Sage.

O'Neill, Maggie. 2001. *Prostitution and Feminism*. Cambridge: Polity.

Onishi, Norimitsu. 2012. "City Moves Homeless, Storing Their Stuff." *New York Times*, 20 June 2012, A12.

Oude Breuil, Brenda. 2008. "'Precious Children in a Heartless World'? The Complexities of Child Trafficking in Marseille." *Children and Society* 22:223–34.

Owens, Lynn. 2013. "Have Squat, Will Travel: How Squatter Mobility Mobilizes Squatting." In *Squatting in Europe*, edited by SqEK, 185–207. Wivenhoe: Minor Compositions.

Parker, Carleton. 1920. *The Casual Laborer and Other Essays.* New York: Harcourt, Brace and Howe.

Parker, James. 2016. "Dear Diary (Volume 1 of 148)." *New York Times Book Review,* 11 December 2016, 23.

Park, Robert. 1928. "Human Migration and the Marginal Man." *American Journal of Sociology* 33 (6): 881–93.

Pepinsky, Harold, and Paul Jesilow. 1984. *Myths That Cause Crime.* 2nd ed. Washington, DC: Seven Locks.

Peters, Kimberly. 2015. "Drifting: Towards Mobilities at Sea." *Transactions of the Institute of British Geographers* 40:262–72.

Petrou, Michael. 2008. *Renegades: Canadians in the Spanish Civil War.* Vancouver: University of British Columbia Press.

Phillips, Stephen. 2003. *Margaret Bourke-White: Photography of Design, 1927–1936.* New York: Rizzoli.

Pickering, Sharon, Mary Bosworth, and Katja Franko. 2018. "The Criminology of Mobility." In *Alternative Criminologies,* edited by Pat Carlen and Leandro Ayres Franca, 150–64. Abingdon, UK: Routledge.

Pinder, David. 2011. "Cities: Moving, Plugging In, Floating, Dissolving." In *Geographies of Mobilities,* edited by Tim Cresswell and Peter Merriman, 167–86. London: Ashgate.

Pogrebin, Robin. 2015. "Pratt to Offer a Degree Focusing in Public Space." *New York Times,* 30 March 2015, C3.

———. 2016. "An Artist's Activism Turns to Migrant Misery." *New York Times,* 21 October 2016, C18.

Postman, Neil. 1985. *Amusing Ourselves to Death.* New York: Penguin.

Povoledo, Elisabetta. 2012. "In Italy, Shantytowns of Refugees Reflect Paradox on Asylum." *New York Times,* 28 December 2012, A12.

———. 2013. "Italy's Immigrant Detention Centers Are Called Inhumane and Ineffective." *New York Times,* 16 June 2013, 12.

———. 2014. "Palace of Squatters Is a Symbol of Refugee Crisis." *New York Times,* 15 June 2014, 6, 9.

———. 2015. "Migrants' Lives in Ruin as Camp Is Razed in Rome." *New York Times,* 17 May 2015, A6.

Powell, Ricky. 2003. "Having a Few Words with the Author of *Evasion.*" *Clamor,* September/October, 51–52.

Precarias a la Deriva. 2004. "Adrift through the Circuit of Feminized Precarious Work." *Feminist Review* 77 (1): 157–61

Presdee, Mike. 2000. *Cultural Criminology and the Carnival of Crime.* London: Routledge.

Prince, Hugh. 1973. "Scepticism, Mobility and Attitudes to Environment." *Antipode* 5 (3): 40–44.

Rafferty, Terrence. 2015. "The Stories She Told." *New York Times Book Review,* 2 August 2015, 1, 19.

Rappert, Brian. 2010. "Revealing and Concealing Secrets in Research: The Potential for the Absent." *Qualitative Research* 10 (5): 571–87.

Reavis, Dick. 2010. *Catching Out: The Secret World of Day Laborers.* New York: Simon and Schuster.

Reclaim the Streets. 2000. "On Disorganization." http://rts.gn.apc.org/disorg
.htm.

Rexroth, Kenneth. 1968. "Stiffs on the Road." *New York Times Book Review*,
21 April 1968, 50–51.

Robbins, Seth. 2015. "Border Drownings Rise as Migrants Take Greater Risk."
Fort Worth Star Telegram Express, 8 April 2015, 3AA.

Robles, Frances. 2016. "Fearing Shift in Status, Cubans Rush for Exits and
U.S." *New York Times*, 10 January 2016, 8.

Rogers, John. 2016. "Anthropologist Follows Trail of Century-Old Hobo Graffiti." Associated Press/*The Big Story*, 30 May 2016. http://bigstory.ap.org
/article/53241721c169476ab44f4d1c34180cc6/anthropologist-follows-trail-
century-old-hobo-graffiti.

Root, Carl, Jeff Ferrell, and Wilson Palacios. 2013 "Brutal Serendipity: Criminological Verstehen and Victimization." *Critical Criminology* 21 (2): 141–
55.

Rosemont, Franklin. 1988. "A Short Treatise on Wobbly Cartoons." In *Rebel
Voices*, edited by Joyce Kornbluh, 425–43. Chicago: Charles H. Kerr.

Ross, Andrew. 2008. "The New Geography of Work: Power to the Precarious?" *Theory, Culture and Society* 25 (7–8): 31–49.

Rubin, Elihu. 2012. "Catch My Drift? Situationist Derive and Urban Pedagogy." *Radical History Review* 114 (Fall): 175–90.

Ryzik, Melena. 2014. "Shadows Return to Ellis Island." *New York Times*,
25 September 2014, C1, C2.

Salgado, Sebastaio. 2000. *Migrations*. New York: Aperture.

Salzman, Jack, ed. 1970. *Years of Protest*. Indianapolis: Bobbs-Merrill.

Sandburg, Carl. 1927. *The American Songbag*. New York: Harcourt, Brace.

———. 1970. *The Complete Poems of Carl Sandburg*. New York: Harcourt
Brace Jovanovich.

Sante, Luc 2010. "The Fiction of Memory." *New York Times Book Review*,
14 March 2010, 17.

Sarfati, Lise. 2012. "On Hollywood." *New York Times*, 25 March 2012, SR8.

Saulny, Susan. 2012. "After Recession, More Young Adults Are Living on
Street." *New York Times*, 19 December 2012, A14, A17.

Saunders, Doug. 2010. *Arrival City*. Toronto: Knopf.

Schept, Judah. 2014. "(Un)seeing like a Prison." *Theoretical Criminology* 18
(4): 198–233.

Schmalleger, Frank. 2004. *Criminology Today*. 3rd ed. Upper Saddle River, NJ:
Pearson.

Sciolino, Elaine. 2015. "Paris, One Step at a Time." *New York Times*, 4 October 2015, ST14–15.

Scott, A.O. 2016. "In the Eye of a Migrant Storm, Struggling to Stay Anchored."
New York Times, 21 October 2016, C10.

Scott, Joanna. 2012. "Self-Portrait in a Sheet Mirror." *Nation*, 11 June 2012,
27–32.

Seigel, Larry. 2008. *Criminology: The Core*. 3rd ed. Belmont, CA: Thompson.

Seligson, Hannah. 2011. "Job Jugglers, on the Tightrope." *New York Times*,
26 June 2011, 1, 6.

Semple, Kirk. 2016. "Haitians Find Door to U.S. Abruptly Shut." *New York Times*, 24 September 2016, A1, A8.

Sengupta, Somini. 2016. "'Road on Fire' for Men Fleeing Drought and War." *New York Times*, 16 December 2016, A1, A12–13.

Sethi, Aman. 2011. *A Free Man*. New York: Norton/Random House.

Shantz, Jeff. 2011. *Active Anarchy: Political Practice in Contemporary Movements*. Lanham, MD: Lexington.

Shenker, Jack, Angelique Chrisafis, Lauren Williams, Tom Finn, Giles Tremlett, and Martin Chulov. 2011. "Arab Youth Anger in the Ascendancy." *Guardian Weekly*, 25 February 2011, 28–29.

Shepard Benjamin, and Gregory Smithsimon. 2011. *The Beach beneath the Streets: Contesting New York City's Public Spaces*. Albany: SUNY Press.

Shubin, Sergei. 2011. "'Where Can a Gypsy Stop?' Rethinking Mobility in Scotland" *Antipode* 43 (2): 494–24.

Shukaitis, Stevphen. 2009. *Imaginal Machines*. Brooklyn: Autonomedia.

Simmel, Georg. (1908) 1971. "The Stranger." In *Georg Simmel: On Individuality and Social Forms*, edited by Donald Levine, 143–49. Chicago: University of Chicago Press.

Slaughter, Jane. 1994. "Staughton Lynd." *Progressive*, February 1994, 33–36.

Smale, Alison. 2015. "Kosovars Who Fought for Land Are Now Eager to Leave." *New York Times*, 8 March 2015, A6–A7.

Smale, Alison, Carlotta Gall, and Gaia Pianigiani. 2016. "On Watch List, Berlin Suspect Slipped Away." *New York Times*, 23 December 2016, A1, A9.

Small, Mario Luis. 2009. "'How Many Cases Do I Need?': On Science and the Logic of Case Selection in Field-Based Research." *Ethnography* 10 (5): 5–38.

Smith, Alexander McCall. 2016. *Chance Developments*. New York: Pantheon.

Smith, Neil. 1996. *The New Urban Frontier: Gentrification and the Revanchist City*. London: Routledge.

Smith, Shawn. 2013. *At the Edge of Sight: Photography and the Unseen*. Durham, NC: Duke University Press.

Snyder, Greg. 2009. *Graffiti Lives*. New York: New York University Press.

Solenberger, Alice. 1911. *One Thousand Homeless Men*. New York: Charities Publication Committee/Russell Sage Foundation.

Sontag, Susan. 1977. *On Photography*. New York: Picador.

Spradley, James. 1970. "The Moral Career of a Bum." *Transaction* 7 (7): 16–29.

Springer, Simon. 2010. *Cambodia's Neoliberal Order: Violence, Authoritarianism and the Contestation of Public Space*. London: Routledge.

———. 2011. "Public Space as Emancipation: Meditations on Anarchism, Radical Democracy, Neoliberalism and Violence." *Antipode* 43 (2): 525–62.

Spyridakis, Manos. 2013. *The Liminal Worker: An Ethnography of Work, Unemployment and Precariousness in Contemporary Greece*. London: Routledge.

Stallabrass, Julian, ed. 2013. *Documentary*. Cambridge: MIT Press.

Stallybrass, Peter. 1993. "Worn Worlds: Clothing, Mourning, and the Life of Things." *Yale Review* 81:35–50.

Steinbeck, John. 1936. *In Dubious Battle*. New York: Penguin.

Steinmetz, Kevin, Brian Schaefer, and Edward Green. 2016. "Anything but Boring: A Cultural Criminological Exploration of Boredom." *Theoretical Criminology* (July 2016). Online edition. http://journals.sagepub.com/doi/abs/10.1177/1362480616652686.

Stephenson, Svetlana. 2006. *Crossing the Line: Vagrancy, Homelessness and Social Displacement in Russia.* Aldershot, UK: Ashgate.

Strand, Ginger. 2012. "Hitchhiking's Time Has Come Again." *New York Times,* 11 November 2012, SR4.

Strasser, Susan. 1999. *Waste and Want: A Social History of Trash.* New York: Henry Holt and Company.

Sykes, Gresham, and David Matza. (1957) 2003. "Techniques of Neutralization: A Theory of Delinquency." *American Sociological Review* 22, no. 6 (December 1957): 664–70. Reprinted in *Criminological Perspectives,* edited by Eugene McLaughlin et al., 231–38. London: Sage.

Tannenbaum, Frank. 1938. *Crime and Community.* New York: Ginn.

Tari, Marcello, and Ilaria Vanni. 2005. "On the Life and Deeds of San Precario, Patron Saint of Precarious Workers and Lives." *Fibreculture* 5. http://five.fibreculturejournal.org/

Terkel, Studs. 1970. *Hard Times: An Oral History of the Great Depression.* New York: Avon.

Thomas, Landon. 2011. "Continuing Money Troubles Take Personal Toll in Greece." *New York Times,* 16 May 2011, A1, A3.

Thomas, W.I. 1923. *The Unadjusted Girl.* Boston: Little, Brown.

Thompson, Hunter S. (1967) 1979. "The Ultimate Freelancer." In *The Great Shark Hunt,* by Hunter S. Thompson, 109–13. New York: Fawcett.

Thrasher, Frederic. 1927. *The Gang.* Chicago: University of Chicago Press.

Tommasini, Anthony. 2014. "Telling Stories, from 'Beowulf' to the Hobo Life." *New York Times,* 24 April 2014, C8.

Toth, Jennifer. 1995. *The Mole People.* Chicago: Chicago Review Press.

Trachtenberg, Alan, Sam Stephenson, and W. Eugene Smith. 2003. *Dream Street: W. Eugene Smith's Pittsburgh Project.* New York: W. W. Norton.

Tudor, Silke. 2001. "Railroaded." *San Francisco Weekly,* 31 October. https://archives.sfweekly.com/sanfrancisco/railroaded/Content?oid=2143279.

Tunnell, Kenneth. 2004. *Pissing on Demand.* New York: New York University Press.

———. 2011. *Once upon a Place: The Fading of Community in Rural Kentucky.* Bloomington, IN: Xlibris.

Turkewitz, Julie, Thomas Fuller, Richard Perez-Pena, and Conor Dougherty. 2016. "Oakland Site Violated Code but Filled Need." *New York Times,* 6 December 2016, A1, A14.

Vaneigem, Raul. (1967) 2001. *The Revolution of Everyday Life.* London: Rebel Press.

Vasagar, Jeevan. 2012. "Public Spaces Fall into Private Hands." *Guardian Weekly,* 22 June 2012, 16–17.

Velarde, Albert. 1978. "Do Delinquents Really Drift? *British Journal of Criminology* 18 (1): 23–39.

Vergara, Camilo José. 1995. *The New American Ghetto*. New Brunswick, NJ: Rutgers University Press.

Villegas, Paulina, and Randal Archibald. 2014. "Mexico Makes Route Tougher for Migrants." *New York Times*, 22 September 2014, A4.

Vitale, Alex. 2010. "The Safe Cities Initiative and the Removal of the Homeless." *Criminology and Public Policy* 9 (4): 867–73.

Vorse, Mary Heaton. (1931) 1970. "School for Bums." In *Years of Protest*, edited by Jack Salzman, 39–44. Indianapolis: Bobbs-Merrill.

Ward, Colin. 1973. *Anarchy in Action*. New York: Harper and Row.

———. 2000. *Social Policy: An Anarchist Response*. London: Freedom Press.

Warner, Nancy, and David Stark. 2014. *This Place, These People: Life and Shadow on the Great Plains*. New York: Columbia University Press.

Weide, Robert. 2016. "The History of Freight Train Graffiti in North America." In *Routledge Handbook of Graffiti and Street Art*, edited by Jeffrey Ian Ross, 36–47. Abingdon, UK: Routledge.

Wheeler, William, and Ayman Oghanna. 2011. "After Liberation, Nowhere To Run." *New York Times*, 30 October 2011, SR1, SR4.

Wilson, Daniel. 2012. "Miraculous Agitations." *Leonardo Music Journal* 22:35–40.

Wilson, James, and George Kelling. 1982. "Broken Windows." *Atlantic Monthly*, March 1982, 29–38.

Wong, Edward. 2011. "The Labyrinth." *New York Times Magazine*, 24 April 2011, 16.

Wright, J.P., and Ed Michael. 2013. "Rank-and-File Railroaders Resist Single-Employee Trains." *Industrial Worker*, January/February 2013, 11.

Wyman, Mark. 2010. *Hoboes*. New York: Hill and Wang.

Xie, Min, and David McDowall. 2008. "Escaping Crime: The Effects of Direct and Indirect Victimization on Moving." *Criminology* 46 (4): 809–40.

Yablonsky, Linda. 2013. "Beautiful Ruins." *New York Times Style Magazine*, 14 April 2013, 88–92.

Young, Alison. 2016. *Street Art World*. Chicago: University of Chicago Press/ Reaktion Books.

Younge, Gary. 2011. "With Slender Job Prospects, Nation's Young Look To Leave." *Guardian Weekly*, 8 April 2011, 13.

Young, Jock. 1971. *The Drugtakers*. London: Paladin.

———. 1999. *The Exclusive Society*. London: Sage.

———. 2007. *The Vertigo of Late Modernity*. London: Sage.

Zellar, Brad. 2014. *House of Coates*. Minneapolis: Coffee House Press.

Zukin, Sharon. 1997. "Cultural Strategies of Economic Development and the Hegemony of Vision." In *The Urbanization of Injustice*, edited by Andy Merrifield and Erik Swyngedouw, 223–43. New York: New York University Press.

———. 2010. *Naked City: The Death and Life of Authentic Urban Places*. New York: Oxford University Press.

FILMS AND VISUAL MEDIA

Ai Weiwei, dir. 2017. *Human Flow*. Gaza: 24 Media Production.

Armstrong, Justin. n.d. *Everywhere Is Nowhere*. https://vimeo.com/38121701. Video, 24:56.

Daniel, Bill, dir. 2005. *Who Is Bozo Texino?* Bill Daniel Studio.

Eastwood, Clint, dir. 1973. *High Plains Drifter*. Universal City, CA: Universal Pictures.

Kish, Albert, dir. 1975. *Los Canadienses*. Montreal: National Film Board of Canada.

Maloof, John, and Charlie Siskel, dirs. 2013. *Finding Vivian Maier*. New York: Ravine Pictures.

Murray, Alison, dir. 2000. *Train on the Brain*. MJW Productions.

Story, Brett, dir. 2016. *The Prison in Twelve Landscapes*. Oh Ratface Films.

Truffaut, Francois, dir. 1959. *The 400 Blows*. Paris: Les Films du Carrosse, Sédif Productions.

Walker, Lucy, Karen Harley, and João Jardim, dirs. 2010. *Waste Land*. London: Almega Projects.

Wellman, William A., dir. 1933. *Wild Boys of the Road*. United States: First National Pictures.

White, Ted, dir. 1999. *We Are Traffic!* San Francisco, CA: Ted White.

Wiseman, Frederick, dir. 1967. *Titicut Follies*. New York: Ziporrah Films.

MUSIC

Bonus, Jack. 1969. "The Hobo Song." *Jack Bonus*. San Francisco: Grunt Records.

Flea, Frusciante, Kiedis, and Smith. 1992. "Under the Bridge." *Blood, Sugar, Sex, Magik*. Los Angeles: Warner Bros.

Garcia, Jerry, and Robert Hunter. 1970. "Brokedown Palace." *American Beauty*. Los Angeles, CA: Warner Bros.

Guthrie, Woody. [193?]. "Hard Travelin'."

Morrissey, and John Marr. 1984. "Reel around the Fountain." *The Smiths*. London: Rough Trade Records.

———. 1987. "Shoplifters of the World Unite." Released as a single. London: Rough Trade Records.

O'Connor, Sinead, and Marco Pirroni. 1990. "Jump in the River." *I Do Not Want What I Haven't Got*. London: EMI.

Parsons, Gram, and Tom Brown. 1974. "Return of the Grievous Angel." *Grievous Angel*. Los Angeles: Reprise.

Prine, John. 1971. "Flashback Blues." *John Prine*. New York: Atlantic.

Puckett, Riley. 1929/1934. "Ragged but Right." San Antonio: Victor/Bluebird.

Rodgers, Jimmie. 1928. "Waiting for a Train." Camden, NJ: Victor Talking Machine Company.

Springsteen, Bruce. 1982. *Nebraska*. New York: Columbia.

Strummer, Joe, and Mick Jones. 1982. "Know Your Rights." *Combat Rock*. Los Angeles: CBS Records.

Waits, Tom. 1976. "Step Right Up." *Small Change.* Asylum Records.
Walker, Jerry Jeff. 1972. "That Old Beat Up Guitar." *Jerry Jeff Walker.* Kensington, UK: Decca Records.

GALLERY/MUSEUM EXHIBITIONS

Ferrell, Jeff, Gavin Morrison, and Fraser Stables. 2016. *American Dirt.* The Reading Room, Dallas, Texas (5 March–2 April).
Hernandez, Anthony. 2016. *Discarded.* Amon Carter Museum of American Art, Fort Worth, Texas (5 March–7 August).
Lee, Zun. 2016. *Fade Resistance: An Exhibition of Found Polaroids.* Gladstone Hotel, Toronto (1–28 February).

Index

"Waiting for a Train," 128
Waiting for Nothing, 83–84, 189
Walker, Jerry Jeff, 195
Walsh, James W., 91–92
Wanderlust, 80
Warner, Nancy, 213
Waters, Todd, 140–141, 236n12
Webb, Alex, 214
Weber, Max, 23, 155
"We Can Be Together," 233n10
Weiwei, Ai, 198, 238n8
Wendy, 141
West Coast Blackie, 234n2
Western Federation of Miners, 89, 236n14

Wheatland Hop Fields' Riot, 82–83, 91, 94, 96
White, Henry A., 127
Who Is Bozo Texino?, 236n9
Wild Boys of the Road, 234n1
Wilde, Oscar, 227
Williams, Hank, 12
Wilson, Daniel, 227

You Can't Win, 14
Young, Jock, 10

Zeke, 105–150, 184, 194

Made in the USA
Monee, IL
06 January 2022